THE CHALLENGES OF PARENTING

About the Author

The author has a Master's degree in Psychology from Jodhpur University and Ph.D. from Barkatullah University, Bhopal. She is presently working as a faculty at the PSS Central Institute of Vocational Education (NCERT), Bhopal— an apex R&D organisation in the area of vocational education in India. Her papers have appeared in *Indian Educational Review, Psychological Studies* and *Indian Journal of Clinical Psychology*. She is a member of National Academy of Psychology (India) and Indian Society of Vocational Education. Currently she is directing a research project on the status of vocational guidance in India. She has prepared resource material for teachers training programme in vocational guidance and counselling and also to facilitate vocational orientation in pupils. Her areas of interest include socialization and parenting, guidance and counselling, development of skills and student motivation.

THE CHALLENGES OF PARENTING

Implications of Maternal Employment for Psychological Development of the Child

Kiran Mathur
Pandit Sunderlal Sharma
Central Institute of Vocational Education
(NCERT), Bhopal

CONCEPT PUBLISHING COMPANY, NEW DELHI-110059

The publication of this monograph is partially supported by financial assistance from National Council of Educational Research and Training, New Delhi.

ISBN 81-7022-865-4

First Published 2001

Published and Printed by
Ashok Kumar Mittal
Concept Publishing Company
A/15-16, Commercial Block, Mohan Garden
New Delhi-110059 (India)

Phones: 5648039, 5649024

Fax: 091–(11)–5648053

E-mail: publishing@conceptpub.com

FOREWORD

The texture of Indian society is changing very fast and in order to cope with the demands of society, planning is needed. Unfortunately, planning in India has been largely confined to the economic part of our life and not much effort has been made to examine other aspects including the possible consequences of economic changes in other spheres. The case of working women–those who are employed in some work outside the four walls of home–clearly points to the problems of this kind. It not only destabilizes the routine life style of home but also challenges the relational equilibrium. Women's act of seeking employment has many connotations including assertion of rights, demonstration of power, having additional sources of income and so on and so forth. There are multiple images of working women which are tied up with the social class. It should be remembered that it was not new for the lower or upper social class women. But it is certainly new to the middle class which is constantly struggling with the question of capability enhancement to meet the ever increasing demands with its limited resources at its disposal. It tries to emulate the needs, style of life and goals held by the elite. It is under pressure to respond to the problems of materialistic and consumeristic life style.

In the above context, the women leaving the traditional frame of reference and joining the work force are bound to experience tensions pertaining to role conflict. Such a woman's life so far was for others (e.g. father, brothers, husband, children) and now she intends to do something for herself. For a woman who has grown in a setting which nurtures a relational self the new self centric image of a working woman may result in the feelings of guilt. At times it is resolved by surrendering the new image and incorporating the new element into the old one and continuing with the new complex image which perhaps has undergone considerable modification. She may become permissive or authoritarian in her attitude and manners but she will not remain the same as she was. Her new or modified image will be reflected most in her relationship with children.

The developmental task of motherhood is still cherished by a majority of the Indian women. In Indian context, climax of being woman is becoming a (good) mother. Working women who are in the transitional phase of identity formation appear to be concerned with the issues of child-rearing. Their new experiences in the outside world inform them about new goals and ideals. A working woman, therefore, questions her role of mother and responsibilities in relation to children. Her own notions of parenting and mothering undergo considerable change. This question becomes more important in the context of contemporary Indian society in which tradition and change coexist. The forces of globalization, market economy and informational revolution have further contributed to the dilemmas and contradictions in life.

The work of Dr. Kiran Mathur addresses some of the key questions emerging in the context of parenting in the lives of working women. She has tried to see the pattern of personality of children of employed and unemployed mothers. Secondly, she examines the way these groups of mothers relate to children. Her work is a meaningful contribution to this important but relatively less explored field of study. Using structured and semistructured techniques a sincere effort has been made in this study to map the different facets of parent-child interaction on the one hand and aspects of personality of children, on the other. The analysis of empirical findings demonstrates that the context of employment has changed the context of parenting in general and disciplining in particular. The important finding is that the nature of parent-child interaction changes qualitatively owing to the change in women's status. Also, the personality related differences in the children of employed and unemployed mothers evince some interesting contrasts. They cannot be explained merely on the basis of status differences. They do indicate the possible linkages with change in parenting style which are worth pursuing.

The present study also provides insight into the preferred

patterns of child-rearing and practices. While social desirability must be there, they do help in deciphering the salient features of child-rearing in the middle class urban families in India. The change from the traditional pattern delineated in our scriptures and often coded in the tales told by the grandmothers is significant. The change is also visible in our society at a concrete level. The parental dilemmas are quite obvious and the problems emerging in the case of children are frequently voiced and brought to our notice through print media and cinema. All this leads us to think more seriously about parenting. The nurture is more important than nature as far as human nature is concerned. Today's demand is to educate parents and empower them as enlightened parents ready to meet the challenges in their life. For long, parenting in the Indian society has been a matter of chance. Now we are moving in a world where parenting is planned. It would be worthwhile if studies like the present one are brought into focus and parents are informed and educated.

I congratulate Dr. Mathur for her effort and hope that she will examine the problems of parenting in other contexts and initiate some work in parental education.

GIRISHWAR MISRA
Professor and Head
Department of Psychology
University of Delhi
Delhi

PREFACE

Indian women are still known more for their role as 'home maker' and 'caretaker' than as a career conscious person. A successful woman is appreciated by the society only if she is also a successful mother and wife. It is a notion among a large number of men and women that maternal employment adversely influences the health and development of their children, because children are neglected and not properly looked after. In recent years, due to spread of education, search for new identity and technological changes, considerably large number of women from the middle and upper middle classes in India are gainfully employed in almost all areas. Many educated women are still not employed due to family constraints, because family still occupies the most important place in their life. It is not correct to say that a working woman cannot handle the diverse roles and responsibilities of a working woman and mother simultaneously. In the developmental context a mother happens to be the central figure in child's home environment. She plays a variety of familial and social roles. A majority of women acknowledge, accept and enjoy child care as the most important aspect of their family role.

However, the challenges emerging out of job demands are leading to significant changes in the family ecology and have important implication for social and personality development of children. In the families of working parents, both the parents are away from home for a considerable period of time. When they return home, mothers are usually busy with discharge of household responsibilities or some child-care duties, either, feeding, cleaning or checking children's homework. On certain days there is hardly any time for family interaction. Family entertainment activities are postponed till the weekends and if some other important and urgent work is to be done during weekends then these are further postponed for the next weekend.

It is generally held that due to mother's employment, there would be differences in the intensity and quality of parent-child interaction and involvement, parental treatment with the child, parental understanding regarding child related matters etc. As both spouses are working, they get less time for each other, which may lead to marital conflict and disharmony. All these factors jointly and differentially influence the personality development of children. On the other hand, double income family means more monetary benefits and more facilities available to all the family members. Maternal employment can influence children's personality development in two ways. On the one hand, it may bring a sense of greater independence, self-esteem, and change in the prevailing sex stereotypes, on the other, it may make the child more apprehensive, generally emotional, reserved or sober. It all depends upon the interaction of many variables such as, family environment, background variables, mother's satisfaction with her diverse roles, treatment of the child and gender and age of the child. Gender and age of the child also determine parental treatment of the child. The way children perceive the parental treatment also has a positive or negative influence on their personality development. This is a very complicated issue. Employment status *per se* does not indicate any particular trend as regards the personality pattern of the child. It is the function of the interaction of a number of variables related to parents, family structure, immediate and broader social context, and type of maternal employment etc.

Women can contribute fruitfully and more effectively at home and at work place if their household and child-rearing responsibilities are shared and supported by their spouse, older children etc. They need sensitivity on the part of their family members especially husband, and employers and colleagues. It should be seen by all concerned that working women are relieved from overburdening themselves. This way their contribution to family and society can be maximised.

This book is organised into eight chapters, which cover introduction to the research problem, overview of concepts and theories, methodology and findings. Maternal employment has become an important aspect of women's lives. Chapter 1 describes the challenges of maternal employment and examines its effects on child development. Empirical studies in this area have been reviewed. Issues related to mothers' employment such as role satisfaction, alternate arrangements, sex-role stereotypes and home environment are discussed in detail. The research questions relating maternal employment to child development and methodological details are provided. Chapter 2 offers an account of the theories of dispositional (traits), cognitive (psychological differentiation) and reflective (self-concept) aspects of personality. The notions of psychological differentiation and self-concept are discussed. The chapter also provides description of the measures used to study various aspects of personality. The findings of the study about the personality of children are analysed and discussed.

In chapter 3, there is an attempt to discuss various disciplinary practices used by parents in child-rearing in view of existing theory and research in this area. The chapter also documents the questionnaire measure developed in the present research to study the use of different disciplinary practices. Children's personality is not only affected by mothers' employment, but there are certain background variables (e.g., age, educational level, socio-economic status of parents, siblings, physical facilities, entertainment facilities) which also contribute to the shaping of personality development. Chapter 4 is an attempt to explore the relationship between various aspects of personality, background variables and disciplinary practices.

Chapter 5 elucidates parents' reaction to child's undersired behaviours and perception of parents' reactions by children. It helps us in knowing the congruence between responses of mothers and children. Parents' marital relationship affects home environment which directly or indirectly influences their interactions with children. Therefore, chapter 6 attempts to study the level of marital adjustment among the employed and unemployed mothers and its relationship with child's personality.

When women start working outside the home due to various reasons, there are certain issues which need attention of women themselves, children and spouses. Chapter 7 includes experiences and views of employed mothers regarding home (family relationship, sharing responsibilities, decision making, etc.) and workplace (timings, transfer, extra work, etc.). Chapter 8 concludes the present work in the light of immediate family background and broader social contexts. It also indicates some of the implications of this work in Indian context and identifies issues which demand further work in this and related areas.

The consummation of this work would not have been possible had it not been for the invaluable guidance, co-operation and inspiration of a number of persons. First and foremost, I am grateful to Prof. Girishwar Misra for his unceasing guidance and help. The comments by Prof. Leela Krishnan and Prof. Pramod Kumar on my doctoral work were helpful in preparing this monograph. I express thanks to them. I would like to place on record my gratitude to Dr. T. Singh for his unflinching and overwhelming help in furnishing this book.

A very special mention has to be made of the support and hortation that I received from my family members–my husband and daughter Priya–who helped me a great deal in accomplishing this work.

I am beholden to all the mothers and children, who were interviewed in connection with this study, for their endurance....

KIRAN MATHUR

CONTENTS

LIST OF TABLES

LIST OF FIGURES

1

INTRODUCTION

The parental practices are facing many challenges in the fast changing world of Indian society, particularly in the urban sector. Change in family structure, especially in middle class families, with disappearance of joint families and preference for small nuclear families, has raised questions for parents about socializing their children. Increasingly, the children in such families find parents and sometimes older siblings as the only adult models. With larger number of women seeking jobs outside their homes, either purely for financial reasons or for self-satisfaction or realization, the situation is further complicated. The spread of education has brought awareness among women about their role in economic and social development of the country. Women are working with men in almost all spheres of life and work. This type of exposure has also influenced the pattern of family interaction, parenting styles and marital adjustment of employed mothers. It is believed that if both parents are working, they get very little time to look after their children. Children are either left in the hands of maid-servant, servant or, if available, in creches. In India, big cities are facing the problem of space and it may be due to the limited space available at home that people simply do not want any intrusion in their privacy by parents or relatives. Help from some relatives (grand-parents, in-laws, etc.) is obtained only during initial period of infancy and babyhood, say about 1 to 2 years. After that, the child is left with a servant or in a creche. This is the time when the child starts learning, while interacting with parents and other members in the family.

However, the general belief is that child care and rearing happen to be only the mother's responsibility. As mother is also away from home for a considerable period of time due to job requirements, when she returns home, besides looking after the child, she also has to execute many household responsibilities. In metropolitan cities like Delhi and Bombay, marriages are facing many problems and the cases of divorce in dual career groups are increasing at an alarming rate. This is perhaps because neither parent wants to take the responsibility of child-rearing alone. Against this backdrop, the present study was conducted to examine the influence of maternal employment on child's personality, marital adjustment and parenting styles. To this end, three aspects of personality were chosen, viz. dispositional (traits), cognitive (psychological differentiation) and reflective (self-concept). To study the parental practices, various aspects of disciplining the child, parent-child interaction and involvement with child were investigated in the groups of employed and unemployed mothers.

Maternal Employment: A Challenge to Indian Families

Human development takes place in a socio-cultural ecology which consists of different systems organised in a nested hierarchy (Bronfenbrenner, 1977). Thus, a child grows in the family environment, the family grows in the environment of the community and the community grows in the context of broader societal functions. All these levels of developmental ecology influence each other and shape the development of a child. In contemporary life, social institutions, individual's roles and their linkages are undergoing important changes and an adequate understanding of child development can be achieved only by studying development in the context of the socio-economic transformations which are taking place.

Rapid socio-economic changes that characterize contemporary Indian society, induce adaptive changes in the family which, in turn, lead to modifications in socialisation and child-rearing practices, as well as changes in family experiences that work as proximal antecedents to the dispositions and characteristics of children and parents. During the last three to four decades, the institution of family in India has undergone phenomenal transformations. These changes involve both structural and attitudinal dimensions which have resulted in altered interrelationships among the members constituting the family, changes in family obligations, decision-making as well as modifications in child-rearing and socialization processes. Sinha (1988) has identified several salient changes in the Indian family that constitute antecedent factors for the development of individual. Sinha has discussed some of the implications of the changing family scene for the socialization process and mental health of individual. According to Sinha (1984;1988) socio-economic changes in Indian society have induced certain changes in family experiences. These changes have significant behavioural and psychological consequences for the individual. Sinha (1988) has viewed the contemporary Indian family as being in a 'transitional' phase where structural changes are not entirely accompanied by psychological changes. People want to live in small nuclear families and particularly in times of crises try to draw strength from the extended family. According to Sinha (1984;1988), this brings ambiguity in setting roles and expectations for the growing child. On the basis of the findings of several studies, he concluded that in the changing family pattern there are unstable and contradictory patterns of child-rearing which generate anxiety and conflict in the growing child. In the changed circumstances, parents are the main socializing agent and elderly people in the family do not play much role in socializing the child. Besides, other external agencies like day care centres, preschools and even peer group are also taking over the socialization role. As a result, Sinha points out that clear cut and consistent role models are not available to the growing child.

Attitudes towards traditional methods of disciplining, toilet training and feeding schedules have shown influences of western thinking, but as the traditional attitudes have not been given over completely, a spurious sense of permissiveness alternates with strictness, which is creating anxiety and confusion in the child. Nuclear family system has further depleted the emotional surround of individuals and thus, made them more vulnerable. Finally, the growing concern for competitiveness, consumerism and materialism are replacing joint family values of sharing, accommodativeness, mutual dependence and conformity with greater feelings of individualism, personal freedom, autonomy, and self-determination. Accordingly, children are being socialized to adapt and adjust to the changing value system and ethos (Bharat, 1992; p. 213).

Status of Women's Employment in India: According to 1971 census, there were 31.3 million women workers in the country. Of these, 80 per cent were in agriculture, 10.5 per cent in industries and the rest in tertiary occupations. Rapid expansion in women's education in the post-independence period has improved the possibility of their employment. Today, there is no profession which women have not entered. Many women are at decision making levels in administration, law, diplomatic services, banks and the media. According to 1991 census, the female work participation rate has increased in the country. This trend appears in Tables 1.1, 1.2 and 1.3.

Table 1.1: Proportion by Sex in Population-Sex Ratio

Level	Female per 1,000 Males of Total Population	
	1981	1991
All India	935	927
Madhya Pradesh	941	931

Source : Census of India, 1991.

Table 1.1 depicts sex ratio in India and Madhya Pradesh in 1981-1991. It suggests that in M.P. the sex ratio is higher, as compared to India both in 1981 and 1991. However, it has decreased in 1991 from 941 to 931. Comparison of male and female workers as given in Table 1.2 suggests that participation of female workers in M.P. is more than that in India. There is not much change in the percentage of female workers in 1981 to 1991 in M.P., whereas in India it has increased from 14.07 to 16.03 from 1981 to 1991.

Table 1.2: Total Workers, Main Workers Marginal Workers and Non-Workers as Percentage to Total Population

Population	Total Workers		Main Workers		Marginal Workers		Non-Workers	
	1981	1991	1981	1991	1981	1991	1981	1991
All India								
Total	36.70	37.50	33.48	34:18	3.22	3.32	63.30	62.50
Male	52.62	51.61	51.62	51.00	1.00	0.61	47.38	48.39
Female	19.67	22.27	14.07	16.03	5.60	6.24	80.33	77.73
Madhya Pradesh								
Total	42.92	42.82	38.41	37.67	4.51	5.15	57.08	57.18
Male	54.48	52.26	53.52	51.51	0.96	0.75	45.52	47.74
Female	30.64	32.68	22.34	22.82	8.30	9.86	69.36	67.32

Source : Census of India, 1991.

From Table 1.3 it is clear that Madhya Pradesh has lower rate in tertiary sector in both male and female workers although it has shown some increase in 1991.

Table 1.3 : Tertiary Rate among Males and Females

India/ M.P	Total		Males		Femal	
	1981	1991	1981	1991	1981	1991
India	43.67	52.19	56.50	64.20	29.85	39.19
Madhya Pradesh	34.23	44.20	48.42	58.42	19.00	28.85

Source : Census of India, 1991.

Table 1.4 depicts employment scenario of males and females in the organised and unorganised sectors during 1971 to 1991. It suggests that the proportion of employment in the organised sector for males has declined from 10.43 per cent in 1971 to 10.23 per cent in 1991. As regards females, the decline in the proportion of employment in the organised sector is more, i.e. from 6 per cent in 1971 to 4 per cent in 1991. Men share 86 per cent of the employment

Table 1.4 : Employment in the Organised and Unorganised Sectors during 1971 to 1991 in (100,000s)

Year	Male			Female			Total		
	Organised sector	Unorganised sector	Total sector	Organised sector	Unorganised sector	Total sector	Organised sector	Unorganised sector	Total sector
1971	155.60	1336.16	1491.76	19.30	294.15	313.45	174.90	1630.21	1805.10
	(10.43)	(89.57)		(6.16)	(93.84)	(17.36)	(9.69)	(90.31)	
1981	200.86	1625.75	1826.61	27.93	427.59	455.52	228.79	2053.34	2282.13
	(11.0)	(89.0)		(6.13)	(93.87)	(19.96)	(10.03)	(89.97)	
1991	229.53	2014.11	2243.64	37.81	859.86	897.67	267.34	2873.87	3141.31
	(10.23)	(89.77)		(4.21)	(95.79)	(28.58)	(8.51)	(91.49)	

Note: Figures in parentheses are percentages with respect to totals.
Source: Gopalan, 1995.

in the organised sector as compared to only 14 per cent of women.

The more significant is the fact that there is a rapid increase in entry of women in employment market in the last decade.

According to the Social Indicators of Development compiled by the World Bank (1994), there are only 25 females in the labour force for every 100 males (age 15 to 64) in India as against a ratio of 38 females for 100 males in the developed countries. In India, the actual labour force is only 56.5 per cent of economically active population. About 78 per cent of the males in this group are in labour force as against only 33.3 per cent of the females. The low proportion of women in the work force is partly due to the fact that lesser number of women seek employment, and partly owing to'the fact that a lot of work done by women is not counted as work in the national statistics.

Maternal Employment In india

In recent years, owing to the spread of education, search for new identity and introduction of technological changes, increasingly larger number of women from the middle and upper-middle classes in India are entering the job-market. Today, they are successfully employed in the different fields of life.

The growing number of educated working women was initially for purely economic necessity to supplement the family income. However, in present scenario, the important factors contributing to women's employment are as follows :

1. Due to latest technologies in household equipments, the time required to carry out household operations has significantly decreased. Therefore, women can spare time from the traditional tedious household chores. Also, this is the time of fastfood and people prefer to have quick food than wasting their time in routine cooking.
2. There is decrement in the number of children and family size. Now educated people do not want more than two children and sometimes even one child. Due to diversified job opportunity for men, they are leaving their parents and living in separate or far away places. Therefore, the usual family size in big and metropolitan cities is not more than 4 members.
3. Previously, women used to work to meet the financial needs of the family, but nowadays due to spread of education, women are also well qualified and want to work because of the greater need for achievement, personal worth, self-esteem and self-image. In addition to these, other attributes associated with women's employment, such as, status aspirations, realization of potential, desire to contribute to social development, high level of energy, achievement orientation towards life and need for social contact also affect their motivation to opt for a job outside the home.
4. The marriages of girls are being delayed. Unlike old days, girls usually do professional courses or post-graduation in any subject. They prefer that before getting married they should be financially independent. Boys also prefer those matches who are already employed. Because girls are employed at the time of marriage, therefore, unless it is very necessary they do not leave their job. Sometimes they try another job at husband's place of posting.

5. Every person wants to live a comfortable and luxurious life, and to have all facilities and entertainment equipments. Added to it is the education of children. These factors also contribute to an increase in the number of more women working outside the home.

6. Last, but not the least, is the ideology of feminism which deplores the economic dependence of women and supports the emergence of individual woman as a strong, independent and free person who may develop herself and realize potential to maximum degree.

In a traditional culture like India, well differentiated gender roles largely determine the division of labour between males and females in the family context. The domestic tasks, household production and child care activities are considered as chief and essential duties of women. In addition, they are often engaged in economic activities that are either home-based or outside the home. However, there are noticeable social class differences in the reasons for and functions of women's employment. While women of the middle and upper strata of society seek employment either for their own sake or for the independence and status it lends, women among the weaker sections of society do so to supplement their family income. With gradual socio-economic transformation and progress taking place in India, education and employment have acquired greater significance for the woman in the enactment of her role as home maker and as an individual participating in diverse social, civic and cultural activities.

Maternal Employment and Child Development : The Changing Scenario

In the context of child development, a mother happens to be the central figure in the child's home environment. She plays a variety of roles at home. Alongwith performing routine activities, she is a model to her daughter and, as Freud noted, is the first love object of the opposite sex to her son. For married working women, the public sphere of work and private sphere of home and family seldom exist as separate and distinct as they are for men. While women and men both have responsibilities in both the spheres, men can usually divide their time and commitment, devoting each week day to their work, and evenings and weekends to their families. In contrast, for women, the areas of responsibility and expectations considerably overlap and can hardly be compartmentalized, particularly when there are children in the family. In the large majority of cases, child care is mainly women's responsibility which women themselves acknowledge, accept and enjoy as the most important aspect of their family role.

The entry of the increasing number of women to the job market is creating changes in the family ecology which has important implications for social and personality development of children. In the recent past, mothers were expected to remain at home to take care of their children, particularly during their early years of development. Many felt that this was the only way a mother could love and properly rear her children during this important phase of life. Today, however, the scene is changing. An increasing number of women have started to work outside the home which has changed the traditional style of house keeping, mothering and child care. Employment of women outside the home has become a fact of modern life. Moreover, there is growing acceptance of the view that a woman can handle the diverse roles and responsibilities of a working woman and mother simultaneously.

It is a general view in the middle class people that when married women are engaged in employment outside the home it brings marital disharmony which, in turn, influences the health and development of their children adversely. It is also held that when the mother is working, children are neglected and not properly looked after. They do not enjoy many facilities which the children of non-working mothers do. They have to sacrifice many things and have to share the burden of household work to help the mother. It is observed that when the mother is working, home duties are not efficiently performed. There are fewer opportunities for mother-child closeness, social life and recreation. Children of these mothers are often found nervous and show difficulty in concentration. It is opined that although school-going children need less child care, they do need love, guidance and a boost in confidence as well as a secure home-base. On the other hand, they also need independence to cope on their own, an opportunity to develop a sense of responsibility and a feeling of competence. When children enter school, the problem of child care decreases considerably. Now the important socialization experiences include more people as peers, teachers and other adults in the community.

EMPIRICAL STUDIES: AN OVERVIEW

Empirical evidence does not show the necessity of full-time presence of mothers at home. Mothering does not have an infinitely positive relationship to the child's mental health. Research findings in this regard indicate that maternal employment *per se* has little effect on child's growth and development. However, maternal employment has obvious repercussions on socialisation and rearing of children, though carefully planned studies in this area are very few. Many feel that in the midst of busy work schedules, conscientious working mothers skilfully do manage to give children love, care and nurturance needed for their growth and development of personality and realization of potentials (Hoffman, 1989).

It is contemplated that educated non-working mother may over-invest in her children bringing an excess of worry and disproportionate encouragement of independence. Non-working mothers are almost at home whole day and available to the child, therefore, sometimes whether children need or not they tend to provide more care. Children may or may not handle it profitably. There is not even compelling evidence that the working mothers spend less time in direct interaction with their children than non-working mothers (Birnbaum, 1975). Maternal employment not only has positive effects on the economic plane, but it may foster healthier psychological development by offering the child a chance to explore a wider world, to relate to other adults, to socialize with peers at an early age and to do more things for himself/herself with less supervision, interference or restrictions (Litovsky, 1986; Schachter, 1981; and Zimmerman & Bernstein, 1983).

Whether a mother's job has benign or harmful influence on child's socialisation depends on the interaction of several factors, such as the nature of substitute or supplementary child care available, social class, nature of mother's work (i.e., sporadically or steadily working), mother's feelings about her job and father's involvement with children. The attitudes of both parents towards dual work status and mother's satisfaction with her work modifies the effects of maternal employment on their children. If a working mother obtains personal satisfaction from employment ; if she does not experience excessive guilt about being away from her children; and if she has adequate household arrangements to prevent her from being stressed by the dual role demands, she is likely to perform similar to or better than the non-working mother. It is agreed that the influence of father, his role, mother's satisfaction, the nature and quality of social support system, parent-child interaction, features of the employment situation and family characteristics are, but, a few variables mediating the influence of maternal employment on children's development.

Several studies in this field have found that there exists as much variability among children of working mothers (WMs) as in children of non-working mothers (NWMs). It has been further suggested that a more profitable approach might be to study the psychological conditions within the family, not only when the parents are at work, but also when they are at home. Although detrimental influence of women's employment on the socialization of the growing child is often hinted at, maternal employment *per se* has little influence and the factors like family circumstances may be more crucial than actual employment status (Eiduson, Cohen & Alexander, 1973). The work status *per se* is not significantly related to maternal attitudes and care-giving behaviours, infant development level, or quality of the mother-infant relationship (Hock, 1980). Mothers who choose to work (or not to work) but live in relatively supportive families apparently do not harm their children by their employment situation (Hoffman, 1984). The amount of time mothers spent with their children and, to some extent, child-rearing attitudes and behaviours of parents are more crucial than the maternal employment status (Easterbrooks & Goldberg, 1985). However, no clear-cut relationship between maternal employment status and child and adolescent development was found (Litovsky & Dusek, 1988; Scarr, Phillips & McCartney, 1989). In a study by Vandell and Ramanan (1992), the effects of early maternal employment (employment during child's first 3 years of life) and recent maternal employment (employment during previous 3 years) on second grade children from low income families was studied. In comparison to mothers who were not employed, the employed mothers had higher mental aptitude and level of education. Both early and recent employment were also associated with the measures of current family functioning. As expected, there was less poverty and more enriched home environment when mothers were employed.

Alternate Arrangements

With the mother being employed, the child has to be put in the care of other people (e.g. neighbours, relatives, maid-servant, creche or some other institutional arrangement). As a result, parental role and involvement in child-rearing and socialization is much less. The effect of this kind of 'limited' parental role has been thoroughly investigated. It is, however, expected that such an early separation of the child from the parents is likely to foster greater individuation, independence and development of autonomous functioning and hinder the inculcation of traditional family and cultural norms.

With regard to the relationship between non-maternal (substitute) child-care and child development, it is generally believed that for the healthy development of a child, maternal care is necessary. However, many studies in this respect have yielded mixed results. It was found that the quality of mother-child interaction and care-taking arrangement was a significant determinant in the adjustment pattern of the children (Hoffman, 1974), and that satisfaction with the substitute child care was positively related with maternal employment but not with the quality of mother-child interaction (Harrell & Ridley, 1975). In mother's absence due to employment status, supervision by some substitute arrangement is necessary. The detrimental effect of mother's absence was significant for older girls who stayed alone after school than the younger children who were supervised by someone at home after returning from school (Trimberger & Mac Clean, 1982). The relation between maternal absence due to employment and quality of infant-mother attachment was found significant in case of first born children of full-time working mothers, and maternal employment negatively affected cognitive and behavioural development of children during first year of life regardless of their gender or economic status. As regards cognitive growth and development of children particularly for girls, grandmother's care was found more beneficial (Barglow & Molitor, 1987; Baydar & Gunn, 1991). Surrogate parenting at an early age may have bearing on the child's personality, because multiple parenting with different rules may confuse and disorient a child. Sometimes the parent in a hurry may break or bend rules which she herself has set earlier. Some children may read it as a signal to bully and blackmail and get their way. The child learns to take advantage of the inconsistency of parenting rules.

Maternal Role Satisfaction

Parental satisfaction with mother's role and with their marriage may prove to be more influential in determining children's perception than maternal employment itself. Insecure attachment among infants of employed mothers seems to be linked with mothers' attitudes, values, and circumstances (Lamb, 1982). On the other hand, children from satisfied middle-class families may not perceive mothers' absence as deprivation and that parents from such families relate to their children in the same basic pattern regardless of mothers' work status (Hamilton, 1982). It is generally contended that a child is probably better off with a working mother who is satisfied than a dissatisfied mother who is at home and works throughout the day and night (Scarr & Hall, 1984). It is agreed that mother's role satisfaction has more of an impact on infant and child development than does work status *per se* and that the influence of maternal role satisfaction is largely through the quality of the parent-child relationship (Lerner & Galambos, 1986).

It is believed that when mother works because she enjoys her occupation or in order to help out the family finances, there is less familial disruption than when maternal employment is motivated by a desire to escape from family responsibilities and from contact with her children. Unemployed mothers (UEMs) who have a sense of satisfaction and competence in their home making role, and employed mothers (EMs) who enjoy their employment, both show strong positive relation with their children than do unhappy full-time housewives who would like to be employed (Hartley, 1966; Hoffman, 1961a; Scott, Yarrow & Heining, 1962).

Mother's role satisfaction has been linked to daughter's career aspirations. Female college students have lower aspirations if their mothers were satisfied in a non-employed role (Parsons, Frieze & Ruble, 1978). It was consistently found that young women who perceived that their mothers were dissatisfied with a non-employed role had stronger career orientation. However, it was also found that dissatisfaction with a career role also led to stronger career orientation in their daughters. Mother's occupational prestige has been shown not to have an egalitarian effect on daughters (Thorton, Duana & Camburn, 1983). Johnson (1996) found that girls whose mothers spent more time in full-time employment expect to return more quickly to employment following child bearing as compared to those girls whose mothers spent more time in part-time employment. However, these influences were not observed for sons. Herzog and Bachman (1982) found little or no effect of maternal employment on a wide variety of gender role attitudes and plans for the future, with respect to family education and occupation, except that maternal employment was strongly related to approval of maternal employment and attitudes about its effects on children. It seems that daughters of employed mothers do not feel they were denied an appropriate mother role; they plan to do likewise in their own families.

Maternal Employment and Sex-role Stereotypes

Development of gender stereotypes among children is the direct result of social learning process. Children imbibe appropriate gender appropriate behaviours through observation of role models. Social rewards and punishment mechanism further reinforce this learning among children. In dual-earning families, the traditional sex-role stereotypes are weak. Generally, when mother is employed, there is more sharing of household responsibilities and child-rearing activities. Father is also equally involved in all the activities at home, and so are the children. In case of daughters of EMs, maternal employment is associated with fewer traditional feminine interests and characteristics. It was also observed that adolescent daughters of working mothers have tendency to admire and respect their mothers than do their counterparts of UEMs (Douvan & Adelson, 1966; Stein, 1973). It is contended that maternal employment not only presents different role models to the child with both parents working and sharing roles, thereby making sex-role stereotypes fade gradually (Zimmerman & Bernstein, 1983), but adolescent children specially like to support women's employment and daughters are usually expected to work outside the home when they get older (Scarr & Hall, 1984). Children of EMs rejected traditional sex-role attitudes to a greater extent (Morgan & Grube, 1987). When both parents work outside the home, the role of the mother may be perceived similar to the role of the father, not only because the mother works but also because the father participates more actively in the family and child-rearing tasks, often regarded as part of the maternal role (Pleck, 1984).

The increasing rate of maternal employment in the last few decades has led to much interest in the effect of maternal employment on children's orientation towards their future familial and employed lives (Bielby, 1978; Keith, 1988; Willetts-Bloom & Steven, 1994). By providing non-traditional female role model with less traditional gender role attitude, it is thought that employed mothers encourage their children to have more egalitarian gender role attitudes and future-expectations. Several studies have found that daughters of employed mothers have more egalitarian gender role attitudes than daughters of non-employed mothers (Thornton, Duana & Camburn, 1983). Maternal employment status has been found to influence daughters' approval of women's and mothers'employment, beliefs regarding women's suitability for politics, and rejection of women's confinement to the sphere of the family (Herzog & Bachman, 1982; Ransford & Miller, 1983). An investigation by Nelson and Keith (1990) revealed significant effect of mother's employment upon development of sex role attitude of adolescents. Dani (1995) in a study, observed that while co-education definitely helps to reduce female stereotypes, mother's employment *per se* does not seem to have much influence on such stereotypes.

Maternal Employment and Home Environment

Children's attitudes towards their working mothers are influenced by their perception of mothers' feelings about employment. It is concluded that daughters of non-working mothers had a close relationship with their fathers, perceived them as happier and more friendly, and experienced less anger and tension in the home environment. It is suggested that non-employment of mothers coincides with less perceived anger, stress and tension between parents (Jenson & Borges, 1986). It is opined that the more hours a mother works, the less time she has to supervise her children. Once such parental perceptions are established, they affect the way parents treat the child. Thus, they could have indirect influence on children's behaviour. Problems have appeared in the case of boys. Fathers reported more problems with their son's behaviour in schools if the mother was working. They rarely described their sons as cooperative or ambitious. Sons of middle class working mothers are generally described as confident. However, among children of employed mothers, relations between fathers and sons seemed strained and boys respected their fathers less.

The preceding review of studies shows that the interaction between the child and parents affects and shapes the growth of personality of children in important ways. The child-parent relationship, however, varies with a number of social, personal and environmental variables. The studies evince social class differences in the quality of parental treatment of children. Also, there is growing evidence that child's behaviour also influences parental behaviour indicating reciprocal relationship between the two. As a part of social change in the Indian context, maternal employment is assuming a decisive role in managing the family affairs. It not only leads to rearrangement of the sequential and temporal organization of family activities but also changes the attitudes and modifies maternal role performance. It was expected that the manner of disciplining and expectations from children would vary with maternal employment. Finally, maternal employment was expected to influence various aspects of child's personality.

RESEARCH QUESTIONS

The available studies indicate that parental perception of children's behaviour, their attitudes and expectations, differ in relation to their employment status. In addition, the impact of maternal employment is found to vary with the developmental stages of children. It has been noted in several studies that substitute arrangement for primary care may prove to be quite effective at the younger age level. The older children, however, show many negative effects if adequate parental interaction is disturbed or disrupted. In fact, as children grow, their expectation and attitudes towards parents also undergo important changes. Against this background, it was proposed to investigate some of the important consequences of maternal employment for certain aspects of personality development of children. It was contended that maternal employment would have diverse influences on family environment, marital relationship, personality and socio-emotional aspects of child behaviour. Maternal employment influences family environment on account of rearrangement and adjustment to accommodate the job demands. Its effect on marital relationship and adjustment is also partly due to the role conflicts and tensions emerging out of employment. If it is felt that the primary duties of housewife and mother are not performed adequately, it might lead to guilt feeling on the part of mother and cause conflicts between wife and husband and yield disharmony in the family.

Thus, taking a lead from past research, the present study intended to examine certain aspects of personality development in relation to maternal employment. However, the study was organized to incorporate macro as well as micro level antecedent variables.

Thus, it was asserted that maternal employment will influence the pattern of child-rearing which, in turn, influences the personality of children. In addition, it was also contended that maternal employment will influence marital relationship of parents which also influences the personality of children. Thus, the differences in children's personality characteristics need to be examined in relation to maternal employment (global variable) as well as child rearing, specifically disciplining techniques (proximal antecedent variable). This would also include an analysis of the similarities and differences in the use of disciplinary practices across the employed and unemployed groups of mothers. To be precise, the research questions addressed in this study were as follows.

1. What is the relationship between maternal employment and personality characteristics, psychological differentiation and self-concept of children? Is this relationship invariant across boys and girls?
2. What is the relationship between different background variables and disciplinary practices used by mothers and personality characteristics and psychological differentiation of children? Are these relationships similar for boys and girls and for different age groups?
3. What are the differences and similarities in the use of different disciplinary practices by employed and unemployed mothers?
4. What is the degree of congruence in the use of disciplinary techniques by mothers and perception of these techniques by children?
5. What is the level of marital adjustment in the employed as well as unemployed groups of mothers and how marital relationship is related to the personality development of children?

6. What is the impact of job on various aspects of family functioning in the group of employed mothers?

The Context of Inquiry

The present study was framed within the ecological perspective on development. According to Bronfenbrenner (1977), ecology provides a useful framework for understanding various aspects of human development. It is related to the contextual mechanisms which influence development, make our research efforts more realistic and help in suggesting some intervention strategies. Sinha (1982) has extended this framework to Indian setting. According to him, the enduring environment of the child or his ecology may be conceived in terms of two concentric layers. The "upper" and the more visible layer contains the home, school, peer groups and so on, each providing three dimensions, namely, physical space and material, social roles and relationship of the child *vis-a-vis* other people and the activities of the child. The "supporting" or the "surrounding" layer embedding the former is provided by the geographic and physical environment and the institutional setting of the child in terms of his social class, caste and the general services and amenities available to him (p.27). The home and its conditions

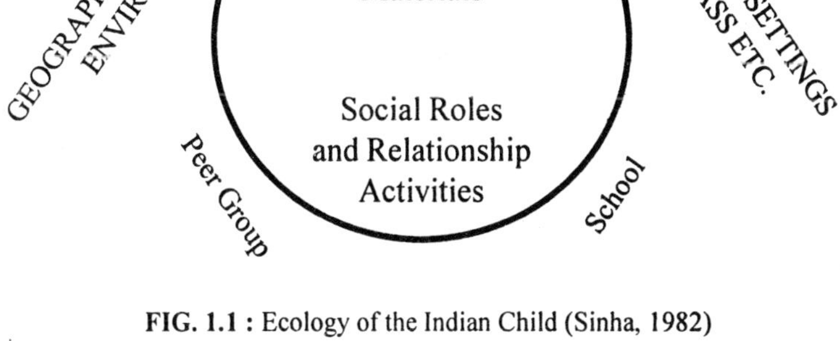

FIG. 1.1 : Ecology of the Indian Child (Sinha, 1982)

i.e., space available to each member of the family, toys, pictorial and cultural artifacts at home, technological devices used for general living constitute the most important visible 'upper layer' influencing the child. According to Sinha (1982), the ecology of child development may be represented in terms of the diagram shown in Fig. 1.1

At home as well as in the school, the nature of interpersonal relationships and activities that are encouraged or inhibited would constitute another kind of influence emanating from the family and the school. The third factor constituting the other visible layer is the nature of interactions and activities prevalent in his/her peer groups right from his/her childhood onward. It may be noted that the visible and the surrounding layer factors often combine and interact with one another and shape not only the economic pursuits and way of life, but also, the socialization processes and interpersonal relationships and the general cognitive and perceptual functioning of the individual. Any difference in one or in combination with others, influences the cognitive and perceptual competence of a child as well as affect his/her motivation, style of coping with problems and the general personality development.

Against this background, the present study was conceived with the assumption that employment status of mothers influences the family environment, relationship between parents, interaction of parents with the child and the techniques used by parents for disciplining the child. These variables ultimately affect the personality development of the child. Thus, employment status of mothers (employed *vs.* unemployed) was used as a broader contextual variable influencing the interaction among the family members as well as parental treatment of children which in turn contributes to the patterning of personality in children. Thus, employment status of mothers influences the development of personality in both direct and indirect ways.

In the present study, maternal employment status was explored by having two levels i.e. employed mothers and full-time housewives. In reference to employment, three types of jobs were included, i.e. clerical, teaching and nursing. This was done to cover a broader range of variation in the type of employment, as different types of jobs require different amount and types of responsibility, carry diverse kinds of workload and lead to differential perception by others.

Sample

A large sample of 200 children and their mothers was drawn from middle class socio-economic background from Bhopal city in Central India. To select the sample the schools (government and private) were contacted. A brief questionnaire about name, age, gender of the child, parents' educational and occupational status, number of siblings, type of family, and family income was prepared and information was collected. On the basis of the predetermined criteria, only those participants (mothers and children) were included in the sample who fulfilled the criteria.

Description of Mother's Sample : On the basis of employment status of mothers, the sample of 200 mothers was broadly divided into two levels, viz. employed mothers (EMs) and unemployed mothers (UEMs). Out of the total sample, 120 mothers were employed outside the home and 80 were full-time mothers. As it was not possible to secure a classified list of all educated employed and unemployed mothers, certain characteristics and conditions were laid down in drawing the sample. Thus, a woman (employed or unemployed) in order to be included in the sample, was required to satisfy the following criteria:

(i) Should have more than one child, of whom atleast one should be between 7 to 12 years age level;

(ii) Should not be a widow, divorcee or separated;

(iii) Should have the monthly family income between Rs. 5000 to Rs. 8000;

(iv) Should belong to a nuclear family; and

(v) Employed mother should have been in service for not less than 5 years.

Table 1.5 presents a summary of different aspects of family background. Mothers' age ranged between 26 to 45 years. In general, the age of EMs was greater (M=36.35, SD=3.91) than the age of UEMs (M=34.40, SD=3.61). The modal age of UEMs and EMs was 35 years. Regarding educational qualifications of mothers, 15 per cent of UEMs and 38 per cent of EMs had education up to matriculation level. About 45 per cent of UEMs and 24 per cent of EMs were graduates, and 40 per cent of UEMs and 38 per cent of EMs were holding a post-graduate degree.

With regard to fathers' educational level and type of occupation it was found that in UEMs' group, 3 per cent fathers and in EMs' group, 23 per cent of fathers had education up to matriculation level. About 17 per cent of fathers in UEMs'group and 32 per cent of fathers in EMs' group were graduates. 55 per cent of fathers in UEMs'group and 32 per cent of fathers in EMs' group were holding post-graduate degree. Professional degree was held by 25 per cent of fathers in UEMs' group in comparison to 12 per cent of fathers in EMs' group. Most of them were professionals employed in private sector (20% in UEMs', and 12% in EMs' group), government sector (38% in UEMs, and 57% in EMs'group) or in banks (37% in UEMs'and 18% in EMs'group). Only 5 per cent in UEMs'group and 4 per cent in EMs' group, fathers were entrepreneurs. In regard to religion, 90 per cent of families in UEMs' group and 71 per cent of families in EMs' group were Hindu. 10 per cent of families in UEMs' group were Sikhs whereas 24 per cent of families in EMs' group were Christians and 5 per cent were Muslims. Monthly family income in UEMs'group was lower (M= Rs. 6328, SD=1101) as compared to EMs'group (M=Rs. 6604, SD=1276).

In EMs' sample, three major occupational categories, namely clerks, teachers and nurses with 40 mothers in each group were selected. It was planned that the group of clerks should include only the clerical staff in public sector organizations or establishments. The teachers should include only those teaching in schools and the mothers in nursing profession should be employed in government hospitals and dispensaries. Thus, an effort was made to select a sample so comprehensive as to include women employed in diverse jobs and belonging to almost similar socio-economic status.

Description of Children's Sample : To elucidate the influence of maternal employment on personality development, children in age group 7 to 12 were included. Because of the other criteria in the selection of mothers' sample, it was not possible to keep equal

Table 1.5 : Main Characteristics of the Parents participating in the Sample

Variables	Unemployed Mothers (N=80)	Employed Mothers (N=120)
Mother's Age		
Mean	34.40	36.35
SD	3.61	3.91
Range (in years)	28 - 43	26 - 45
Mother's Education		
Matric	12(15)	46(38)
Graduate	36(45)	28(24)
Post-graduate and above	32(40)	46(38)
Father's Education		
Matric	2(3)	28(23)
Graduate	14(17)	40(33)
Post-graduate	94(55)	38(32)
Professional course	20(25)	14(12)
Father's Occupation		
Private Sector	16(20)	15(12)
Govt. Sector	30(38)	69(57)
Bank Service	30(37)	21(18)
Entrepreneurs	4(5)	5(4)
Religion		
Hindu	72(90)	85(71)
Muslim	0(0)	6(5)
Christian	0(0)	29(24)
Sikh	8(10)	0(0)
Monthly Family Income (in Rs.)		
Mean	6328	6604
SD	1101	1276
Range	3000 to 8000	3000 to 8000

Note : Figures in parantheses are percentages.

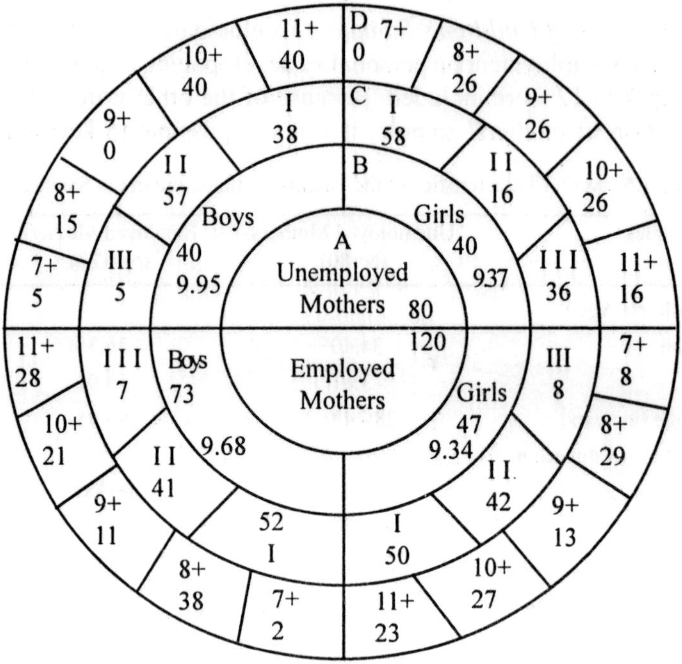

A Employed Status of Mothers
B Gender and Age
C Percentage of Children according to their ordinal position
D Percentage of Children in Age Group.

FIG. 1.2 : Sample Distribution : Children

number of boys and girls and match their ordinal position and the number in the families of both UEMs and EMs. However, age of children was the main criterion. Table 1.6 and Fig. 1.2 report the main characteristics of children's sample.

The sample of children (N=200) aged between 7 to 12 years in UEMs (M= 9.68, SD=1.15) and in EMs (M=9.28, SD= 1.61). They were enrolled in various private or government schools located in Bhopal city. Mean age for boys and girls in UEMs' group was 9.95 (SD = 1.17) and 9.37 (SD = 1.04) years, respectively. In EMs' group, the mean age of boys and girls was 9.16 (SD = 1.78) and 9.34 (SD= 1.29) years, respectively. Regarding ordinal position, 38 per cent of boys and 58 per cent of girls in UEMs' group were first born as compared to 52 per cent of boys and 50 per cent of girls in the group of EMs. 57 per cent of boys and 16 per cent of girls in the group of UEMs and 41 per cent boys and 43 per cent of girls in the group of EMs were holding second ordinal position. Rest of them were last born. (Fig. 1.2)

Table 1.6 : School related Features of Children

Variables	Unemployed Mothers			Employed Mothers		
	Boys (N=40) f (%)	Girls (N=40) f (%)	Total (N=80) f(%)	Boys (N=73) f (%)	Girls (N=47) f (%)	Total (N=120) f (%)
Grades						
II	2(5)	4(10)	6(8)	12(17)	8(17)	20(17)
III	6(14)	4(10)	10(12)	17(23)	13(28)	30(25)
IV	6(14)	14(35)	20(25)	14(19)	7(15)	21(17)
V	6(14)	6(15)	12(15)	16(22)	3(6)	19(16)
VI	12(33)	6(15)	18(23)	11(15)	13(28)	24(20)
VII	8(16)	6(15)	14(17)	3(4)	3(6)	6(5)
School Timings						
Morning shift	26(67)	10(26)	36(45)	62(85)	36(77)	98(81)
Day shift	4(9)	6(10)	10(12)	2(3)	0(0)	2(2)
Morning to Evening shift	10(24)	24(63)	34(43)	9(12)	11(23)	20(17)

Note: Figures in parentheses indicate percentages.

Information collected on the basis of the Background Information Schedule is presented in Table 1.7. It suggests that about 60 per cent of unemployed mothers had a part-time servant whereas about 50 per cent of employed mothers did not have any help in performing household chores. Almost equal number of employed and unemployed mothers reported that they live in multi-storied buildings. Regarding availability of physical space for children at home, about 62 per cent of employed mothers reported 'average space' available for studying, playing and living, whereas 32 per cent of unemployed mothers reported 'more than sufficient' space available. Entertainment facilities like books, games etc. available at home, were equally reported by both the groups. Availability of T.V. was reported by all mothers in both the groups except 3 per cent in employed mothers' group. Availability of V.C.R. was reported by more mothers in unemployed group. Relationship of these background variables with children's personality was investigated.

Table 1.7: Facilities Available to the Child at Home

Physical Facilities	Unemployed Mothers (N = 80) f (%)	Employed Mothers (N=1 20) f(%)
Help in Household		
No Servant	20 (25)	55 (46)
Part time	48 (60)	60 (50)
Full time	12 (15)	5 (4)
Type of House		
Independent	22 (28)	39 (32)
Multi-storied	44 (55)	63 (53)
Block type	14 (17)	18 (15)
Availability of Physical Space		
Average	12 (15)	74 (62)
Sufficient	42 (53)	36 (30)
More than sufficient	26 (32)	10 (8)
Entertainment Facilities		
Average	24 (30)	24 (30)
Sufficient	44 (55)	44 (55)
More than sufficient	12 (15)	12 (15)
Television		
Yes	80 (100)	117 (97)
No	0 (0)	3 (3)
V.C.R.		
Yes	36 (45)	24 (20)
No	44 (55)	96 (80)

Note: Figures in parentheses indicate percentages.

Measures

The following measures were used in the present study:

1. Background Information Schedule
2. Parental Disciplinary Practices Questionnaire
3. Semi-Projective Measure of Parental Practices
4. Marital Adjustment Inventory
5. Questionnaire for Working Mothers
6. Early School Personality Questionnaire (ESPQ)
7. Story-Pictorial Embedded Figure Test (SP-EFT)
8. Who Am I ? Test

The detailed description of the measures used to collect information is given in respective chapters.

Procedure : After obtaining the consent, the schedule with important demographic information was presented to all mothers individually. The instructions were read thoroughly and mothers were asked if they had any doubt. The mothers were requested to be candid and honest in answering questions and their anonymity was assured. It was also impressed upon them that there were no 'right' or 'wrong' answers. It was desirable that their answers should reflect true feelings and reactions with regard to particular issues. Each mother was assured that the information provided by her would be kept strictly confidential and would be used for no purpose other than that of research. After ascertaining family related data, mothers were asked about questions related to disciplining their child. They were asked to select the most suitable answer category, which they used most frequently while treating their children. After completing this questionnaire, another questionnaire (semi projective technique for parental practices) was presented. Marital Adjustment Inventory was also completed by all mothers. Employed mothers were asked to complete one more questionnaire regarding information about their family and job related aspects.

In case of children's sample, each child was contacted individually and rapport was established through a light conversation. First, the Early School Personality Questionnaire (ESPQ) was presented. Instructions were given and after making sure that children had followed the instructions, questionnaire was given individually. Then, the Story Pictorial Embedded Figure Test (SP-EFT) was also presented with proper instructions. Responses were recorded carefully. To know about "Who Am I ?", the children were asked to give as much information as they can about their identity, parents, siblings, friends, school, hobbies etc. Semi-projective technique for parental practices was presented to children also to get an idea about the perception of children regarding parental disciplinary techniques. All the participants were thanked for their cooperation.

2

CHILDREN'S PERSONALITY

Whenever and wherever we see children in spontaneous play in their homes, in nursery schools or on playgrounds, we are struck with the range of individual differences in behaviour, characteristics and motivation displayed by them. We find some children are very active, outgoing, independent, explorative, curious, aggressive and adventurous, others seem passive, dependent, shy and withdrawn. Each child manifests a unique personality, that is, an enduring organization or pattern of characteristic and ways of thinking, feeling, relating to others, and adapting to the environment, a pattern that is manifested in a wide variety of situations and settings. Child development comprises of both personality and social development. Development of a child depends on heredity and the context in which (s)he lives. A child does not grow in a vacuum, but (s)he is continuously influenced by the surroundings/environment. In the early stage, family influences his/her development, after that school and peer group come in the contact and child learns to cope with different situations. Child is not only responding to different stimuli/ forces exerting pressure upon him/her, but he/she is also influencing and manipulating the environment though he/she has to behave in a particular manner or according to the situation but sometimes he/ she creates the situation. The family, home, and other contexts are crucial for the child's personality and social development.

The acquisition and modification of children's personalities and social behaviours are regulated by many factors, including temperament, the values of the social class or ethnic group to which they belong, rewards and punishment in the home, interactions with peers and exposure to behaviour and standards through the mass media. Each culture, sub-culture or ethnic group has its own typical media. Each culture, sub-culture or ethnic group has its own typical personality–a particular set of valued motives, ideals and ways of interacting with people–which is characteristic of its members. Personality is a product of hereditary potentialities and environmental forces. The individuality of an individual emerges out and is crystallized by the cultural environment–the consistently operating psycho-cultural forces around the growing individual. The present study investigated the personality pattern of children of employed and unemployed mothers. It is generally opined that employment of mothers plays an important role in shaping of the personality of their children. It is a general view that working mothers are sharing household duties as well as working outside the home, they get little time and opportunity to interact with their children. They are not able to look after their children properly, and this adversely affects the personality development of their children. It may be other way also. As children of working mothers are separated from their mothers at a comparatively early age, they become more independent and several positive personality traits develop. With this in view, the dispositional, cognitive and reflective aspects of the personality were taken into account while studying the personality development of children of working and non-working mothers.

Personality : A Conceptual Analysis

In everyday speech, the word "personality" takes on any number of different meanings. In psychology too, it has been defined in many ways, depending on theoretical preferences and any definition of personality cannot be generally applied. In his seminal work, Allport (1937) defined 'personality' as "the dynamic organization within the individual of those psychophysical systems that determine his 'unique adjustment' to his environment". Eysenck (1959) viewed 'personality' as "the enduring organization of a person's character, temperament, intellect and physique which determines his unique adjustment to his environment". Similarly, behaviourists, humanists, and cognitive theorists have offered still other definitions of personality which emphasize different aspects of one's life and experience.

Forgus and Shulman (1979) have stated that different theories emphasize different aspects of personality which include (1) the underlying motives and strategy of human behaviours; (2) the organization of behaviour into an overall system; (3) the relationship of the parts of the system to the whole; (4) the process of selection by which a person chooses particular ways of perceiving, evaluating and responding to life situations; (5) the prediction of behaviour; and (6) maladaptive behaviour and how to remediate it.

Psychoanalytic thinking has been a major influence not only on personality theory but on many diverse areas, particularly on child-rearing. Freud believed that personality represents a compromise between the needs of an individual and the demands of the society. The id, the ego and the super ego constitute the building blocks of personality and represent the dynamic interaction of specific processes.

The psychoanalytic theory characterised personality development by five psycho-sexual stages: oral, anal, phallic, latency and genital. Similar to Freud, in some respect, the foundation of Jung's personality theory is 'psyche' which consists of the ego, the personal unconscious and the collective unconscious. Jung distinguishes stages of development according to values. In childhood, 'survival' values are the uppermost, while the adolescent lays greater stress on 'sexual' and 'self-assertive' values. Adult values become more culturally oriented, less impulsive and more 'introspective'. The older adults put emphasis on the 'spiritual' values. Adler's 'individual psychology' is much more concerned with the uniqueness of the individual. Erich Fromm believes that personality development represents interaction between the individual and his or her cultural context.

Freud emphasised childhood experiences, whereas Jung examined the powerful effects of human social history on the individual. Jung argued that the collective experience of the human race resides in the unconscious of every individual. Adler, like Jung, rejected Freud's emphasis on sexuality and argued that consciousness was at the centre of personality development. Adler viewed social rather than biological forces crucial in the process of personality development. Erich Fromm worked on the relationship between culture and personality, recognizing fully both the positive and negative aspects of culture. The constant interplay between the individual as a creator of society and the society as source of nourishment for the individual were considered significant. Erickson (1968) modified Freud's theory by incorporating the importance of culture and social history. He described personality development in eight stages : (1) Early Infancy, (2) Later infancy, (3) Pre-school, (4) School, (5) Adolescence, (6) Young Adult, (7) Middle Adult, and (8) Maturity. Erickson's theory permits to compare cultures and social situation to a greater extent than Freud's theory.

Following behaviouristic approach, Dollard and Miller (1950) emphasized learning as a major psychological process shaping the development of personality. Bandura (1962) working with children stressed the role of models and imitation in the learning. Human beings often model their behaviour after another person, they act like other human beings, and learn how to do this by observing others of their kind. This kind of learning has been called 'modelling' or 'imitation' or 'observation'. Observations may be direct or indirect–through books, films and television. The behaviour of individuals in interaction may be analyzed in terms of three systems: the personality system, the social system and the cultural system. Analysis in terms of personality considers properties of individuals such as attitudes, traits, feelings, habits, needs and motives, as well as the way in which the individual conceives of himself/herself and the world around him/her. Such analysis emphasizes the differences between one individual and another and attempts to identify the distinguishing characteristics of a person, whether they be attitudes, motives, habits or whatever. Cognitive social learning theorists emphasize the interaction of the individual and his or her environment as well as expectancy and self-control. Thus, Rotter (1954) believed that the study of personality should focus on the interaction between the individual and his environment. He argues that in order to predict behaviour, one must know a person's expectations and values (s)he puts on the available reinforcement. The source of reinforcement is an element of particular interest in the learning and acquisition of social cognition.

Existential/phenomenological theories explain personality in terms of the importance of person's consciousness, freedom to think, feel and act, and the necessity of the values for meaningful human life. Kelly's (1955) theory emphasized individual personal constructs through which reality is approached and understood. Rogers believed in self-actualization which is the basic motive for living, learning and growing. Rogers (1964) contended that people organize their experiences around a stable feature self-concept. Maslow (1968) suggested that personality is an individual's unique expression of his/her needs. The personality strives for health and maturity, through attention to increasing abstract needs and development of values.

Aspects of Personality Chosen for the Present Study

Although personality is one of the central concepts in psychology, it has proved to be one of the most difficult concepts to define. As indicated earlier, the difficulty is largely due to the variation in the underlying theoretical perspectives involved in the diverse construals of personality. In fact, different theories of personality are rooted in different metaphors and bring into focus diverse and often incompatible aspects of personality. It seems that personality is a multifaceted construct and no one approach is better or more comprehensive than the other. In the context of this diversity, it was decided to focus on three important features of personality, namely, dispositional, cognitive and reflective. The dispositional aspect emphasizes the characteristics of traits which are supposed to provide a description of the core of personality structure. The cognitive aspect as noted in psychological differentiation essentially represents the interactive aspects of personality or the way people respond to the environment. Finally, the reflective aspect refers to the self-concept. Human beings construct their self-concept and represent it, which becomes part of the personality and influences the functioning of the individual. These three aspects of personality are briefly described below.

Dispositional Aspect of Personality : Traits

Traits are generalized habits, combination of two or more habits. They are organized and recur in consistent and recognizable forms. Many kinds of traits compose an individual. Two general classes of traits are, 'unique traits' which occur in only one person and 'universal or common traits' which appear in the behaviour of many persons. Common traits are shared within a culture. These traits enable common cultural identity, sharing of values and beliefs, and eventually contribute to the similarity among persons of the same culture. Common traits help us to make comparisons among people. Traits are motives or needs, the prime movers of personality, and responsible for behaviour.

Trait psychologists have been more precise about categorizing people on the basis of empirically derived traits. Lamberth, Rappaport and Rappaport (1978) define trait as a 'relatively enduring personality characteristic that has a generalized effect on behaviour in diverse settings'. A trait should have three basic qualities: (1) It should be rather long lasting, (2) It should affect the behaviour of the individual, and (3) It should affect the behaviour in diverse situations. Traits are generally thought of as dispositions to act in certain ways rather than as characteristic that always cause a person to behave in a particular way.

For Cattell (1976) the basic unit of the study of personality is the trait. A trait is a "mental structure," that is inferred from behaviour. A mental structure is a fundamental concept and accounts for behavioural regularity or consistency. According to Cattell, the principal factors that emerge (through repeated measurements) are called 'source traits' of personality because they operate as underlying sources of the observed behaviours. Source traits are basically independent of each other, and thus 'orthogonal factors'. Factors that are not independent of each other, i.e. 'oblique factors' can also be identified. These factors seem to go together because of the overlap of several influences, referred to as "surface traits". Surface traits are clusters of trait elements that appear to hang together; whereas source traits are the underlying mental structure that determine these surface manifestations.

Cattell considers source traits more important than surface traits. Surface traits are produced by the interaction of source traits and generally can be expected to be less stable than factors. According to Cattell, identification of 'source traits' is more important in understanding personality development. These traits can further be broken down into 'environmental mould traits' (those that emphasize environmental conditions) and 'constitutional traits' (those that emphasize constitutional factors). Cattell, as a strong trait theorist, recognizes that both environmental and constitutional factors influence personality.

Cattell contemplates that any trait may represent the outcome of the operations of environmental factors, hereditary factors, or some mixture of the two. He further suggests that surface traits must represent the outcome of both environmental as well as hereditary factors. Source traits may be divided into those that reflect hereditary or constitutional factors and those derived from environmental factors. Cattell has avoided the use of term 'innate' as it is known that the source is physiological and within the organism, which will mean inborn only in a certain fraction of cases. He agrees that 'environmental-mould' traits spring from the moulding effects of social institutions and physical realities which constitute the cultural pattern. The traits may be general or specific. 'General traits' affect behaviour in a variety of situations. 'Specific traits' affect behaviour in more narrow, circumscribed situations. He identified 16 primary factors and developed tests to measure these traits.

In recent years there has been some reports which indicate weak effects of parental influence on personality of children. Such findings are not conclusive and difficult to interpret because they differ in methods used, age groups of children and environment of various confounding factors. Taken together they do not compel to rule out parental influence on children's personality.

Maternal Employment and Children's Personality : Empirical Studies

Several studies have been conducted to study the relationship between maternal employment and development of children's personality. It has been observed that full time mothering is not always beneficial for the personality development of children. Full time mother care during pre-school years may enhance intelligence in children but such children were also found conforming, fearful and inhibited in their adolescence (Moore, 1975). Mother's working status presents the child with a special situation which makes the child more competent and sensitive to mother's working (Owen & Landsdale, 1978). Children of working and non-working mothers did not show difference in the language development but intelligence level was significantly higher in the toddlers of non-working mothers. As regards social status, the children of working mothers, were more peer-oriented and self-sufficient while children of non-working mothers solicited more help and protection and were also more jealous. As compared to their counterparts, girls spoke to adults more often (Schachter, 1981). Children of working mothers showed greater sense of personal worth and belongingness and better interpersonal relations in the family and also at school (Gold & Andres, 1978b; Hoffman, 1974). On the other hand, no significant difference was observed between the children of working and non-working mothers on dependence, anxiety, psychosomatic symptoms or social behaviour (Hoffman, 1984; Morgan & Grube, 1987). If mothers do not feel guilty about leaving their children behind alone while at work, the employment status of mothers encourages self-sufficiency and independence in their children at an early age (Hock, 1978).

In Indian context, it was found that although the male children of working mothers are socially more participative than children of non-working mothers, they tend to be higher on nervousness (M.B. Prasad, & A.Prasad, 1975). It was also observed that the children of WMs were more independent, more adjusted and well-behaved (Juneja, 1979), and showed increasingly greater incidence of non-traditional sex role among daughters of highly educated and professional mothers (Dixit & Vishnoi, 1980; Ghadially & Kazi, 1979). In a study by Mehrotra and Anjula (1992), it was found that college students belonging to employed mothers were mostly characterized by worries, short temperament, fantasy, nervousness or over excitedness. On the other hand, students belonging to full-time mothers showed carelessness, too much dependence on others and moodiness. Development of behavioural problems in the children did not show any impact of maternal employment (Vanaja & Vankatramaiah, 1990). Children of working mothers showed better social and personality adjustment (Gold & Andres, 1978b; Hoffman, 1974). Similarly, high achievement and positive adjustment was observed in the girls of working mothers (Hoffman, 1974; Query & Kuruvilla, 1975; Rommer & Cherry, 1978; Smokler, 1975). Maternal employment has a positive effect on the adjustment of girls than boys. For boys, adjustment level is high when mothers are non-employed (Litovsky, 1986).

Children of double income groups (both parents working) are called *Latchkey kids* because when they come home they have to use the key around their necks to get into the deserted home. Such children feel lonely and have nobody to talk to about their day in school and at home. It was also reported that children of working mothers generally tend to mature faster, are smarter, more independent and learn to fend for themselves. But each child's reactions differ depending on child's temperament, age, gender, school, surrogate parent, father's role etc. (Chadha, 1997).

Psychologists say that generally children of working mothers do not face any emotional or behavioural problems. However, about 25-30 per cent are affected by such problems. In children in rural areas where women go out to work, such problems are not observed. They are better adjusted as compared to their urban counterparts, particularly those whose parents are professionals. It could be because younger children in rural areas are mostly staying with mothers or they have someone to look after them at home. Bhagat (1997) says that an obvious benefit of a double income household is a better life style, but there are more subtle benefits too. Children of working mothers become self-reliant and learn to deal with strangers and difficult situations on their own. They manage to solve their fights themselves and never feel the need to go to parents for every little thing. Some parents take the children into confidence, and discuss the situation with them. If children know that mother's job means additional resources to meet their growing needs, they accept the situation happily. A few, on the other hand, do not accept the fact and develop emotional and behavioural problems. It was also observed that children of working mothers mature at an early age as compared to the children of non-working mothers.

Cognitive Aspect of Personality : Psychological Differentiation

Psychological differentiation is rooted in the concept of cognitive style. A cognitive style represents another way of conceptualizing the hierarchical organization of personality. Cognitive style is considered as a perceptual pattern which contains valuable information about an individual's self-concept, world view, typical instrumental responses and ideals (Forgus & Shulman, 1979). According to Witkin, Oltman, Raskin and Karp (1971) cognitive style represents, "the characteristic, self-consistent modes of functioning which individuals show in their perceptual and intellectual activities. These cognitive styles are manifestations in the cognitive sphere of still broader dimensions of personal functioning which cut across diverse psychological areas. "

In their seminal work, Witkin, Dyk, Faterson, Goodenough and Karp (1962) reported that subjects differed markedly in their reliance on visual and bodily cues in the judgement of the vertical (upright) dimension. While visual cues were generally dominating, some subjects also used bodily cues as well. These more differentiated people were referred to as "field independent" and others as "field dependent". Other researchers have indicated that the freedom from a restricted perceptual set or modality is the part of a larger class of organization, i.e., the articulation or differentiation of the field. In general, the less restricted an individual is, the more articulated and differentiated will his/her perceptual discrimination be. Thus, independent individuals are more accurate and adaptive in their perception.

The field dependence-independence cognitive style has received greatest research attention over the years. First and foremost reason of its popularity is the theoretical framework of psychological differentiation. Furthermore, this approach to cognitive style is not content loaded; its structural properties extend to the broader areas of human behaviours and various subsets of the human population. Also, effective procedures for its assessment are available.

Witkin *et al.* (1962) used the concept of differentiation to identify the formal properties of a system. According to them, "degree of differentiation is an important characteristic of the structure of any system, whether psychological, biological or social. In a broader sense differentiation refers to the complexity of a system's structure. A less differential system is in a relatively homogeneous structural state, a more differentiated system in a relatively heterogeneous state" (p. 9).

The theory of psychological differentiation posits that differentiation system has a number of sub-systems to take care of different functions. A less differentiated system lacks such segregation of functions; it is in a homogeneous state. The degree of differentiation is indicated in three different domains; self-nonself segregation, field-independence segregation of psychological function and neuro-psychological functions (Berry, 1976).

Self-nonself segregation implies that differentiated individual distinguishes his own needs, goals and attributes from those of others. Field independence, thus, denotes a greater degree of autonomy from external referents, including social referents. Such a conceptualization of the construct of field-independence implies its subsidiary construct; restructuring skills and limited interpersonal competence. Witkin and Goodenough (1981) assert that field-independent individuals, because of their greater autonomy from external referents, demonstrate a wide variety of restructuring skills, but limited interpersonal skill because of their autonomy from external referents (Witkin & Goodenough, 1977). On the contrary, field-dependents show an interpersonal orientation and gravitate towards social structures.

Child Rearing Antecedents of Psychological Differentiation

Witkin (1976) has reported a number of developmental and dispositional correlates of this style. He found that democratic socialization methods were more likely to produce field-independence in children than autocratic methods. Democratic parents permit their children more freedom of choice and greater participation in decision making. Autocratic parents are more likely to command than to interact. Working on studies of child-rearing practices and attitudes of mothers, Dyk and Witkin (1965) and Witkin *et al.* (1971) found that mothers of field dependent boys encouraged continued connection with them. They emphasized conformity, discouraged aggressive behaviour and used severe training methods. Thus, they hypothesized that child-rearing practices which encourage separate and autonomous functioning foster the development of differentiation and a field independent cognitive style, while child-rearing practices emphasizing reliance on parental authority are likely to make for less differentiation and a more field-independent cognitive style.

The results of Berry (1966) and Dawson (1967) also confirm this trend; 'field dependent' boys were not allowed to set their own standards, were severely punished for aggressive and assertive behaviours, were punished according to their parents' whims and moods and were generally disciplined in an authoritarian manner. Greater parental involvement reinforces field dependence in their children (Dawson, 1967). Dyk (1969) reported that mothers of field dependent children used relatively non-specific modes of comforting their children. Parental strictness was associated with field dependence. The parents of field dependent children discouraged separation (Claeys & Deboeck, 1976; Edgerton, 1976) and strongly dominated family interactions as compared to parents of field independent children who shared power. Witkin *et al.* (1971) summarized general findings and noted that interactions between parents and child that encourage separation and autonomous functioning lead to field independence. However, autonomous functioning in the child is not always related to the child's level of field independence. Coats, Lord and Jakabovics (1975) found that children who tend to play in isolation were independent than those who were socially orientated in their play.

Gender Differences in Psychological Differentiation

Consistent sex differences have repeatedly been found in the field-dependence-independence dimension. Males tend to be more field-independent than females. In several cross cultural studies, small but consistent sex differences have been reported but it is also suggested that these differences may not be present before the age of eight or in geriatic samples. There are also some normative gender differences in differentiation. For instance, in Indian society, females are not only reinforced to be more dependent but also to be more conforming, that is, to take the cues for their behaviour from the environment rather than from themselves. This also accentuates field-dependence.

Psychological Differentiation and Family Structure

Family structure also influences psychological differentiation. In nuclear family, interaction between parents and with their children is also different from extended type of families. In a nuclear family, the child encounters only the close family members which may enhance strong and intense personal bonds with his/her parents. Active participation of parents and greater concentration and intensity of interaction between parents and children may contribute to a clear and distinct self-identity and functioning in an individualized way which constitutes a very important feature of psychological differentiation. Further, since there are not many family members in a nuclear family, the child is generally on his/her own, which makes him/her autonomous and independent. The atmosphere in a nuclear family is more permissive and the child is less severely disciplined and less harshly treated. Because of fewer family members, supervision is also less protective which also helps him/her to develop his/her self-identity and acquire an articulated body concept.

Studies indicate that in nuclear families, father's presence fosters field independence and greater differentiation (Busse, 1969; Dawson, 1967; Dreyer 1975). With an increase in the spectrum of father's role, the mother's role is limited only to child care which helps the child to separate from the mother. This leads to individualized development and autonomous functioning and contributes to greater differentiation. Witkin *et al.* (1974) have reported that nuclear family structure was associated with field independence. Ponnuswami (1977) tested two samples of Indian-American origin children and mothers, living in India, to find out whether mother-child interaction, as a socio-cultural variable influenced field dependence and independence as conceived by Witkin *et al.* (1954). The results showed that mother-child interactions were pertinent to the determination of cognitive style of children in the American sample. Only the importance of socio-cultural deprivation factors in the socialisation process was noted.

In Indian setting few studies have been conducted in this area. Field-independent individuals could construct a social situation at cognitive level, their better restructuring skills could then be used to out perform field independent people in this situation. Responses of field independent people in this situation may be indicative of their superior restructuring skills rather than of social skills (Sahoo, 1982). With this rationale, Sahoo (1982,1986) found greater effective sensitivity of the field-independent people in a socially involving setting and a greater effective sensitivity of the field-independent people in a socially non-involving (cognitive) setting. Regarding environmental influences on psychological differentiation, studies have shown that environmental disadvantages make an individual less differentiated (Majeed & Ghosh, 1979; Sinha, 1978). It is opined that disadvantaged children are usually analytical and impulsive while advantaged children are less analytical and more reflective. School environment also plays an important role in enhancing psychological differentiation. Superior schools as compared to ordinary schools facilitate pictorial perceptual skills in children (Mishra & Gupta, 1978; Sinha, 1977). Sinha and Mishra (1987) did not find the supporting results. Misra and Tiwari (1992) found that influence of ecological setting was significant for the girls characterized by greater differentiation among the urban than the rural girls. The study further indicated that the quality of home environment was significantly related to cognitive differentiation in boys as well as in girls. Also, boys of superior schools showed greater differentiation with advancing age. Other studies did not support the significant relationship between environment and psychological differentiation (Ghosh & Massey, 1979; Mishra & Tripathi, 1980).

Reflective Aspect of Personality : Self -Concept

Self-esteem is central to good psychological adjustment, personal happiness, and effective functioning in children and in adults. Generally, self-concept or self-esteem are used to refer to individuals' judgement about themselves, and their attitudes towards themselves. Children generally show high self-esteem and confidence about their abilities to accomplish their goals, academic competence and relationships with parents and peers. For many theorists, the integrator of personality is considered to be the self. Thus, Sullivan speaks of self-system, Rogers of self-concept and Jung labels the self as the final integrator of personality structure.

The concept of self, the core of the personality pattern is made up of beliefs and attitudes toward self. It is conceptualised as a structure consisting of three major components; the perceptual, the conceptual and the attitudinal. The self-concept takes many forms; the basic, which includes the person's perception of his appearance, abilities, role and status in life, values, beliefs and aspirations; the transitory or the concept a person holds of himself only temporarily before replacing it with another self-concept; the social or "mirror image" in which the person sees himself as he believes others see him; and the ideal self-concept or the person's perception of the kind of person he would like to be.

According to James (1892) and Cooley (1902), everyone possesses a global self-concept over and above more specific self-judgements in the different domains of life. However, their theoretical formulations suggest very different determinants of one's global sense of self. For James, the origins of one's overall sense of esteem lay in how one weighed one's competencies, but this overall sense of esteem did not involve the averaging of one's competencies. Rather, he suggested that one places a different value on success within various domains of one's life, a factor that leads to a very different personal equation for each individual. Cooley (1902) focused primarily on the social origins of the self, highlighting the incorporation of the attitudes of significant others. In contrast to James, who focused singularly on the individual's evaluation of the level and importance of one's perceived competencies, Cooley postulated that the origins of the self were primarily social in nature. Thus, the origins of self resided in the attitudes which significant others held towards the self. According to him, the individual is motivated to appraise other's attitudes towards the self, opinions that one then imitates or incorporates and that become one's own sense of self. Thus, Cooley termed these reflected appraisals as 'looking glass' self; since significant others constitute the social mirror into which one gazes for information that come to define the self. Mead (1934) elaborated on this theme in his concept of the "generalized others" which represented the pooled or collective judgements of significant others towards the self.

Coopersmith (1967) has concluded that self-concept is a unidimensional construct, best assessed by combining an individual's self-evaluations across items tapping a range of content. Items are given equal weight, and it is summed that, the total score resulting from such a combination adequately reflects an individual's sense of self across various areas of his/her life. This unidimensional view of the self-concept has been challenged by many theorists. According to them, such an approach marks important evaluative distinctions that individuals make about their competence or adequacy in different domains of their life. Proponents of this approach put forward models, and adopted measurement strategies, that identify the particular domains of self-evaluation, assessing each separately (Harter, 1985a; Mullener & Laird, 1971; Shavalson, Hubner & Stanton, 1976), thus, providing a profile of self evaluations, across those domains identified by a given investigator.

Rosenberg (1979) emphasized global self-esteem, namely the general regard one holds for self as a person. He acknowledged that such a global judgement is the product of a complex combination of discrete judgements about the self. Harter (1985a) represents an integration of two approaches in which the need to consider a multi-dimensional nature of self-evaluative judgements as well as the individual's overall sense of worth is emphasized. It is critical to appreciate the fact that global self-worth is a construct, in and of itself, namely an overall judgement about one's worth as a person. Therefore, it cannot be assessed by combining domain specific judgements, but is assessed by its own independent set of items, questions that measure the construct of self-worth to which the child likes oneself as a person, likes the way one is leading one's life, and is happy with the way one is. By conceptually and empirically separating domain specific judgements of competency or adequacy from the more global judgements of one's worth as a person, the relationship that specific competencies bear to global self-worth can be determined. A summary of the most salient dimensions of the self-concept at each of the five developmental periods as selected by Harter (1985) is presented in Table 2.1.

During the middle childhood, the structure of self-concept changes in that not only are domain differentiated, but the ability to make judgements about one's self-worth emerges. Harter (1985b) on the basis of self-profile for children, revealed that children between the age of eight and twelve clearly differentiate the five domains, e.g. Scholastic Competence, Atheletic Competence, Peer Social Acceptance, Behavioural Conduct and Physical Appearance. In addition to these emerging discrimination, children's response to items asking about their global self-worth indicate that this concept takes on meaning in middle childhood. Because of the complexity of the human representational system, we can view ourselves as objects and can, therefore, assign a wide range of qualities to ourselves. We can identify, locate, evaluate, interpret, interact with, study and learn more about ourselves. We want others to like, respect or recognize us; we want things for ourselves ; we want to be safe and feel capable. As we grow, we continually appraise ourselves and our behaviours with respect to these and other wants. In this process we become more or less aware of our self through various aspects of our being and behaviour. Shulman (1973) has described aspects of self as follows :

1. *Bodily sense :* (What is me ?) This is the awareness of self as a physical entity with specific boundaries.
2. *Self-identity :* (What am I ?) This is how the person locates himself in his world. Self-identity moves through stages.

Table 2.1: Domains of the Self-concept at Each Period of the Life Span

Early Childhood	Middle/Late Childhood	Adolescence	College	Adult
Cognitive competence	Scholastic competence	Scholastic competence	Scholastic competence Intellectual ability Creativity Job competence	Intelligence Job competence
Physical competence	Atheletic competence Physical appearance	Atheletic competence Physical appearance	Atheletic competence Physical appearance	Atheletic competence Physical appearance
Peer acceptance	Peer acceptance	Peer acceptance Close friendship Romantic relationships	Peer acceptance Close friendship Romantic relationships Relationships with parents	Sociability Close friendship Intimate relationships
Behavioural conduct	Behavioural conduct	Conduct/Morality	Morality Sense of humour	Morality Sense of humour Nurturance Household management Adequacy as a provider
	Global self-worth	Global self-worth	Global self-worth	Global self-worth

3. *Self-image :* (Who am I ?) This is how the person evaluates himself. So the self-image is a judgement the person places on himself in positive or negative fashion. Developmentally, self-image is a self fulfilling prophecy, since it leads to behaviour which confirms the self-image. The level of self-esteem depends upon the self-image.

4. *Self-interest :* (What is good for me ?) We judge that certain things are good for us and some bad. It is, however, different from selfishness.

5. *Self-Ideal :* (What do I strive for ?) We strive to be that which is our self-interest, which enhances our self-image and confirms our self-identity. Self ideal is a relatively permanent aspect of self, although ways of trying to achieve it may change over time.

All these aspects of the self form a self-concept which includes all the views the person holds about himself/herself, whether or not (s)he is.

Parent-child Relationships

Parental attitudes toward the child affect his/her self-concept. Pattern of parental reward and punishment for child's behaviour is crucial in the development of child's self-concept. If parental discipline does not satisfy the needs of the developing child, child may develop negative personality characteristics. Parents may be detached, indifferent, neglecting, rejecting, over-protective and indulgent and possessive. Parents may be liberal, cooperative, accepting, sufficiently protective and controlling. Any combination of these characteristics is possible. Many psychologists observe that children with high self-esteem tend to have parents who are also high in self-esteem. Such parents show consistency in encouraging and supporting their children. Such parents are self-confident, emotionally stable, self-reliant, resilient, effective in their child-rearing practices, and compatible with each other. Mothers of such children are more accepting and supportive, expressing their acceptance through everyday manifestations of concern and affection. These mothers also enforce established rules consistently, preferring rewards and non-coercive treatment in efforts to alter their children's behaviour. It suggests that democratic family environment plays crucial role in developing self-esteem and confidence in children.

The studies of maternal employment and development of personality and other psychological functions, which are usually undertaken by the researchers, have often taken global variables as antecedent and specific (micro) variables as dependent variables. Such relationships are difficult to interpret and do not lead us very far in terms of the understanding of the phenomena under study. The present study investigated the pattern of personality in the children of employed and unemployed mothers. The analysis of personality included traits, psychological differentiation and self-concept.

Measures

Following measures were used to study various aspects of personality of children

Early School Personality Questionnaire (ESPQ) : Early School Personality Questionnaire developed by Lal (1987) was used to measure children's personality. It is the Hindi adaptation of Cattell's (1966) measure. It has been standardized for the children aged 7 to 12 years. ESPQ measures 13 personality traits. (A brief description of all the factors is given in the 'Results' section). The ESPQ contains 80 items. There is no time limit for completion of the questionnaire. Each question has two answers, the children have to mark only one answer. On the basis of scoring stencils, the total number of responses in each trait were counted and according to that each child's personality was analyzed. The index of reliability of this test ranges from 0.70 to 0.88 and validity co-efficient ranges from 0.43 to 0.60. The maximum score in each factor is 6, except in factor B where maximum score is 8. The ESPQ has been found useful in measuring personality traits of children by many investigators in Indian situation.

child's psychological differentiation, each child was administered the SP-EFT developed by Sinha (1984) within the rationale of task requirement of Witkin's EFT and validated against CEFT. The reliability coefficient of the test is 0.80 and validity against CEFT is 0.47. The test consisted of 3 sets of pictures for practice and 8 sets as test series. Each set was comprised of a simple and a complex picture. The subject was presented with the simple figure and was asked to identify the objects depicted therein. If the subject faced any difficulty, (s)he was helped to identify and count the objects depicted therein. Then, the complex picture in which the objects were hidden was presented. In the background of picture presentation, a story which described the circumstances leading to the holding of objects in complex picture was told and the subject was asked to locate the hidden figure(s). No time limit was imposed for this purpose. However, the subject was asked to indicate as soon as (s)he discovered all the hidden figures. The subjects were asked to use plastic stylus to trace the figures. The number of simple figures correctly disembedded and the time taken to discover them were noted. After the practice series, the test series was presented in a time limit of 90 seconds for each card. Responses were recorded in terms of the total number of pictures disembedded and the time taken in disembedding.

Who Am I ? Test : With a view to attain a perspective on self-construals of children, an open-ended interview of children was undertaken. This was largely along the line of 'who am I' (Kuhn & McPartland, 1954) test. The children were asked about themselves. How they perceive their qualities, their relationship with parents, siblings and peers, views about school, hobbies and what they want to be when they grow up? Children were simply asked to tell as much as they could about themselves. Younger children were helped and prompted to give information as they could not express themselves efficiently. The older children were asked to write about themselves. The obtained responses were coded and categorized in meaningful categories. Six broad categories emerged which consisted of personal identity, personal qualities, parent-child interaction, sibling and peer interaction, hobbies and aspirations.

Results

Personality development is determined by a set of multiple factors, both contextual as well as specific experiences. The present study attempted to explore some of the aspects of children's personality in relation to mother's employment status, and sex and age of the child. Mother's employment status also influences the family environment and adoption of specific disciplinary methods. This chapter presents a synoptic picture of the findings and discusses them in relation to theory and research in this area.

Personality Dispositions

With a view to precisely determine the degree of variation in scores on each of the personality traits of ESPQ, the scores for the four groups of children subjected to separate 2 x 2 (Gender of child x Employment Status) factorial ANOVAs. The summary of these analyses is presented in Tables 2.2, 2.3 and 2.4. The results regarding maternal employment status revealed that the children of employed mothers significantly differed from the children of unemployed mothers on four factors i.e., A,C,G and O. The children of EMs were found relatively more outgoing than the children of UEMs. Relatively more ego strength, conscientiousness and placidity were observed in the children of UEMs. Factor J (Restrained/Vigorous) showed marginal difference, showing that the children of UEMs were relatively more vigorous.

Table 2.2 shows the means and standard deviations of the scores of all the four groups of children on 13 personality traits . Figures 2.1 to 2.5 graphically represent the personality profiles of these children. A close perusal of the pattern of these data suggests that personalities of children of EMs shared a considerably similar pattern with the children of UEMs, although certain differences did emerge as regards to the strength of some personality traits.

Factor-A: Outgoing Vs Reserved On this factor, a high score means that the child likes to meet people, is social, altruistic and is active and energetic, whereas a low score means that a child is selfish,

Table 2.2 : Means and Standard Deviations of Scores on ESPQ Personality Factors as a function of Mother's Employment Status and Gender of the Child

	Personality Factors	Children of UEMs (N = 80)		Children of EMs (N=120)	
		Boys (N=40)	Girls (N=40)	Boys (N=73)	Girls (N=47)
A	Outgoing/Reserved	3.43 (1.00)	3.47 (0.68)	3.71 (0.91)	4.23 (0.88)
B	More Intelligent/ Less Intelligent	5.95 (1.25)	5.89 (1.33)	5.71 (1.19)	6.26 (1.23)
C	Ego Strength/ General Emotionality	4.52 (1.10)	4.52 (1.14)	3.99 (1.32)	4.04 (1.20)
D	Affected by Feelings/ Emotionally Stable	3.19 (1.43)	3.47 (1.70)	3.63 (1.47)	3.55 (1.40)
E	Assertive/Humble	2.24 (1.31)	1.21 (1.06)	2.41 (1.41)	1.38 (1.35)
F	Happy-Go-Lucky/Sober	2.38 (1.17)	2.26 (1.33)	2.29 (1.23)	1.94 (1.19)
G	Conscientious/Expedient	4.62 (1.36)	4.79 (1.40)	4.25 (1.19)	4.21 (1.07)
H	Venturesome/Shy	3.33 (1.21)	3.32 (1.08)	3.10 (1.05)	3.13 (1.35)
I	Tenderminded/ Toughminded	4.29 (1.08)	4.05 (0.94)	4.08 (1.17)	4.28 (1.27)
J	Restrained/Vigorous	2.10 (1.23)	2.58 (1.27)	2.58 (1.22)	2.79 (1.38)
N	Shrewd/Forthright	1.76 (0.75)	1.42 (0.82)	1.63 (1.10)	1.55 (1.16)
O	Apprehensive/Placid	1.33 (1.17)	1.84 (1.35)	2.34 (1.35)	2.30 (1.41)
Q-4	Tense/Relaxed	2.57 (1.26)	2.05 (1.19)	3.48 (4.97)	2.45 (1.16)

Note : SDs are in parentheses.

does not like meeting people and is usually self-centred. On this factor the children of EMs scored significantly high (M = 3.97) as compared to children of UEMs (M=3.45), $F(1,196) = 15.98$ $p < .01$ and girls ($M = 3.85$) in comparison to boys ($M = 3.57$), $F(1,196) = 4.71$ $p < .05$. It suggests that children of EMs showed greater outgoingness than their counterparts. Girls in comparison to boys showed relatively more outgoingness. Girls of EMs as compared to other children, scored highest (M = 4.23) on this factor.

The above differences may be explained by observing the special conditions faced by the children of EMs, where they get greater opportunity to meet people and have to observe many household liabilities. Since mothers are usually absent for a longer period from home because of their job requirements, children sometimes feel parents' absence and whenever someone comes to their house or they get an opportunity to go out, they do try to avail such an opportunity. Similarly, they also know that if they will help someone, only then they will get help. Because of mothers being engaged in jobs outside home, their children have to be more energetic and active in reciprocating with others.

Factor-B: More Intelligent Vs Less Intelligent A high score on this factor indicates that the child is more intelligent and *vice versa.* As regards employment of mothers, the children of UEMs had a mean score of 5.92 and of EMs 5.98, showing no significant difference in the mean scores. However, girls in EMs' group, as compared to other children, scored highest (M = 6.26) showing relatively higher level of intelligence.

A number of studies have shown that girls generally benefit intellectually when their mothers are employed but that boys

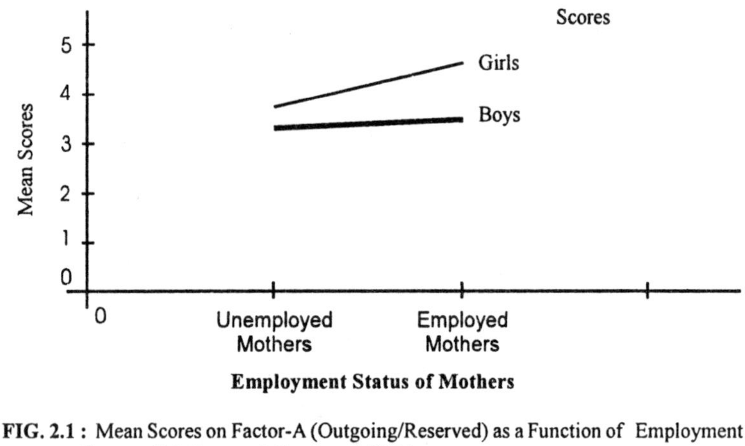

FIG. 2.1 : Mean Scores on Factor-A (Outgoing/Reserved) as a Function of Employment Status of Mothers and Gender of Children

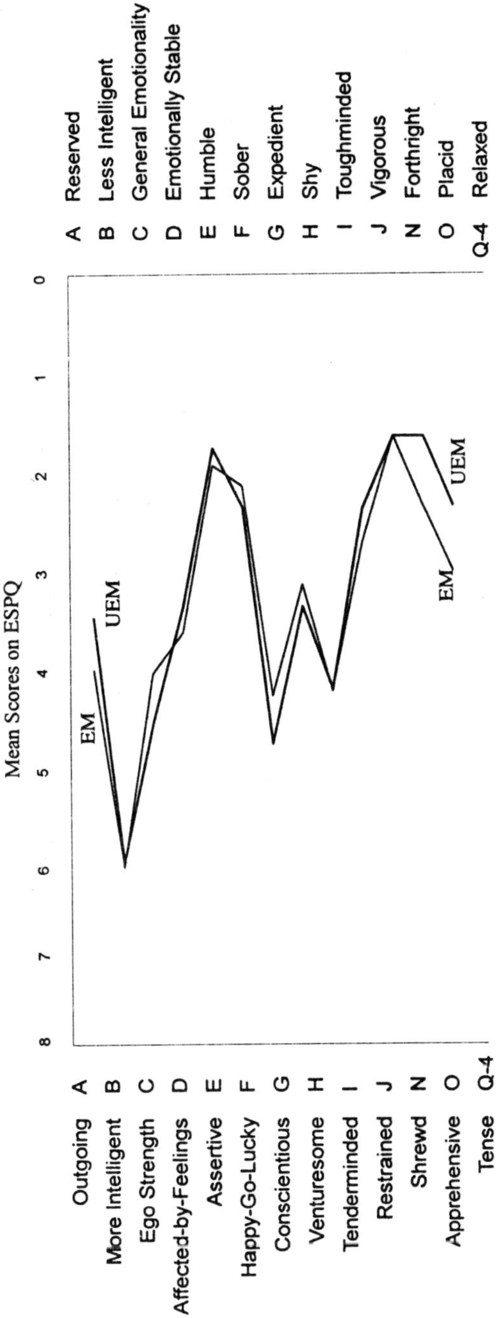

FIG. 2.2 : Personality Profile of Children of Employed and Unemployed Mothers on ESPQ

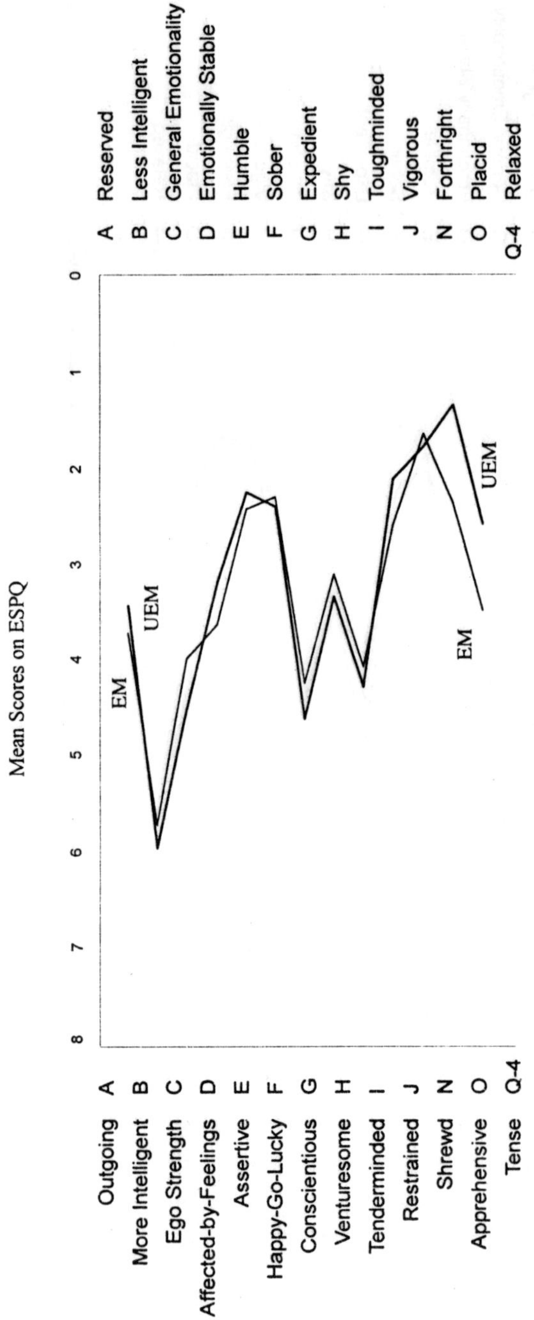

FIG. 2.3 : Personality Profile of Boys on ESPQ

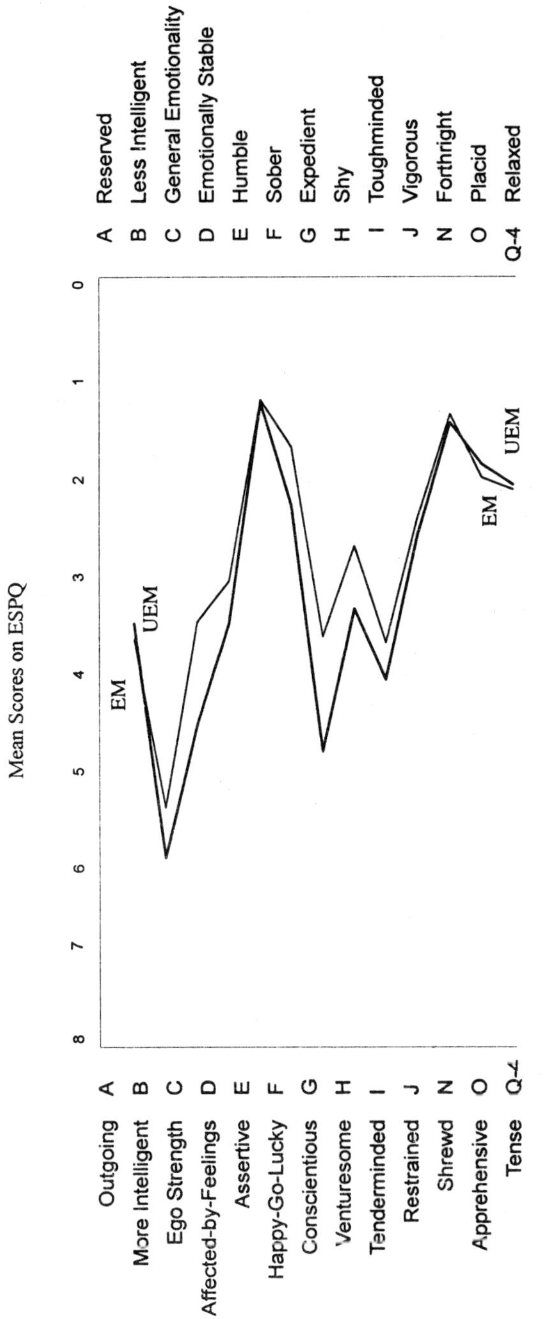

FIG. 2.4 : Personality Profile of Girls on ESPQ

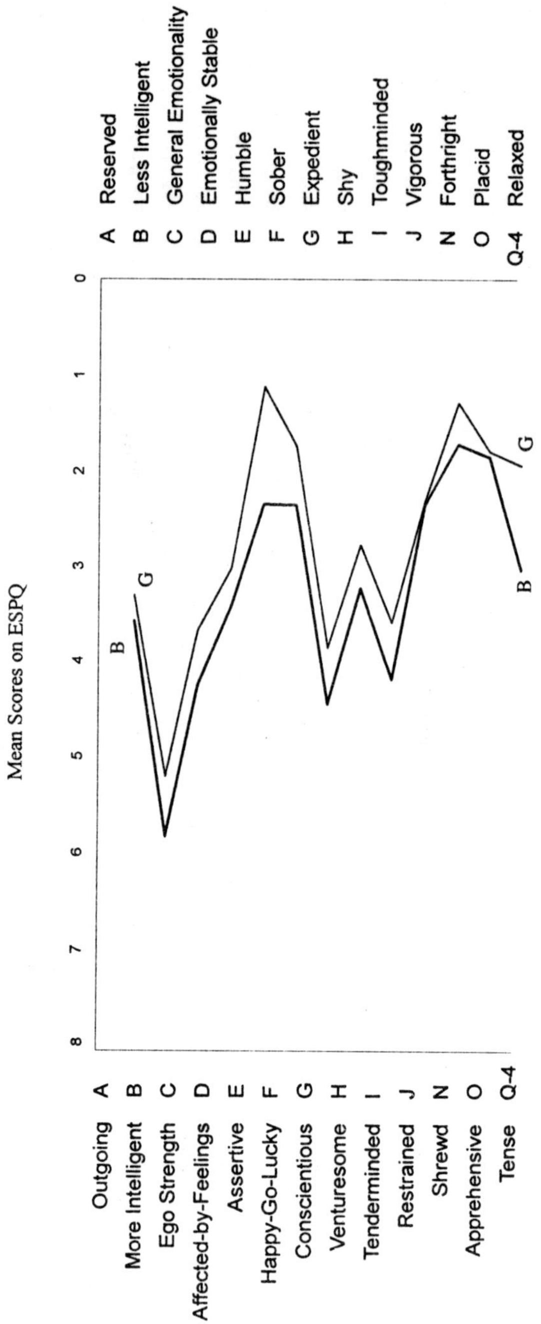

FIG. 2.5 : Personality Profile of Boys and Girls on ESPQ

sometimes suffer. For instance, Stucky, McGhee and Bell (1982) found that daughters get more attention in families with employed mothers whereas boys receive more attention in families with full-time mothers. The positive image of daughters and praise for self-reliance in girls who are probably seen as emulating their mothers is replaced by complaints about non-compliance and aggressiveness in boys by almost half of the full-time WMs.

Factor-C: Ego Strength Vs General Emotionality Children scoring high on this factor are full of ego strength, are mentally and socially mature, calm and mentally stable. Such children interact effectively with other children and do not find any problem in social adjustment. In contrast, children scoring low are governed by emotions, are immature and mentally unstable. They cannot repress their frustration or control emotional responses. Effect of employment of mothers was significant for this factor. Children of UEMs scored significantly high ($M = 4.52$) as compared to children of EMs ($M = 4.01$), thus, children of UEMs showed greater ego strength than their counterparts, $F(1,196) = 8.15$ $p < .01$. Boys in EMs' group evinced relatively less ego strength ($M = 3.99$) as compared to other groups.

Due to job demands, EMs hardly get spare time. The amount of time they get is usually spent on child's studies as it assumes greater significance for the school-going children. In children's minor disputes with peers and siblings, parents usually do not interfere and generally children have to solve their problems on their own. In case of the EMs, the children are allowed to express anger towards friends. This might have contributed to the low scores of their children on this factor.

Factor-D: Affected-by Feelings Vs Emotionally Stable High score on this factor means the child gets irritated or provoked by minor things. Children getting low scores are usually emotionally balanced. Children of EMs scored 3.59 and the children of UEMs 3.33, showing similar pattern on this factor.

Table 2.3 : Mean Scores on 13 Personality Factors of ESPQ as a Function of Main Effects of Maternal Employment and Gender of children

Personality Factors		Children		Children	
		UEMs (N = 80)	EMs (N=120)	Boys (N=113)	Girls (N=87)
A	Outgoing/Reserved	3.45	3.97	3.57	3.85
B	More Intelligent/ Less Intelligent	5.92	5.98	5.83	6.07
C	Ego Strength/ General Emotionality	4.52	4.01	4.25	4.28
D	Affected-by-Feelings/ Emotionally Stable	3.33	3.59	3.41	3.52
E	Assertive/Humble	1.73	1.90	2.33	1.30
F	Happy-Go-Lucky/Sober	2.32	2.11	2.34	2.01
G	Conscientious/Expedient	4.71	4.23	4.44	4.50
H	Venturesome/Shy	3.33	3.11	3.22	3.22
I	Tenderminded/ Toughminded	4.17	4.18	4.19	4.17
J	Restrained/Vigorous	2.34	2.69	2.34	2.69
N	Shrewd/Forthright	1.60	1.60	1.70	1.49
O	Apprehensive/Placid	1.60	2.32	1.84	2.07
Q-4	Tense/Relaxed	2.31	2.97	3.03	2.25

Factor-E : Assertive Vs Humble Children scoring high on this factor are usually very active, bold and of aggressive nature. Such children can face many problems, but if this characteristic is utilized properly, then they can get success.in their life. Children getting low scores are usually of very simple type. Children of EMs (M = 1.90) and UEMs (M = 1.73) showed humility more as compared to assertiveness. Maternal employment did not show significant effect for this factor. However, gender difference was observed, as girls (M = 1.30) in comparison to boys (M = 2.13) showed greater amount of humility.

Factor-F : Happy-Go-Lucky Vs Sober High score on this factor means that the child is full of excitement, optimism and self-confidence, whereas low score means the child is of serious or depressed type. Almost all children except girls in EMs' group (M = 1.94) scored average, thus, showing more sobriety. Children of

UEMs and EMs scored mean scores of 2.32 and 2.11, in order.

Factor-G: Conscientious Vs Expedient High scorers on this factor are usually intelligent, thoughtful, hard-working and dependable. Social and adult values are quite developed in the thinking and behaviours of such children. Low scorers are usually of average ability and are undependable. Children of EMs scored 4.23 whereas children of UEMs scored 4.71 showing significant difference regarding this factor $F(1,196) = 6.70$ $p < .01$. Children of UEMs were found relatively more conscientious as compared to the children of EMs.

We know that most of the time children of EMs are on their own, looking after themselves. As the family structure is usually nuclear, there is less accessibility to adult models who can tell them what is correct and what is incorrect. Parents can directly guide only those behaviours which a child displays in their presence. In contrast, children of UEMs by and large remain in mother's focus of attention. For them, mother is more frequently available to guide and explain the logic of socially desired behaviours.

Factor-H: Venturesome Vs Shy High score on this factor means the child is social and extrovert, can interact effectively with others, is quite bold and independent. Low score means the child is usually introvert, nervous and always frightened. In general, all children scored (UEMs, 3.33; EMs, 3.11) average level on this factor showing average characteristics of venturesomeness and shyness.

Factor-I: Tenderminded Vs Toughminded A high score on this factor means that the child is sympathetic to others, escapist and dependable. On the other hand, a low score implies that the child is more independent and carefree. On this factor, children of UEMs and EMs scored a mean score of 4.17 and 4.18 respectively. It shows that almost all children showed greater tendermindedness.

Factor-J: Restrained Vs Vigorous Children scoring high on this factor are usually individualistic, selfish and critical of others, whereas low scorers are broadminded, active and tolerant. On this factor, a marginally significant difference between the mean scores of children of UEMs was found. Children of UEMs scored 2.34 and EMs scored 2.69, thus, children of UEMs showed relatively greater degree of vigorousness than the children of EMs.

Factor-N: Shrewd Vs Forthright Children scoring high on this factor have insight and efficiency to face social situations, understand the opportunity and take advantage of it whereas low scorers are simple, emotional and of average mental ability. Children of UEMs and EMs scored a mean score of 1.60 showing more characteristics of forthrightness.

Factor-O: Apprehensive Vs Placid Children scoring high on this factor are usually mentally scared and insecure. They are irritable and anxious. Children scoring low are full of self-confidence. Factor O clearly showed differences in the personality pattern of children of UEMs (M= 1.60) and EMs (M= 2.32). Although both groups scored below average but children of UEMs scored significantly low on this factor suggesting children of UEMs to be relatively more placid than children of EMs, $F(1,196) = 14.04$ $p < .01$.

Factor-Q-4: Tense Vs Relaxed High score on this factor means that the child is usually suffering from tension, frustration and pessimism. Low scorers are calm and quiet and show social maturity. Children of UEMs (M = 2.31) and EMs (M = 2.97) scored average on this factor showing mixed characteristics of tense and relaxed personality.

When mothers work outside the home, there is hardly any adult character at home to look after the children. As the urban society is not safe and secure against any mishappening, parents usually warn their children and ask them to be extra cautious. Such type of physical and psychological environment may be less helpful in the development of such characteristics in these children. Though it is not necessary that UEMs are always available to the child, the child is often assured that whenever (s)he would need the mother, she would be available. This might develop self-confidence, a feeling of security and placidity in the child. On the other hand,

EMs are always out at a fixed time and may not be available when children need them.

Table 2.4 : Summaries of 2 x 2, Maternal Employment, Status × Gender, ANOVAs Performed on the ESPQ Scores of Children

Personality Factors	Employment Status of Mothers		Gender		Interaction	
	MS	*F* (1,196)	MS	*F* (1,196)	MS	*F* (1,196)
A Outgoing/Reserved	12.81	15.98**	3.78	4.71*	2.67	3.33
B More Intelligent/ Less Intelligent	0.17	0.11	2.77	1.76	4.24	2.70
C Ego Strength/ General Emotionality	12.26	8.15**	0.04	0.03	0.03	0.02
D Affected by Feelings/ Emotionally Stable	3.17	1.40	0.50	0.22	1.52	0.67
E Assertive/Humble	1.40	0.80	49.65	28.33**	0.00	0.00
F Happy-Go-Lucky/ Sober	2.08	1.34	2.59	1.67	0.64	0.42
G Conscientious/ Expedient	10.59	6.70**	0.22	0.14	0.49	0.31
H Venturesome/Shy	2.13	1.54	0.00	0.00	0.03	0.02
I Tenderminded/ Toughminded	0.00	0.00	0.02	0.01	2.15	1.64
J Restrained/Vigorous	5.57	3.38	5.69	3.45	0.87	0.58
N Shrewd/Forthright	0.00	0.00	2.05	1.99	0.82	0.80
O Apprehensive/Placid	25.21	14.04**	2.53	1.41	3.60	2.00
Q-4 Tense/Relaxed	19.22	1.96	28.28	2.79	3.10	0.31

$*p < .05$; $**p < .01$

Gender Differences and Children's Personality

Sex of an individual is related to certain endocrinal hormones giving rise to the characteristics of masculinity-femininity which are socially nurtured and often treated as key elements of one's personality. In almost all societies, interaction of boys and girls including play, differed considerably. Conventionally, almost in every society different patterns of behaviour are expected for the person of each sex. Being treated differently and sharing diverse interactions with significant others in the family, school and other social settings, it becomes natural that boys and girls may develop diverse personality characteristics. With regard to gender differences, the results of the present study yielded significant main effects for two factors, i.e. Outgoing Vs Reserved (Factor A) and Assertive Vs Humble (Factor E). Thus, girls were found relatively more outgoing and humble (*M*=3.85,1.30) than the boys (*M*=2.13, 2.33). On factor J (Restrained Vs Vigorous), marginally significant difference was found, showing girls as more vigorous (*M* = 1.30) as compared to boys (*M* = 2.13). On rest of the factors, there was no significant gender difference. The interaction of ME and gender was marginally significant for factor A, Outgoing Vs Reserved. Figure 2.1 shows that while boys and girls of UEMs showed a similar pattern, the girls of EMs were relatively more outgoing than boys.

The girls were found significantly more outgoing than boys (Factor A). Also, it was found that as compared to girls of UEMs, girls of EMs scored higher on this factor. Many studies (e.g., Gold & Andres, 1978; Scarr, 1984; Stein, 1973) have reported that daughters of EMs are less bound by the sex role stereotypes and usually expect to work outside the home when they get older. From the very beginning, EMs, perhaps, socialize their daughters in this framework which enhances the characteristics like outgoing, warm, social and easy-going nature. Males are brought up in such a psycho-social environment which encourages and requires them to become comparatively more dominant than females. The role adoption of this kind starts quite early in life from childhood itself. As a result, boys are usually found to be more dominant or assertive and less submissive than girls of their own age group. In the present study, boys scored relatively higher than girls on factor E (Assertive Vs Humble).

Chronological Age and Personality Traits

Chronological age as related to the development of specific personality traits did not emerge as a dominant variable in the present sample. The age of the children showed positive relationship with factors A, B, C, D, E, G, J, N and Q-4. It suggests that older children as compared to younger children showed more outgoingness, intelligence, general emotionality, affected-by-feelings, sobriety, conscientiousness, vigorousness, shrewdness and relaxedness. However, in case of girls of UEMs, child's age was positively related to factor A, showing greater outgoing tendency with advancing age. It suggests that as compared to younger ones the older girls like to meet people more, are usually more social, altruistic, active and energetic. It can be said that usually children (specially girls) of UEMs do not get much opportunity to meet people, but as they grow older and start going out and join the school they also start taking interest in such matters. Girls of EMs generally come in contact with many people in parent's absence. They are usually found more social, talkative, and active as compared to boys. This characteristic is facilitated more with increasing age in the case of girls of UEMs. Age was also found related with factors J and N, in case of boys of EMs showing relatively greater vigorousness and shrewdness with increasing age. Such children are broad-minded, active and tolerant and also evince insight and efficiency in social situations. They display more understanding to take the advantage of available opportunities. The circumstances provided by mothers' employment may lead the older boys to become more vigorous and shrewd. When boys grow older, mothers prefer to assign greater responsibility to them outside the home as compared to girls.

Psychological Differentiation

Psychological differentiation was considered as a cognitive facet of personality. It primarily reflects the way an individual interacts with his/her environment. Present findings have shown that employment status of mothers is associated with performance on the Story-Pictorial EFT. Children of EMs emerged to be more psychologically differentiated as compared to their counterparts. This trend was statistically significant for both the measures, i.e. disembedding score (DS) as well as time score (TS) on EFT.

Table 2.5 indicates the distribution of scores obtained by

children in different groups on SP-EFT. All the children, except girls in UEMs' group, scored relatively higher. It shows that boys of UEMs appeared to be more differentiated as compared to girls of UEMs.

Table 2.6, shows the mean scores of boys and girls of UEMs and EMs on the measure of psychological differentiation. A close perusal of mean scores reveals that disembedding of pictures was at a higher level in the children of EMs (Girls, *M*= 33.74; Boys, *M* = 34.45) as compared to their counterparts from the group of UEMs (Girls, *M*= 32.32; Boys, *M*= 33.33). In general, boys in both the groups showed greater disembedding and, therefore, greater differentiation than girls.

Table 2.5 : Distribution of Disembedding Scores on SP-EFT for Boys and Girls

Class Intervals	Children of UEMs		Children of EMs	
	Boys (N=40) f(%)	Girls (N=40) f(%)	Boys (N=73) f(%)	Girls (N=47) f(%)
38 - 42	8(19)	4(11)	21(29)	7(15)
33 - 37	22(52)	14(37)	35(48)	25(63)
28 - 32	8(19)	18(47)	12(16)	13(18)
23 - 27	4(10)	2(5)	5(7)	2(4)

Table 2.6 : Performance of Children on SP-EFT

Groups		Disembedding Scores (DS)		Time Scores (TS)	
		M	SD	M	SD
UEMs	Boys	33.33	4.67	529.29	121.02
	Girls	32.32	4.04	536.95	101.20
EMs	Boys	34.45	4.50	520.12	131.62
	Girls	33.74	3.39	537.43	91.61

With a view to determine the degree of variation in psychological differentiation, scores on the SP-EFT for the four groups of children were subjected to 2 x 2 (Gender x Mother's Employment Status) factorial ANOVA. The summary of this analysis is presented in Table 2.7. It is clear that the main effect of employment status of mother was significant for disembedding scores. The children of EMs showed greater DS (*M*=34.25) as compared to their counterparts (*M*= 32.85). The main effect of gender was also significant. Boys evinced greater differentiation (*M*= 34.16) as compared to girls (*M*= 32.93). The interaction of mother's employment status and gender was found significant, F (1,196) = 12.06 $p < .01$. The effect of mother's employment was greater in the case of girls than boys. The girls of EMs were relatively more differentiated than the girls of UEMs. The extent of such an effect was lesser for boys.

Studies by Witkin, Dyk, Faterson, Goodenough and Karp (1962) have shown that if a child gets greater opportunity to explore his/her immediate world and freedom in going out independently, the chances are greater that (s)he will become more differentiated. EMs' children usually have to stay alone at home and most of the time have to perform their work by themselves. Thus, they get more chance to face diverse situations on their own. This may promote independence in such children. This special situation may contribute to differentiation and field-independence. It is evident from several studies (Wiggins, Renner, Clore & Rose, 1971; Witkin, 1963) that independence also influences psychological differentiation. In several studies (Hock, 1978; Mody & Murphy, 1988; Moore, 1975; Schachter, 1981) it was found that the children of EMs were usually found more independent as compared to their counterparts. The present finding in this regard, is also in line with these studies.

Witkin *et al.* (1974) and Holtzman, Diaz, Guerrero and Swarty (1975) found that the nuclear family structure was associated with field-independence, where fathers play an important role in interactions and thus, provide a suitable model to their boys. Thus, father's presence fosters field-independence and facilitates greater differentiation (Busse, 1969; Dawson, 1967; Dreyer, 1975). Pleck (1984) has contended that when both parents work outside the home, father also participates more actively in family chores and shares the burden of child-rearing which also favours differentiation in their children. With an increase in father's role, the mother's role is limited only to child care which helps the child in separating him/her from the mother. This leads to individuation and facilitates autonomous functioning and differentiation. The atmosphere in a nuclear family is more permissive and the child is less severely disciplined and less harshly treated. (S)he is under the supervision of his/her parents and siblings and is not hampered by excessive protection and care available from others. Thus, the child gets opportunity for developing his/her self-identity and acquiring an articulated body concept. In the present study, only nuclear families were included, and as it is clear from the above studies, this type of family structure facilitates independence, which is further enhanced by maternal employment.

Table 2.7 : Summary of 2×2, Maternal Employment Status × Gender ANOVA Performed on the Disembedding Scores of Children

Source of Interaction	*df*	*Ms*	*F*
Mother's Employment (A)	1	93.31	5·97*
Gender (B)	1	71.89	4·60*
A× B	1	188.53	12·06**
Within Cell	196	15.64	

*$p < .05$; **$p < .01$.

Psychological Differentiation and Gender

In their early work, Witkin, *et al.* (1954) found females to be more field dependent than males. In the present study, boys scored higher on EFT than the girls in EMs' as well as UEMs' groups. There are normative differences regarding gender differences in differentiation. The reason behind them may lie in diverse socializing methods employed for boys and girls. In Indian society the socialization of a girl child is considerably different from that of boys. Girls are not only reinforced to be more dependent, but also to be more conforming (Sinha, 1981). It means that instead of taking cues from themselves, they are expected to depend more on the environment, which further contributes to field-dependence. The present results are in line with the findings of Sinha (1980) and Misra and Tiwari (1992).

Psychological Differentiation and Children's Age

Previous studies indicate clear age-related changes in field-dependence over the life span. Witkin, Goodenough and Karp (1967) had suggested that development curves for field independence, covering 8 to 24 years period, show a marked, continuous increase between 8 to 15 year's age range, although the rate of change in this period slows down with advancing age. Present findings have shown similar trends. Positive relationship between age and DS and negative correlation between age and TS implicate that field-independence increases with age. An increase in DS and decrease in TS with increasing age, is in line with the findings of Berry (1976), Chandra (1974), Witkin, Goodenough and Oltman (1979). Sinha and Misra (1988) suggested that role of biological and experiential factors can be associated to field-independence with increasing age. Misra and Tiwari (1992) found significant age related changes in scores on SP-EFT. Also, the differences were related to the type of schooling and environmental conditions.

Self-Concept

Because of the complexity of the representational system, human beings can view themselves as objects and can, therefore, assign a wide range of qualities to self. People identify, evaluate and interpret their views of 'self'. As we grow older, we continually appraise ourselves and our behaviours with respect to the sense of self. With this in view, children in the present study were simply asked to respond to an open ended question "who am I?" The obtained responses on the measure of self-construal were coded and categorized into six broad categories. Separate analyses of responses were performed according to mother's employment status, children's age and gender. Table 2.8 reports the responses given by children in six broad categories as detailed below.

Identity: This category included all the referents of self such as name, age, gender, date of birth and child's daily routine. It was found that in the EMs' group about 45 per cent boys and about 70 per cent girls mentioned these characteristics. In UEMs' group, almost all children, between 7 to 9 years age reported these features, compared to 60 per cent to 69 per cent of older children in the same group. It is quite clear that younger children in both the groups reported more about these identity characteristics. In contrast, home address, name and job of parents were equally reported by the children of both groups.

Personal qualities: Children were asked to indicate their notions about behavioural and dispositional qualities. The positive qualities mentioned by them included: " helping", "obedient", "liked by others", " punctual", "friendly with others" etc. A very few children mentioned negative qualities also such as "naughty", "lazy", "disobedient", "careless" and "teasing others". It was noted that the younger children and especially girls reported larger number of positive qualities.

Parent-child interaction: Children of EMs expressed more love for mother, whereas children of UEMs reported equal feelings for both the parents. All the children reported that both the parents care for them equally. About parental treatment of negative behaviour, children of UEMs, especially at the younger age level, reported greater incidence of punishment. In the EMs' group, older boys and younger girls reported greater incidence of punishment.

Sibling and peer relationship: In regard to sibling interaction, children reported about liking, helping, sharing and playing with siblings. A small number of them also mentioned disliking and quarrels. Almost all the children reported a common response pattern, but children of UEMs reported relatively more healthy relationship with their siblings. Disliking was almost equally reported in all the groups. Better peer relationship and more number of friends were reported by the children of UEMs (53 per cent as compared to 28 per cent in EMs' group).

Table 2.8: Aspects of Self Awareness in Children by Maternal Employment, Gender and Age

Aspects of Self Concept	Employed Mothers					Unemployed Mothers				
	Boys		Girls		Total	Boys		Girls		Total
	(N=26) 7-9	(N=47) 10-12	(N=24) 7-9	(N=23) 10-12	(N=120)	(N=8) 7-9	(N=32) 10-12	(N=20) 7-9	(N=20) 10-12	(N=80)
	f (%)	f (%)	f (%)	f (%)	f (%)	f (%)	f (%)	f (%)	f (%)	f (%)
Personal Identity										
Self	12 (46)	21 (45)	19 (79)	15 (65)	67 (56)	8 (100)	22 (69)	20 (100)	12 (60)	62 (78)
Address	3 (16)	1 (2)	0 (0)	3 (13)	7 (6)	0 (0)	0 (0)	2 (10)	1 (5)	3 (4)
Parents	2 (7)	6 (13)	2 (8)	5 (21)	15 (13)	0 (0)	1 (3)	0 (0)	2 (10)	3 (4)
Personal Qualities										
Positive	13 (50)	37 (79)	24(100)	23 (100)	97 (80)	8 (100)	14 (44)	20 (100)	20 (100)	54 (68)
Negative	4 (15)	5 (11)	5 (21)	2 (9)	16 (13)	1 (3)	1 (3)	0 (0)	0 (0)	2 (3)
Parent-Child Interaction										
Loves one parent	6 (23)	13 (28)	1 (4)	5 (22)	25 (21)	0 (0)	2 (6)	0 (0)	0 (0)	2 (3)
Loves both parents	2 (8)	10 (21)	7 (29)	3 (13)	22 (18)	5 (63)	7 (22)	10 (50)	6 (30)	2 (31)
One Parent cares more	1 (4)	3 (6)	2 (8)	2 (8)	8 (7)	0 (0)	4 (13)	1 (5)	0 (0)	5 (6)
Interaction with siblings										
Liking	10 (38)	21 (45)	19 (79)	12 (52)	62 (52)	6 (75)	16 (50)	20 (100)	8 (40)	50 (68)
Disliking	9 (35)	29 (62)	9 (38)	14 (62)	61 (51)	5 (63)	15 (47)	17 (85)	7 (35)	44 (55)

(Contd.)

Table 2.8: *(Contd.)*

Aspects of Self Concept	Employed Mothers					Unemployed Mothers				
	Boys		Girls		Total	Boys		Girls		Total
	(N=26)	(N=47)	(N=24)	(N=23)	(N=120)	(N=8)	(N=32)	(N=20)	(N=20)	(N=80)
	7-9	10-12	7-9	10-12		7-9	10-12	7-9	10-12	
	f (%)	f (%)	f (%)	f (%)	f (%)	f (%)	f (%)	f (%)	f (%)	f (%)
Interaction with Peers										
Liking	2 (8)	10 (21)	6 (25)	15 (65)	33 (28)	6 (75)	16 (50)	12 (60)	8 (40)	42 (53)
Quarrels	7 (27)	12 (26)	5 (21)	4 (17)	28 (23)	2 (25)	6 (19)	10 (50)	5 (25)	23 (29)
More friends	4 (15)	7 (15)	2 (8)	4 (17)	17 (14)	7 (88)	7 (22)	7 (35)	5 (25)	26 (33)
Less friends	2 (8)	7 (15)	2 (8)	3 (13)	14 (12)	0 (0)	3 (10)	4 (20)	2 (10)	9 (11)
Schools										
About school	5 (19)	19 (40)	14 (58)	9 (36)	47 (39)	8 (100)	26 (81)	20 (100)	17 (85)	65 (81)
Positive ratings	24 (92)	23 (28)	24(100)	13 (57)	84 (76)	8 (100)	28 (88)	20 (100)	16 (80)	72 (90)
Negative ratings	4 (15)	7 (15)	2 (8)	1 (4)	14 (12)	3 (38)	4 (13)	3 (15)	2 (10)	12 (15)
Hobbies										
Swimming & Cycling	4 (15)	4 (9)	6 (25)	6 (26)	20 (17)	2 (25)	2 (6)	3 (15)	1 (5)	8 (10)
Playing	16 (62)	37 (79)	11 (46)	9 (39)	63 (53)	8 (100)	18 (56)	16 (80)	4 (20)	46 (58)
Artistic	1 (4)	17 (36)	13 (54)	13 (57)	44 (37)	3 (38)	9 (28)	10 (50)	4 (20)	26 (33)
Music	2 (8)	3 (6)	1 (4)	6 (26)	12 (10)	0 (0)	1 (3)	4 (20)	4 (20)	9 (11)
Love for plants & animals	4 (15)	9 (19)	6 (25)	2 (57)	21 (18)	1 (13)	9 (28)	1 (5)	1 (5)	12 (15)
Reading	9 (35)	24 (51)	10 (42)	11 (48)	54 (45)	7 (88)	12 (38)	11 (55)	6 (30)	36 (45)
Watching TV	2 (8)	8 (17)	4 (17)	6 (26)	20 (17)	2 (25)	4 (13)	2 (10)	1 (5)	9 (11)
Aspirations	6 (23)	39 (83)	5 (21)	15 (65)	60 (50)	3 (38)	4 (13)	8 (40)	12 (60)	27 (34)

Note : Figures in parentheses are percentage.

Almost all children considered the school very important for them while telling about themselves. More positive ratings were given for school studies and teachers by the younger children of EMs and by all children in case of UEMs.

Hobbies and aspirations: Regarding hobbies, most children reported swimming, playing, painting and drawing, love for music and dance, watching TV, outing, love for plants and animals, reading and studying etc. Almost all children in UEMs' and EMs' group reported similar hobbies, only 'playing' showed a difference according to child's age level and mother's employment status. Younger children, especially in UEMs' group reported (boys 100% and girls 80%) that they spend spare time in 'playing' any game, Boys of EMs also gave preferences for 'playing'. Children also reported about their future plans. Main preference among many alternatives (e.g. Teacher, Social Worker, Judge, Police officer, Engineer, Army officer, Pilot, Cricket player and IAS) was for 'doctor'. Older boys of EMs reported varied preferences. Younger group could not tell much. Girls in both the groups reported almost similar trends.

Conclusion

The results revealed that maternal employment has an important influence on the personality development of children. As regards dispositional aspect of personality, significant differences in the personality traits of children of UEMs and EMs were found, especially in case of factors A, C, G and O. Children of EMs were relatively more outgoing, apprehensive, generally emotional, and expedient as compared to children of UEMs. In contrast, children of UEMs showed greater reservedness, ego strength, conscientiousness, vigour and placidity. A common pattern was shared by children of both groups on other personality factors. Statistically significant differences in the mean scores on factors A and E depicting relatively greater outgoingness and humility in girls of both the groups. Girls were also found to be more vigorous and relaxed. The interaction of maternal employment status and gender was significant for Factor A. Girls of EMs appeared to be more outgoing than boys of EMs, boys and girls of UEMs were similar on this factor. On the rest of the factors, boys and girls in both the groups seemed quite similar. Except F, H, I and O, other factors were found related with child's age. Older children showed greater outgoingness, intelligence, general emotionality, affected-by-feelings, sobriety, conscientiousness, vigorousness, shrewdness and relaxedness.

As regards cognitive aspects, it was found that children of EMs were relatively more field-independent as compared to the children of UEMs, and boys in comparison to girls displayed greater psychological differentiation. Interaction between maternal employment and gender was also seen. Girls of EMs showed greater differentiation than that of UEMs. Children's age was also related positively with psychological differentiation, where older children showed more field-independence.

Reflective aspect of personality showed marginal influence of employment of mothers and gender of children. It was found that children of UEMs reported relatively more about their identity, whereas in addition to personal identity, children of EMs reported more about their parents. More children of EMs as compared to children of UEMs, reported about positive qualities and some of them mentioned their negative qualities also. Regarding age difference, more younger children than older ones reported about identity, parental treatment, liking and disliking the 'siblings' and 'playing' as a main hobby. Older children reported more about disliking the siblings, artistic and reading hobbies and more aspirations. As regards gender differences, girls reported more about parents, liking friends and artistic hobbies. Almost similar response pattern was obtained on other aspects.

3

DISCIPLINARY PRACTICES

At birth, the individual's survival depends on mother, the primary care taker. Due to limited physical and mental capabilities during the first few years of life, the place of family in child's life becomes central. The family is the first socializing agency in her/his life. Parents, siblings and relatives are the first people with whom the child has social interactions. They become the first ones to teach him/her to live with other persons, and his/her status and role within the family. Parents and others help the growing child in learning the basic principles of social control and self-control. It is, therefore, the family which plays an important and powerful role in shaping a child's personality. Each family has certain social norms, and it expects the child to conform to these. The family provides the first social environment for the developing child where s(he) learns to deal wisely and effectively with everyday problems in a friendly atmosphere.

In recent years, the structure and functioning of Indian family system has been undergoing significant changes. The traditional joint families are gradually being replaced by nuclear type families and allocation and enactment of child rearing responsibilities are changing on account of demands, such as, maintaining higher standards of living and enjoying the benefits of modern life. It also affects the socialization of the child. The term socialization refers to the process by which the individual acquires those behaviours, beliefs, standards and motives that are valued by her/his family and the cultural group to which (s)he belongs. At birth, infants possess an enormously wide range of behavioural potentialities. They can theoretically, at least, become aggressive or self-effacing, selfish or generous, atheistic or deeply religious, concerned about or indifferent to intellectual achievement, honest or dishonest. Generally, children adopt only those personality characteristics and responses which are considered appropriate or at least acceptable, by their own social, ethnic and religious group. Many people and institutions contribute significantly to the child's socialization, but parents and siblings are the principal and most influential agents especially during the early years. The parents and siblings have maximum interaction and contact with the child during this period. The interaction is intense and frequently regulates and modifies the child's behaviour.

In the context of personality development, it has generally been observed that, in addition to genetic factors, child rearing practices play a vital role. In particular, the disciplining practices are considered more important. As a result, considerable attention has been paid by psychologists and the students of child development to the study of disciplining methods used in training children, which seem to be proximal actecedents of personality development.

In the changing family scenario joint families are gradually transforming into smaller nuclear families where parent-child relationship is very different. In a traditional joint family, the role and responsibility of bringing up children was not confined to the mother only but was shared by other family members, usually by an aunt, grandmother and, invariably, by an older sibling too. There were many adults for the child to interact with and therefore, demands on any one individual were not so intense. In joint families, multiple parenting makes the children more loving and trusting. Their vocabulary also develops very fast. In such a family context, for the first few years, the child lived in a world of its own. There were very few expectations from child to achieve any specific goal. Anandalakshmy (1986) described 'childhood' in traditional joint families as a period of joy, freedom, and a time to celebrate the joys of no responsibility. Kakar (1981) analysed the adult-child interaction in this context as an interplay–the interplay which as a paradigm of growing up emphasized the adult-child unit and concerned itself with mutual learning and mutual pleasure, not concentrating solely on 'the child' and his movement towards adulthood, unlike western cultures.

The nuclear family may be understood as a group comprising of husband, wife and their unmarried children. The term 'elementary family' is sometimes used to denote the most basic family structure with the minimum of essential components of a family, namely, parents and their children. In today's families, because of the highly intimate parent-child relationships, the interactions are intense in nature. Expectations and unsatisfied needs usually create considerable tension among family members. Also, the child in the family has fewer adults and siblings to interact with. In the contemporary middle class nuclear Indian families, particularly in urban areas, the childhood is characterized by limited space and time, and fewer siblings and friends to play with. Due to subsequent rise in competitive values, parental aspirations and expectations regarding children's education have also become very high. As a result, children start going to school at an early age thus, curtailing their freedom due to long hours of school, pressures of home work and the hectic life-style of parents. With this busy schedule of family members, children hardly get time and opportunity for active play.

Mother's employment invariably adds further to the stress in the family in many ways. Thus, changing social milieu and home environment, high expectations of parents along with the demand of school extract their heavy toll from the child. Kumar (1993), while analysing childhood in Indian society, rightly draws attention to the conflict in the socialization of the child by two contradictory forces. One, that of school, media and consumer products emphasizing child's autonomy and his specialized status, the other that of parental/adult authority. Children in different contexts perceive things in different ways. They have their family values and socialization pattern. Exposure to external world provides a different set of role models. Children in contradictory situations get confused and are not able to decide which one to follow. In case of working parents children have limited scope to interact with the parents, and therefore, cannot get rid of their confusions.

Dimensions of Disciplining: An Overview

Discipline is often considered as essential for the growth and development of child. In the absence of discipline, the child's world remains too "unstructured" to permit adjustment. If there are no rules to the game of living, a child will not be able to learn to play it. It is a very important instrument in the process of socialization in which parents guide the child in the direction of what is socially acceptable in his/her culture (Hurlock, 1978).

Generally, 'discipline' is treated as synonym of punishment. According to this view, discipline is used only when a child violates the rules and regulations set down by parents, teachers or adults in charge of the affairs of the community in which (s)he lives. Since long, it is believed that children need discipline but there have been changes in the attitude about why they need it. In the past, it was believed that discipline was necessary to adhere to the standards that society established and would tolerate no deviations from them. Today, it is recognised that the child needs discipline, if (s)he has to be a happy and well adjusted person in the society. Discipline also helps children to satisfy certain needs and thus, adds to their happiness and to good personal and social adjustments. Hurlock (1978) has summarized some of the many needs, fulfilled by discipline (p. 380) :

1. It gives the child a feeling of security by telling him what he may or may not do.
2. By helping the child avoid frequent feelings of guilt which lead to unhappiness and poor adjustment. Discipline enables him to live according to the standards approved by the social group.
3. Through discipline, the child learns to behave in a way that leads to praise, which he interprets as an indication of love–essential to successful adjustment.
4. Appropriate discipline serves as an ego-bolstering motivation which encourages the child to accomplish what is required.
5. Discipline helps the child to develop a conscience, the 'internalized voice', that guides him in making his own decisions.

We know that children differ in their rate of maturation, and therefore, discipline that is developmentally appropriate for one child may not be appropriate for all children of the same age. Younger and older children need different explanations of why certain forms of behaviour are acceptable and others are not. Discipline is most likely to be needed in connection with routine activities, such as eating, going to bed or preparing for school and is least likely to be needed when the child is free to play as (s)he chooses. And finally, older children need discipline less often than young children. As the child grows older (s)he can communicate better and thus, understands the need of conformity.

Discipline consists primarily of habit formation. The principles of learning involved in habit formation are essential in discipline, if it has to be successful. Regardless of the techniques of discipline used, the omission of any of the elements of learning may result in unfavourable attitudes on the part of the child and in a behaviour that will not be socially approved. The essentials of discipline include, rules, consistency, punishment and reward. Early studies on the techniques of discipline may be classified under two major types: (1) Power-assertive discipline, which includes physical punishment; and (2) Love-oriented discipline, which includes showing disappointment, isolation, withdrawal of love, praise and contingent giving of affection and reasoning. Maccoby and Martin (1983) have classified the techniques of disciplining in a four-fold scheme consisting of : (1) Authoritarian-Autocratic style, (2) The Indulgent-Permissive style, (3) The Authoritative-Reciprocal style, and (4) The Uninvolved-Indifferent style. A brief description of these styles as stated by Maccoby and Martin (1983) is given below:

Authoritarian-Autocratic Style: All kinds of authoritarian disciplinary styles are characterized by strict rules and regulations to enforce desired behaviours. Such techniques include severe punishment for failure to come up to the expected standards and little or no recognition, praise or other signs of approval when the child meets the expected standards. Authoritarian discipline always means control through external force in the form of punishment, especially corporal punishment. The main features of these techniques include the following :

1. Fairly severe punishment, often physical, is likely to be employed when children deviate from parental requirement.
2. Direct or verbal orders are given.
3. Power assertion is more than needed.
4. Physical control is exercised, such as, arousing fear by threatening.
5. No reward or incentive is offered.
6. Directive teaching style is practised.

Baldwin (1948,1949) has reported two major parenting dimensions as predictive of children's characteristics, i.e. democratic/autocratic and permissive/controlling. It was found that children of autocratic parents were low in social interaction with peers and tended to be dominated by their peers during the interaction that did occur. In addition, they were found obedient, not quarrelsome or resistive and lacked spontaneity, affection, curiosity and originality. Baumrind (1967) has reported that parents of unhappy and socially withdrawn nursery school age children were authoritarian. In a subsequent longitudinal study, Baumrind (1971) found that high parental demand was associated with higher social assertiveness in girls, higher social responsibility in boys and cognitive competence in children of both sexes. High parental responsiveness was associated with higher cognitive competence and somewhat higher level of social assertiveness in boys and greater degree of social responsibility in children of both sexes. The negative impact of authoritarian child-rearing method was somewhat stronger for boys than girls. Pre-school children of authoritarian parents showed relatively little independence and obtained middle-range scores on social responsibility. These relations were stronger for boys than girls. Boys also showed higher rates of anger.

It was found that power assertive child-rearing techniques were associated with low scores on the measures of conscience. It seems that the children of authoritarian parents tend to lack social initiative. Though they do not differ in behaviour from children of other types of parents, yet, on contrived measures of resistance to temptation, projective tests and parental reports show lesser evidence of 'conscience'. In discussing what is the 'right' behaviour in situations of moral conflict, they are more likely to have an external, rather than internal, moral orientation. Boys show low motivation for intellectual performance. In a number of studies authoritarian parenting is found to be associated with low self-esteem and external locus of control. Further, the parents of aggressive children tend to be authoritarian but children of authoritarian parents are not necessarily aggressive. The aspects of family interaction, crucial in determining whether a child of authoritarian parents will be subdued or 'out of control', have yet to be satisfactorily identified.

The Indulgent-Permissive Style: Permissive discipline involves very little or no use of discipline. It does not usually guide the child into socially approved patterns of behaviour and does not employ punishment. The child often has no limits or boundaries set on what (s)he may do; (s)he is permitted to make her/his own decisions and act on them in practically any way (s)he wishes. The main features of this type of child-rearing may be summarized as follows:

1. Giving little or no punishment and avoiding assertive authority or imposing control or restrictions wherever possible.
2. Covering or overlooking children's mistakes, thus giving over protection.
3. Encouraging dependency by often doing children's work.
4. Excessively using material rewards and incentives to make children work.

Baumrind (1967, 1971) characterized permissive parents as

tolerant, having positive attitude towards the child's impulses, including sexual and aggressive impulses, and using little punishment. If possible, they hardly impose any control or restriction on asserting authority. Such parents make few maturity demands (e.g. manners or carrying out tasks), allow children to regulate their own behaviour and make their own decisions when at all possible, and have few rules governing the child's time schedule. Olweus (1980) has reported that permissive parents occasionally react with harsh punishment when they find themselves unable to tolerate children's continued outbursts. Some parents allowed their children to show aggressiveness because it takes much effort to stop them. This, perhaps, reflects parental inattentiveness and indifference, rather than commitment to children's rights.

According to Maccoby and Martin (1983), permissive parents are different from uninvolved-indifferent parents. Instead of neglecting their children, they use permissiveness as an act of indulgence. It seems that permissive child-rearing practice has more negative than positive effects because it is related to children being aggressive, impulsive and lacking independence in the ability to take responsibility.

The Authoritative-Reciprocal Style: According to Maccoby and Martin (1983) the authoritative-reciprocal parenting is "a pattern of family functioning in which children are required to be responsive to parental demands, and parents accept a reciprocal responsibility to be as responsive as possible to their children's reasonable demands and points of view" (p. 46). Reciprocity highlights a 'two way communication process' between the parent and the child, in which each is responsive to the other's demands, but parents are expected to respond only to the 'reasonable demands' from their children. Its main features are as follows.

1. Parents apply psychological control, such as, by arousing guilt in the child or instilling anxiety.
2. Psychological punishment such as withdrawal of love is a more common practice.

3. Physical punishment is mild and rare and often followed by reasoning.
4. Parents use psychological rewards such as praise, recognition of work than material rewards or incentives to motivate children to work. Power assertion is just enough to secure compliance.
5. Suggestions are given instead of direct verbal orders or directions, leaving the child with some freedom of choice.

Comstock (1973) and McEachern (1973) have noted that children with high self-esteem tend to perceive their parents as exercising fairly high level of firm control. Moral development is another area in which reciprocal relationship enhances mature functioning in children. Hoffman and Saltzstein (1967) and Hoffman (1970) contended that parents of "humanistic" type did not exercise firm control but at the same time showed a good deal of warmth and were not punitive.

Authoritative-reciprocal pattern of child-rearing is associated with such personality characteristics of children as independence, social responsibility, ability to control aggression, self-confidence and high self-esteem.

The Uninvolved-Indifferent Style: The uninvolved parents try to spend the least possible time and effort while interacting with children and are likely to reflect a desire to keep the child at a distance. They tend to orient their behaviour primarily towards the avoidance of inconvenience. Thus, they respond to the immediate demands from children in such a way as to terminate them. Here the term 'uninvolved' means the degree to which a parent is committed to his or her role as parent, and to the fostering of 'optimal child development'. Variability in involvement above and beyond this base level is considerable. Parents may be highly involved in other activities and have little time or attention to spare for the child as compared to the parents who are totally involved in their parenting role. Main features of the technique are:

1. Parents are low in demand and exercise very little control.
2. They are indifferent to their children's mistakes.

Egeland and Sroufe (1981a, b) have indicated some extreme implication of low level of parental involvement in their study of a group of abusive parents. They distinguished several aspects of these parents' behaviour, such as, physical abuse, hostilty, verbal abuse, neglect and psychological unavailability. Psychological unavailability and neglect involved parents being detached, emotionally uninvolved, often depressed and uninterested in the child. Martin (1981) tried to determine the correlates of high or low parental involvement in a more normal sample, and defined involvement as the extent to which mothers set plan of action or routine according to their own preferences. Follow up studies revealed that maternal involvement was associated with a decreased child demand and coerciveness in the interval from 10 to 42 months, but that child demand had no detectable influence on maternal involvement during that interval.

In a longitudinal study Pulkkinen (1982) noted considerable difference along the dimensions of child-centred *vs* parent-centred child-rearing methods. The features of child-centred methods were similar to the features of reciprocal or authoritative parenting. At the age of 14, children reared by child-centred methods were, on an average, responsible, achievement oriented, competent in social relationships, likely to maintain good relationship with their parents and held future orientation. In contrast, children of parent-centred homes were impulsive and unintegrated in school and their friends were often disliked by the parents. They were more likely to be hedonistic and lacked frustration tolerance and emotional control.

It is concluded that the levels of parental involvement must be linked to the child's developmental level and it should be high when the child is relatively immature and should decrease gradually as the child becomes more able to function independently (Maccoby & Martin ,1983). However, there are reasons to believe that continued parental involvement in the child's life and decisions positively monitors development during adolescence (Patterson,

1982; Pulkkinen, 1982).

Dekovic and Janssens (1992) revealed that authoritative/democratic and authoritative/restrictive behaviour of parents appeared to be predictive of both the child's prosocial behaviour and his/her sociometric status. Fischer and Crawford (1992) examined the association between the parent-child relationship and the adolescents' co-dependency, and found that daughters of authoritarian fathers had higher co-dependency scores than did daughters of permissive fathers, whereas sons of authoritarian fathers reported higher levels of co-dependency than did sons of uninvolved fathers. Also, the exercise of control on the part of fathers, untempered by perceptions of parental warmth or support, was related to higher co-dependency scores in their offsprings. Parenting style of mothers was unrelated to co-dependency scores. Hart, Dewolf, Michele and Burt (1992) explored relations among parents' self reported disciplinary styles, pre-schoolers' playground behavioural orientation and peer status and revealed that children of more inductive parents, (i.e. less power assertive) exhibited fewer disruptive playground behaviour. In addition, daughters and older pre-schoolers of inductive mothers were more preferred by the peers. However, few significant relations were found between parental discipline and child behaviour/peer status. Age related patterns of behaviour also indicated that older pre-schoolers who engaged in more prosocial and less anti-social and disruptive playground behaviour were more preferred by peers.

Patterns of Child-rearing in India : An Overview

The socialization of the Indian child begins in a relatively stress–free and carefree environment in the company of multiple adults, especially, female adults. Although she is helped by other women in the family, the mother is the primary agent of socialization (Kakar, 1978; Tandon, 1981). According to Kakar (1978), the main emphasis during infancy is on avoidance of frustration and enhancement of pleasurable mutuality between the mother and the infant. Saraswathi and Dutta (1988, 1990) suggest a warm and nurturant family environment experienced by the growing child in

Indian context. There are minimal demands placed on the child to function independently and to master developmental skills. There is a relaxed pace of toilet training and generally no harsh methods are used for such training. The infancy stage is delayed and the child remains dependent on the mother for a longer period. Kakar (1978) says that the Indian child is usually deeply attached to the mother. Kakar contended that due to prolonged infancy the later stages are not sequential but compressed into one when the child is at once confronted with the tasks of ...... "separation and individuation, of autonomy and initiative, of wilful self-definition and oedipal rivalry". This is sometimes an unpleasant experience for the child especially, the male, because he is suddenly pushed out from the female domain into the domain of males and masculine work. In nuclear families the experience of psychological separation from mother may not be as painful for the child because the process of separation starts a little early and is facilitated by the reality of nuclear composition. In such families, there are not many nurturant figures available to start with.

In Indian context, the disciplining techniques used in socializing the child are most often harsh and strict. Ross (1961) found that more than half the total number of respondents had experienced very strict discipline at home. Physical punishments were reported by less than half the total number, a higher percentage being that of boys. Other forms of punishment were deprivation of food, sarcasm, swearing, threats or nagging, of which "nagging" was considered the worst form of punishment. However, Ross reported absence of resentment or ill feelings among children towards their parents probably because "right" and "wrong" behaviours were clearly spelt out. Children understood the reasons and accepted them uncritically. Saraswathi and Datta (1990) found scolding and threats to be common and predominant modes of punishment among families in rural and urban settings in Gujrat. Some amount of reasoning and explaining was also used as a form of disciplining. The goal of disciplining was stated to be teaching children proper conduct to gain respect and social status. In yet another study, Saraswathi, Thakkar and Kaur (1979) found beating and physical punishment as frequent forms of power assertion in working class families, while scolding and threatening were more common among middle and upper-middle class families. Withdrawal of love and services like food are also common (Beals, 1967). Reward and praise are used infrequently. It was thought that the child may get spoilt and think too much of himself or herself (Minturn & Lambert, 1964). As a result of the authoritarian style of parenting and use of threat in disciplining, children learn to avoid displeasing the parent and eventual punishment rather than imbibe the norms (S. Malhotra & A. Malhotra, 1985).

While studying personality development of children in relation to child-rearing practices among different socio-economic classes Joshi and Tiwari (1977) revealed that although socio-economic status does affect child-rearing practices, it influences the development of different personality traits in children. According to them, middle class mothers, who use praise and reward to inculcate obedience and desirable behaviours, are more punitive (spanking) and less consistent in their threatening and punitive behaviours than mothers of upper social class. Extent of parental approval for disciplining techniques for children is greater in middle class homes than in the upper class homes. Mostly fathers are disciplining agents for children in the middle class homes.

Relationship between attitudes of mothers towards child-rearing as a function of age was investigated by Seth and Khanna (1978). They found that as compared to older mothers (mothers above 40 years), younger mothers (below 30 years) tend to experience more marital conflict and more approving of the activities of their children. In a study of sex differences in child's perception of parent-child relationship, it was found that parent-child mutual acceptance and democratic practices of parents affect parental perception, and girls perceived their parents in a more favourable way than boys, (Wadekar & Palsane, 1987). Family background factors such as family size, family pattern and individual's birth-order affected children's perception of maternal acceptance and the incidence of perceived maternal acceptance was greater in small families than in large ones (Sandhu & Bhargava, 1987).

The relationship between social responsibility and parental disciplinary practices was studied by Singh and Fatmi (1980). The results showed that in the case of males, the use of induction as disciplinary technique by mothers had a positive relationship with social responsibility. However, for females, a relationship between social responsibility and power assertion by father and love withdrawal by mother was recorded. Other disciplinary techniques adopted by parents showed no relationship with social responsibility in both males and females. In a study by Singh and Sowaid (1976), it is indicated that guilt (over hostility) was positively related to love-oriented discipline and negatively related to power-assertive discipline. No definite relationship between hostility and power-assertive or love-oriented discipline was observed. Similarly, no consistent relationship emerged between conflict over hostility and love-oriented or power-assertive discipline. Ojha and Singh (1988) observed that parents' restrictive, rejecting and neglecting attitudes gave rise to the feeling of insecurity in their children, while permissive attitude reduced it. Over-protection by parents fostered dependence proneness while their neglecting attitude was negatively linked with dependence proneness and father's restriction was positively associated with dependence proneness. Chatterjee and Shah (1981) studied the relationship between adjustment and perceived parental behaviour among male and female students. A positive correlation was found between emotional and social adjustment scores of females and their perception of mothers and to a lesser extent of their fathers as nurturant and affectionate.

Anxiety in school children has been found positively related to authoritarianism, anxiety and rigidity in fathers, and the use of strict discipline (Hassan, Enayatullah & Khalique, 1977). Similarly, restrictive and rejecting behaviour on the part of parents was associated with authoritarianism in children (Ojha, 1977).

Agarwal and Saksena (1977) had reviewed the literature and suggested that child's emotional development is influenced by parents' child rearing attitudes and practices and by the parent's personality. They also suggested that parents should be exposed to training programmes in order to avoid children from being adversely affected. Parental warmth and affection showed a positive relationship with a sense of competence in their children. A similar attitude on the part of teachers also helped children to develop a sense of confidence and personal worth. It was pointed out that such attitudes should be accompanied by firm and consistent discipline both at home and in the school, in order to enable the children to develop maturity (Sharma, Saraswathi & Gir,1981). Mothers of children with high separation anxiety scored high on child-rearing dimensions, such as, fostering dependency, encouraging verbalisation, marital conflict and approval of the child's activity (Barar S. & Barar S.S., 1990).

Saraswathi and Sundaresan (1979) studied the relationship between parental disciplinary techniques and children's moral maturity in a sample of 12-13 years old. They found class-differences as well as gender differences. In the upper-class group, power-assertion was negatively correlated and induction was positively correlated with moral maturity among boys, whereas only the first correlation was significant among girls. In the working-class, the correlations were low. The upper-class subjects reported that love-withdrawal was rarely used as a disciplinary technique, and that power-assertion was the most commonly used technique, followed by induction. In case of the boys of working-class, the use of power assertion was very frequent. In another study Saraswathi, Thakkar and Kaur (1979) also reported similar findings.

Child-rearing antecedents of self-esteem as a personality variable have been examined by many researchers. In a study Kapur and Gill (1986) compared socially advantaged and disadvantaged children and found that in both the groups, parental acceptance was positively related with positive self-esteem while parental rejection was associated with negative self-esteem in children and was stronger in the socially advantaged group. Gupta (1990) found a positive relationship between parental machiavellianism and offspring's self-esteem.

Minturn, Boyd and Kapoor (1978) reported changes in socialization practices of Rajput mothers of Khalapur from 1955 to 1975. It was found that due to alterations in status, mothers in the 1975 sample exercised a more direct control over the care and discipline of their children. These mothers, with education, trained their children for greater responsibility and assertiveness, allowed them to cry more, and were more severe in dealing with boys than were mothers in the 1955 sample. In a comparative study of the child-rearing practices of Satnamee and non-Satnamee mothers and personalities of their children, it was found that the Satnamee children were breast-fed for a longer period and their toilet training commenced at a later stage. On the ESPQ, the Satnamee children were found comparatively languid and slow, socially clumsy, vague and contented (Joshi & Daharwal, 1977).

Tiwari and Misra (1977) studied the development pattern of achievement motivation (n-ach) in relation to prolonged deprivation, parental attitude towards independence training, demands for mastery and independence and restrictions on independence activities. The findings indicated that the strength of N-ach varied significantly as a function of deprivation level. It was also found that parents of high achievement and low anxiety group reported a significantly higher degree of independence attitude and indicated more early demands and fewer early restrictions compared to parents of other groups. The results also demonstrated that the strength of n-ach increased with age at all deprivation levels. Anandalakshmy and Bajaj (1981) described the physical and ecological environment in which the child grows up and the differences in the rearing practices of male and female children. The results showed no evidence of direct and simple relationship between the parents' efforts to socialise the child and the child's competence behaviour. Individual factors, situational events and specific life experience within the framework of the eco-cultural environment of the community were found to be salient in the socialisation process.

The traditional Indian family has an authoritarian structure and it stresses conformity and de-emphasizes autonomy and independence. Family structure has a significant influence on the interaction among family members (Begum, 1975; Bisht & Sinha, 1981; Gore,1978; Mehra, 1974; Menon, 1974; Roland, 1978; Sharma, 1971). A positive influence of parents' educational level, socio-economic status and size of the family on personality development of children has been observed in many studies (Begum, 1975; Mehra, 1974; Menon, 1974; Sharma, 1971). Singh and Sharma (1978) reported that secure parent-child relationship helped the child in coping rather than defending from the situation. Children from such backgrounds learnt social competence and displayed the feelings of independence and responsibility for their acts. Over-protection and permissive child-rearing help in developing unbound trustfulness, gullibility and dependence so that individuation and autonomy were rendered difficult (Bassa, 1978). Interparental conflicts with regard to child rearing problems have an adverse effect on child's adjustment and scholastic achievement (Kakkar, 1970) and parental techniques that encourage internalization of behaviour codes were effective in controlling aggressive behaviour (Sharma, 1971). Kalra (1979) has observed that parental aspiration and praise influence the personality development of individual from infancy onwards.

In a recent study by Lavakare and Hiswanker (1995) the effect of parent directed intervention on child's personality dimensions and parental approach towards the child was studied. Two types of interventions were planned, viz. (a) face to face discussion, (b) a letter form material. The effect of intervention was evident in both child's as well as in mothers' approach in both types of interventions. They further found that letter-form material appeared superior than face to face discussion type. Lavakare and Hiswankar also quoted a few studies related to parent-child interaction and development of the child (Bornstein & Lemb, 1992). In recent years there have been studies on the effect of skill training (Werkerle & Wolfe, 1993), training in competence in child-rearing (Wolfe & Werkerle, 1993), and training in approaches (Eisenstadt *et al.*, 1993). Most of these studies focused on parents' discipline, health and expectations, (Lavakare, 1994), maltreatment of the child (Belsky, 1993) and over-protection (Mak, 1994) indicated that there is a relationship between parents' behaviour and child's behaviour and there is a strong need for intervention. Ojha and Pramanick (1995) have studied parental behaviour as related to some personality traits of adolescents and found that both mother's and father's behaviours, in general, were significantly related with hostility, self-esteem and self-disclosure. Child's perception of parental rearing behaviours is a crucial determinant of his/her personality (Eastburg & Johnson, 1991; Paris & Prank, 1989; Ritcher, Eisenmann & Ritcher, 1991).

Passi (1998) has observed that if the parents are authoritarian type, in all likelihood, the children are going to develop into aggressive and hostile adults with feelings of frustration wrought over them. In a study on juvenile delinquency, Sanyal (1998) contemplated that parents must understand their moral responsibility in adopting adequate parental care such as continuous awareness of child's needs, familiarity with his/her activities, acquaintance with his/her friends and adequate overall supervision. Simply disciplining the child is not sufficient, it is very important that a child should be treated as an individual, parents should participate in his/her activities, and should also know about the friends. All these can go a long way in the healthy development of a child. Parents usually blame media and surroundings for misbehaviour among children. They seldom realise that their own behaviour is the determinant of such behaviour. Emotional abuse and neglect play even greater role in developing delinquency if they are allowed to continue very frequently. Sanyal further adds that parental treatment such as screaming at the child and excessively criticising or generally ignoring the child have harmful effect on the self-esteem of the child. While analysing the determinants of delinquent behaviour in children, Sanyal says that inconsistent and physically harsh discipline in the home may lead to more delinquency than consistent and adequate form of discipline. If a child receives severe punishment, (s)he shows more resentment and aggression. She further says that if a child lives with hostility, (s)he learns to fight, if (s)he lives with fear, (s)he learns to be apprehensive, if (s)he lives with jealousy (s)he learns to feel guilty.

According to Bhagat (1997), children should be encouraged to pursue constructive hobbies and participate in cultural programmes, to keep them away from developing undesirable traits. Bhagat also says that parents should listen to the children in a non-directive manner.

It is evident from the preceding review that parenting has been conceptualized along several dimensions in which *authority* and *involvement* emerge as very crucial. However, exact practices employed by parents evince considerable variety. In particular, there are cultural, subcultural, social class and age related variations in the preference and use of disciplining practices. The studies of employed mothers have been confined to limited aspects of disciplining practices and the relationships of those practices with personality and related variables are inconclusive and have often led to contradictory findings. This confusing state of understanding in this area suggests that more comprehensive treatment of child rearing practices and their relationship with personality variables are needed. In this context, the cultural factors should receive greater attention. With this in view, the present study was aimed at examining the pattern of disciplining practices used by working and non-working mothers. It is hypothesized that due to dual roles working mothers may have very little time to think about child's behaviours and follow appropriate disciplinary techniques. On the other hand non-working mothers are generally at home and children usually remain in their focus of attention. They may have more opportunity to understand child's behaviours. Because of the different perceptions of working and non-working mothers about their children's behaviour, their disciplinary pratices may differ in many ways.

Measures

Questionnaire of Parental Disciplinary Practices : A questionnaire measure of how parents discipline their children and interact with the child, the way they participate in child's activities and look after the physical, emotional, psychological and intellectual needs of the child, was prepared in Hindi language on the basis of a review of past research (Bhogle, 1978, 1981; Joshi & Tiwari, 1977; Nanda, 1991; Pal & Sharma, 1981; Saraswathi & Sundaresan, 1979; Sinha, 1981). The items relating to these aspects were first scrutinized by a group of experts according to their importance and relevance in disciplining the child in the Indian context. Its preliminary form was then administered to a small group of employed and unemployed mothers(n - 30). This questionnaire was open ended. After obtaining responses from all the respondents, the least frequent and ambiguous items were eliminated. After making necessary changes, the measure was finalized.

The main questionnaire consisted of items related to different aspects of disciplining the child and child's interaction with parents, siblings and peers. The present investigator's ratings correlated significantly with the ratings made by another researcher. The values of correlations for the different areas of the measure ranged between .58 to .87. The questionnaire had 7 sub-parts as detailed below.

Aspects of Disciplining: It contained 12 items, namely, teaching cleanliness, expected obedience, reaction to disobedience, reaction to obedience, expected discipline, operative level of discipline, techniques to inculcate positive habits, incidence of lying, reaction to lying, reaction to child's insistence, reaction to losing something in the school, consistency in mother's reaction to child's negative behaviour and persistence of negative behaviour.

Parental Involvement with the Child : A total of 6 items related to parent-child relationship were included. They consisted of parental understanding regarding child related matters, expression of love and affection towards the child, parental participation in child's different activities, intimacy with either parent and cause of intimacy with either parent, and amount of spare time spent with the child.

Quality of Maternal Interaction : This part of the questionnaire contained 12 items which mainly dealt with aspects like degree of understanding between mother and the child, trust in child's activities, monitoring child's activities, sharing matters with mothers, mother's use of spare time with the child, helping the child in spite of being busy, helping the child in simple work, judging child's ability, degree of satisfaction with child's performance in school and promotion of physical games and exercises.

Independence to the Child : It consisted of 2 items, i.e. freedom in going out independently and in expressing disapproval to parents.

Interaction with Siblings : It contained 3 items like incidence of quarrel with siblings, sharing with siblings, and helping the siblings.

Interaction with Peers : It included 4 items, e.g., relationship with neighbouring children, freedom in expressing anger towards friends, sharing thoughts related to peers with mothers and mother's reaction to quarrelling with friends.

Perceived and Desired Characteristics of Children : To know mother's liking and disliking a particular characteristic of the child and the most desired characteristics, following open-ended questions were presented to mothers :

— What characteristics of your child do you like the most ?
— What characteristics of your child do you dislike the most?
— What characteristics do you desire to inculcate in your child?

The responses for disciplinary items were obtained along categories like 'physical punishment', 'scolding', 'no talking', 'depriving' and 'explaining'. Reaction to positive behaviours by mothers were categorised in terms of 'indifference', 'encouragement', 'praise', 'reward', 'giving love and affection' and 'according to situation'. Other response categories included 'less than average' to 'more than average', and depending upon the content of the items.

Results

Aspects of Disciplining the Child : In order to study the various facets of disciplining, mothers were asked to give their responses regarding different aspects of disciplining the child. The responses are presented in Table 3.1.

Table 3.1 : Responses of Employed and Unemployed Mothers on various Aspects of Disciplining the Child

Aspects of Discipline	Unemployed Mothers (N=80) f (%)		Employed Mothers (N=120) f (%)		(df) χ^2
Teaching Cleanliness					
According to situation	0	(0)	5	(4)	
Explaining	14	(18)	19	(16)	
Forcing to do	8	(10)	18	(15)	
Depriving	38	(47)	32	(27)	
Scolding	20	(25)	35	(29)	
Physical punishment	0	(0)	11	(9)	(5) = 17.93**
Degree of Expected Obedience $					
Average	14	(17)	19	(16)	
Above average	38	(48)	53	(44)	
Complete	28	(35)	48	(40)	(2) = 0.51
Reaction to Disobedience $					
Physical Punishment	0	(0)	11	(9)	
Scolding	20	(25)	35	(29)	
Depriving	38	(47)	32	(27)	
Forcing to do	8	(10)	18	(15)	
Explaining	14	(18)	19	(16)	
According to situation	0	(0)	5	(4)	(5)=17.93**
Reaction to Obedience					
Encourage	10	(13)	19	(16)	
Praise	28	(35)	40	(33)	
Reward	2	(2)	3	(3)	
Love	38	(48)	42	(35)	
According to situation	0	(0)	6	(5)	
Indifferent	2	(2)	10	(8)	(5)=9.00

(Contd.)

Table 3.1 : Contd......

Aspects of Discipline	Unemployed Mothers (N=80) f(%)		Employed Mothers (N=120) f(%)		(df) χ^2
Degree of Expected Discipline					
Complete	0	(0)	39	(32)	
Above average	38	(48)	60	(50)	
Average	26	(32)	21	(18)	
Below average	16	(20)	0	(0)	(3)=54.66**
Operative Level of Discipline					
Complete	0	(0)	17	(14)	
Above average	10	(12)	45	(38)	
Average	40	(50)	55	(45)	
Below average	30	(38)	3	(3)	(3)=58.05**
Techniques to Inculcate Positive Habits $					
Scolding/Depriving	0	(0)	11	(9)	
Example of ideals	4	(5)	49	(42)	
Example of neighbours	44	(55)	32	(26)	
Example of family members	8	(10)	2	(1)	
Explain with love	12	(15)	2	(1)	
Reward	12	(15)	2	(1)	(5) = 67.86**
Incidence of Lying Behaviour $					
Frequent	0	(0)	7	(6)	
Sometimes	32	(40)	37	(31)	
Rare	46	(58)	71	(59)	
Never	2	(2)	5	(4)	(3)=6.23
Reactions to Lying $					
Being indifferent	0	(0)	3	(3)	
Physical punishment	4	(5)	7	(5)	

(Contd.)

Table 3.1 : Contd.....

Aspects of Discipline	Unemployed Mothers (N=80) f (%)		Employed Mothers (N=120) f (%)		(df) χ^2
Scolding/Depriving	14	(18)	3	(3)	
Explaining	62	(77)	107	(89)	(3)=13.65**
Reaction to Child's Insistence $					
Scolding	0	(0)	11	(9)	
Depriving	2	(2)	5	(4)	
Explaining	70	(88)	80	(67)	
Fulfil on Condition	6	(8)	22	(18)	
Immediate fulfilment	2	(2)	2	(2)	(4)=14.68**
Reaction to Losing Something in School by the Child $					
Scolding	16	(20)	24	(20)	
Depriving	0	(0)	7	(6)	
Explaining	28	(35)	61	(51)	
Encourage to keep things properly	36	(45)	28	(23)	(3)=14.41**
Consistency in Mother's Reaction to Child's Negative Behaviours					
Always	4	(5)	10	(8)	
Mostly	48	(60)	41	(34)	
Sometimes	22	(27)	54	(45)	
Less	6	(8)	15	(13)	(3)=12.97**
Persistence of Negative Behaviour $					
Frequently	12	(15)	14	(12)	
Sometimes	44	(55)	76	(63)	
Rarely	24	(30)	30	(25)	(2)=1.41

* $p < .05$; ** $p < .01$.

$ - Reverse the scoring

1. Teaching cleanliness : In early years of life, children learn discipline through keeping their body and surroundings clean. Mothers in both the groups reported a variety of techniques for teaching cleanliness. More mothers in unemployed group (47%) reported 'depriving from something' (eating, playing, watching TV etc.) as compared to only 27 per cent of EMs, in case child did not show compliance. On the other hand almost equal number of mothers in both the groups (25% and 29%) reported 'scolding'. Other response categories included 'explaining' and 'forcing to do'. 'Physical punishment' was reported only by EMs' group. More UEMs reported 'depriving' the child from something or 'scolding', whereas EMs reported almost all techniques depending upon the situation. The results suggest a significant difference in the responses of both groups, $\chi^2(5) = 17.93, p<.01$. It seems 'explaining' does not work when children are taught cleanliness.

2. Degree of expected obedience : What is the expectation of parents about the level of obedience in their children? Some parents are very strict and expect total compliance in their children whereas others consider time, age and mood of the child. It was observed that almost all mothers expected a considerably high degree of obedience on the part of their children.

3. Reactions to disobedience : When children disobey the parents or the elders in the family, the parents either punish or scold the child for disobeying or explain the importance of obeying. Disobedience was disliked by UEMs and reacted to by 'depriving' (47%) more and also 'scolding' (25%), whereas EMs used 'scolding' (29%) and 'depriving' (27%) almost equally. In addition, 'explaining' and 'forcing to do' were used by a small number of mothers in both the groups. EMs reported use of 'physical punishment' (9%) also. The results showed that the EMs and UEMs differed significantly in this regard, $\chi^2(5) = 17.93, p < .01$. On this aspect, more UEMs reported 'depriving from something' as compared to their counterparts. Generally, UEMs remain at home and whenever child disobeys, they can immediately react to it. But in case of EMs such incidents are less noticed, because they are away for a relatively longer hours. Sometimes they come to know later but they may ignore it. It seems that mothers considered this aspect more important and therefore, instead of 'explaining' they used relatively harsh techniques.

4. Reactions to obedience : Generally, parents check the negative behaviours by punishment or by induction. It is also very necessary to reinforce the positive or desired behaviour. Therefore, obedience shown by children should also be acknowledged. It was reported by mothers in both groups that the enactment of obedience on the part of children was reciprocated by 'love' and 'praise'. The, compliance to obedience was responded to in a similar fashion by employed and unemployed mothers.

5. Degree of expected discipline : Besides obedience, discipline is needed in every aspect of day-to-day life, such as completing routine activities in time, being punctual, organised, systematic etc. Therefore, it is necessary to know as to how much discipline is expected by the parents and whether employed and unemployed mothers differ in this regard. The level of expected discipline as expressed by EMs was significantly greater than their counterparts, $\chi^2(5) = 54.66, p < .01$. EMs showed their concern regarding child's future success and, therefore, expected a higher level of discipline. If someone wants to be successful in life, one should be disciplined. It does not mean that UEMs do not consider it very important. Actually daily routine and other activities in EMs' life follow a systematic pattern and except weekends they cannot afford slight deviation in this regard. This is why they reported 'complete' or 'above average' level of discipline.

6. Operative level of discipline : Although parents may expect a very high level of discipline in their children, it may not be necessary that their children are also disciplined upto that level. The comparison of responses reported by both the groups showed that the operative level of discipline was also significantly greater in the case of EMs. About 38 per cent of EMs reported that children are above average in discipline and about 14 per cent reported complete discipline. In contrast, only 12 per cent of UEMs reported above average level of discipline. In case of UEMs 38 per cent reported that their children are 'below average' in discipline as compared to only 3 per cent of EMs, χ^2 (3) = 58.05, p <.01.

7. Techniques to inculcate positive habits : To inculcate socially desired habits in their children, parents either punish their children for showing negative behaviour or they use positive techniques like citing examples of ideals, neighbours or family members and explain the reasons for developing good habits. To promote positive habits in children, about 40 per cent of EMs as compared to only 5 per cent of UEMs used "citing examples of ideals", whereas, 55 per cent of UEMs as compared to 26 per cent of EMs used 'examples of neighbours'. 'Scolding' and 'depriving' were used by a very few EMs (9%). In UEMs' group, 'explaining' and 'reward' were also used by a considerable number of mothers (30%), $\chi^2(5) = 67.86, p < .01$. More EMs reported 'citing examples of ideals'. It may be possible that EMs also had their own ideals or they know that children are more fascinated by the legendary figures. UEMs reported greater use of life experiences. Generally, parents have a tendency to compare their children with their peers. Perhaps UEMs thought that children can learn better and faster when compared with their friends.

8. Incidence of lying and reactions to it: To escape punishment or parents' annoyance, children sometimes lie. Higher incidence of such behaviour may suggest that parents use negative techniques for disciplining the child. Responses of both the groups indicated that mothers did not perceive their children lying in a substantial manner. However, they did admit that sometimes children do lie (40% UEMs, and 31% EMs). Mother's responses to lying behaviour included a variety of techniques among which 'explaining' was reported by most of them in both the groups (77%, 89%). 'Physical punishment' was used by a very small number of mothers in both the groups.

9. Reaction to insistence : When children insist upon something, parents react differently. Sometimes parents immediately fulfil their demand and sometimes either the child is threatened to be 'deprived of something' or 'scolded'. In response to 'insistence by the child' the dominant response of mothers was 'explaining' (88% and 67%). However, 'fulfilling on condition' and 'scolding' were more frequent in the case of EMs (18% and 9%) than UEMs (8% and 0%), χ^2 (4)= 14.68, $p < .01$.

10. Reaction to losing something in school : Children of this age group sometimes lose their belongings in the school. What do mothers do to check this behaviour and promote responsibility in their children ? 'Losing something in school' was responded to by EMs with 'explaining' (51%) followed by 'encouraging to keep things properly' (23%) and 'scolding' (20%) in the order. UEMs used techniques like 'encouraging to keep things properly' (45%) followed by 'explaining' (35%) and 'scolding' (20%). EMs and UEMs significantly differed on this aspect, $\chi^2(3)$=14.41, $p < .01$.

11. Consistency in mother's reaction to child's negative behaviour: For proper personality development of children, consistency in mother's reactions to child's behaviour is very necessary. Inconsistency in parental behaviour may confuse the child and (s)he may not be able to learn the socially desired behaviour. Regarding this aspect, the UEMs appeared to be relatively more consistent in their reactions (65%) as compared to their counterparts (42%), χ^2 (3) = 12.97, $p <.01$. Relatively less consistency reported by more EMs can be 'explained' by considering the situation with EMs. Parents' reaction to child's negative or positive behaviour depends upon the time, mood and condition or preoccupation of parents. Sometimes parents are so tired that they do not want to pay much attention to what child did in their absence. Sometimes parents' experiences at the work place may be reflected in their treatment with the child. Sometimes parents are in a good mood and react mildly to an undesired behaviour. UEMs are having children in their focus of attention, therefore, they can show relatively more consistency in their reactions.

12. Persistence of negative behaviour : Inspite of 'punishment' or 'explaining' by parents, children tend to show negative behaviour more often. Mothers in both the groups reported that their children sometimes repeated the negative behaviour (UEMs, 55% and EMs, 63%). The trend was similar in both the groups.

Parental involvement with the child For healthy personality development, a child needs attachment with parents. To this end, degree of parental understanding regarding child's matters, expression of love and affection towards the child, parental participation in child's activities, mother's feelings about the amount of spare time spent with the child, mothers' perception of child's intimacy with parent and cause of intimacy were included. Responses on these variables provide information about the nature of family environment. Table 3.2 presents the aspects of parental involvement which are described in following sections.

1. Degree of parental understanding regarding child's matters : There are several matters related to child, from daily routine to studies, hobbies, play activities etc. Parental understanding regarding these matters is very important so that a child may easily know what to do and what not to do? Sometimes parents have adequate understanding regarding child related matters. When parents do not hold such understanding, child is the sufferer. EMs reported relatively greater understanding (52%) in comparison to UEMs (38%). About 52 per cent of UEMs showed average understanding, χ^2 (2) = 10.55, p <.01.

2. Expression of love and affection towards the child : Every parent loves his/her child, but sometimes one parent expresses more affection by way of fulfilling child's wishes, playing with him/her or by participating in his/her daily routine. Comparison of responses of EMs and UEMs suggested that a common trend regarding 'expression of love and affection' was found across both the groups.

3. Parental participation in child's activities : Generally, it is believed that mothers participate more in child's daily routine and fathers in studies, taking the child outside the home, and during play (outdoor/indore games). When mothers are also working

Table 3.2 : Responses of Employed and Unemployed Mothers Regarding Parental Involvement with the Child

Various Aspects of Parental Involvement	Unemployed Mothers (N=80) f(%)		Employed Mothers (N=120) f(%)		$(df)\chi^2$
Degree of Parental Understanding regarding Child's Matters					
Mostly complete	30	(38)	62	(52)	
Average	42	(52)	36	(30)	
Below average	8	(10)	22	(18)	(2)=10.55**
Love and Affection towards the Child's $					
None	0	(0)	6	(5)	
Father	32	(40)	46	(38)	
Mother	36	(45)	57	(48)	
Both	12	(15)	11	(9)	(3)=5.52
Parental Participation in the Child's Activities By $					
None	0	(0)	6	(5)	
Father alone	32	(40)	46	(38)	
Mother alone	36	(45)	57	(48)	
Both Parents	12	(15)	11	(9)	(5)=5.52**
Child's Intimacy with $					
Mother only	40	(50)	49	(41)	
Father only	20	(25)	35	(29)	
Both equally	20	(25)	36	(30)	(2)=1.64
Cause of Intimacy $					
Not specific	22	(28)	46	(38)	
Spends more time with the child	20	(25)	11	(9)	
Not Strict	28	(35)	38	(32)	
Need gratification	6	(8)	11	(9)	
Gives Company	4	(5)	14	(12)	(4)=12.11
Amount of Spare Time Spent with the Child					
More than Sufficient	8	(10)	2	(2)	
Sufficient	44	(55)	48	(40)	
Insufficient	28	(35)	70	(58)	(2)=14.35**

** $p < .01$

$ = Reverse the scoring

outside the home then the pattern of parental participation in the families becomes important. It is important to note the extent of sharing of fathers in child's activities. About 40 per cent of UEMs as compared to 38 per cent of EMs reported that father also participated almost equally in child's activities. However, more mothers, about 48 per cent of EMs and 45 per cent of UEMs reported greater participation by the mothers.

4. Child's intimacy and cause of intimacy with either parent : Due to some reason or the other, children are more intimate or close to either father or mother. In this study children's intimacy with parents was almost similar in both the groups. Approximately 50 per cent of UEMs and 41 per cent of EMs reported that children shared intimacy with their mothers, and with fathers it was 25 per cent (UEMs) and 29 per cent (EMs) respectively. Rest of them reported that children shared intimacy with both the parents equally. However, the causes of intimacy varied in their emphasis. It was found that while 'being not strict' was an important reason reported by approximately 32 per cent of EMs, the UEMs felt that 'spending more time' was crucial. 'Providing company' was another important reason in EMs' group. It is also important to note that a considerable number of mothers could not specify any definite reason in this regard.

5. Amount of spare time spent with the child : It is generally opined that qualitative interaction with the child is more important than the quantitative. Mother's satisfaction with the amount of time spent with the child is also very important. Full-time housewives may spend whole day with their children but it is important to know that how much interaction is actually taking place. EMs may spend relatively less amount of their time with children but interaction with the child may be more intense. What is the feeling of mothers regarding the amount of spare time they spend with their children? The amount of time spent by parents with the child was viewed insufficient by 58 per cent of EMs as compared to only 35 per cent of UEMs. About 55 per cent of UEMs felt 'sufficient' and 10 per cent 'more than sufficient' whereas in case of EMs only 40 per cent of mothers expressed their satisfaction with the amount of time available with the child, $\chi^2(2) = 14.35, p < .01$.

Maternal Interaction with the child Mothers, as compared to fathers, spend more time with the child participating in routine activities and fulfilling child's needs and demands. Such interaction requires understanding between the mother and the child, faith in child's activities, appreciating child's abilities with reference to his/her agemates and degree of satisfaction with child's interests etc. Table 3.3 presents the responses of UEMs and EMs regarding these aspects.

1. Mother's use of spare time with the child : If mothers, employed and unemployed, get spare time, how do they spend it with their children? Whether they themselves take the decision or child's wish is also considered? The pattern of responses in using spare time with the child showed significant differences. About 73 per cent of UEMs in comparison to 58 per cent of their counterparts reported that they usually 'go out'. The dominant mode was 'outing' followed by 'play'. More EMs (17%) also considered 'child's wish', $\chi^2(2)=10.26\ p<.01$.

2. Understanding between mother and the child : It is said that mothers have clear understanding about behaviour of their children, but sometimes they also do not understand the cause behind a particular behaviour of the child. The results indicate that EMs as well as UEMs shared considerable degree of understanding with the child. More than 75 per cent of mothers in both the groups expressed the view that they had mutual understanding with their children.

3. Trust in child's activities and monitoring child's activities : Mothers believe that child can do a particular activity by himself/ herself. It suggests that mothers consider their children mature enough to take an activity independently. Monitoring child's activities shows mothers' concern about their children. The responses of EMs and UEMs indicated that almost all mothers;

Table 3.3 : Responses of Employed and Unemployed Mothers Regarding Quality of Maternal Interaction with the Child

Various Aspects of Mother Child Interactions	Unemployed Mothers (N=80) f(%)		Employed Mothers (N=120) f(%)		$(df)\chi^2$
Mother's use of Spare Time with the Child $					
In Playing	20	(25)	30	(25)	
In Going out	58	(73)	70	(58)	
According to child's wish	2	(2)	20	(17)	(2)=10.26**
Degree of Understanding Between Mother and Child					
Complete	40	(50)	64	(53)	
Above average	24	(30)	26	(22)	
Average	14	(18)	27	(23)	
Less than average	2	(2)	3	(2)	(3)=2.02
Trust in Child's Activities					
Complete	12	(15)	10	(8)	
Mostly	44	(55)	57	(48)	
Average	22	(27)	42	(35)	
Less	2	(3)	11	(9)	(3)=6.60
Monitoring Child's Activities					
Always	36	(45)	62	(52)	
Mostly	26	(33)	27	(23)	
Sometimes	14	(18)	29	(24)	
Rarely/Never	4	(5)	2	(2)	(3)=5.02
Sharing with Mother $					
Good things only	14	(18)	38	(32)	
Bad things	2	(2)	15	(12)	
Both	64	(80)	67	(56)	(2)=13.63**
Mother's Attention in Different Matters $					
Studies only	40	(50)	58	(48)	
All matters	40	(50)	62	(52)	(1)=0.05

(Contd.)

Table 3.3.: Contd.....

Various Aspects of Mother Child Interactions	Unemployed Mothers (N=80) f	(%)	Employed Mothers (N=120) f	(%)	$(df)\chi^2$
Helping the Child while Busy $					
After completing the work	0	(0)	2	(2)	
Keep the child busy	12	(15)	23	(19)	
Ask to wait	44	(55)	36	(30)	
Child's need	24	(30)	48	(40)	
Immediate help	0	(0)	11	(9)	(4)=17.98**
Helping the Child in Simple Work $					
Do not help	2	(3)	22	(18)	
Consider child's mood	52	(65)	38	(32)	
Consider child's need	22	(27)	55	(46)	
Immediately help	4	(5)	5	(4)	(3)=26.14**
Judging Child's Ability in Comparison to Other Children					
Excellent	4	(5)	12	(10)	
Good	48	(60)	54	(45)	
Average	28	(35)	54	(45)	(2)=4.79
Degree of Satisfaction with Child's Interest, Ability and Habits					
Complete satisfaction	0	(0)	5	(4)	
Average	22	(28)	32	(27)	
Less than average	56	(70)	76	(63)	
Dissatisfied	2	(2)	7	(6)	(3)=4.85
Reaction to Child's Performance in School $					
Encourage	24	(30)	37	(31)	
Praise	54	(68)	46	(38)	
Reward	2	(2)	10	(8)	
According to the situation	0	(0)	27	(23)	(3)=28.90**
Promotion of Physical Games and Exercises $					
Indifferent	0	(0)	13	(10)	
Forcing to do	2	(3)	17	(14)	
Own initiative	16	(20)	79	(66)	
Explaining	58	(73)	3	(3)	
Reinforcement	4	(5)	8	(7)	(4)=114.11**

* $p < .05$; ** $p < .01$.

$ - Reverse the scoring

irrespective of their employment status, had confidence in their children's ability to perform activities. As far as monitoring the child's activities was concerned, almost all mothers (75 per cent) felt that the children are monitored most of the time.

4. Sharing matters with mothers : Usually children report their good and socially desired actions and behaviours to their parents. It may be due to child's fear about getting punishment for negative behaviours (e.g. punishment in school, quarrels with siblings, peers etc. damaging something at home). For healthy personality development, children should share all matters either with mother or father. Considerably large number of UEMs (80%) in comparison to 56 per cent of EMs reported that their children usually share all matters (good or bad) equally. About 32 per cent of EMs reported that children mostly share good things only. The employment status emerged to be associated significantly with sharing matters with mothers, χ^2 (2)=13.63 $\underline{p} < .01$.

5.Mothers' maximum attention to child related matters : The age group of children taken in the study has the tendency to tell each and everything to their parents after they come back from school or play. Do the parents pay attention to the matters related to studies only or to all the matters equally ? About 50 per cent of mothers in both the groups reported that they pay attention to children's studies only, whereas about 50 per cent of mothers reported that they try to pay attention to all matters equally.

6. Helping the child in spite of being busy and helping in simple work: Sometimes mothers are very busy and child demands help from mother or father. There are instances when child even wants assistance in doing simple work also. Responding to the need for help by the child, busy UEMs usually asked them 'to wait for sometime' (55%). Also, they responded to the severity of 'child's need' (30%). A small number of them reported 'keeping the child busy in some other work' (15%). On the other hand, 'severity of child's need' emerged to be the most important factor for EMs (40%). This was followed by 'asking them to wait' (30%) and 'keeping them busy' (19%), $\chi^2(4) = 17.98$, $p < .01$. Helping in simple work depended on 'child's mood' (65%) and 'need' (27%) for the UEMs, while 'need' was a predominant factor for EMs (46%) followed by 'child's mood' (32%). The employment status significantly influenced the responses of mothers, $\chi^2(3) = 26.14$ $p < .01$. A close perusal of the responses in case of EMs suggests that child's need is more important for them. They try to attend the child first and then other things.

7. Judging child's ability in comparison to other children : Parents usually compare the child's abilities with other children (siblings, peers etc.). In this regard mostly mothers in both the groups rated the child as 'average' or 'good'. Mothers in unemployed group (60%) as against the EMs (45%) rated their children at a slightly higher level. About 35 per cent of UEMs and 45 per cent EMs judged their children as 'average' on intellectual level.

8. Degree of satisfaction with child's interests, abilities and habits: Parents' satisfaction with child's interests, abilities and habits helps children to develop confidence. It helps them to perform better also. Mothers in both the groups expressed considerably low level of satisfaction. About 75 per cent of mothers in both the groups expressed less than average level of satisfaction. Only 28 per cent of UEMs and 27 per cent of EMs showed average level of satisfaction. It suggests that both groups expect more from their children. They reported that today's world is a competitive world and to adjust in this fast changing world children should have more abilities and a different pattern of interests and habits.

9. Reaction to child's performance in school : How parents react to child's performance in school? Generally parents praise or encourage the child to perform better. Reward is usually given when the child performs extraordinarily. Mothers' reaction to children's performance varied greatly in both the groups. UEMs (68%) used 'praise' most frequently followed by 'encouragement' (30%). In contrast, EMs used 'praise' and 'encouragement' almost equally (38% and 31%), and their responses were also moderated by situational characteristics (23%), which were not mentioned by any of the unemployed mothers, $\chi^2(3)=28.90, p<.01$.

10. Promotion of physical games and exercises for the child : Nowadays, due to increased competition on, parents are more worried about the mental or intellectual development of their children. Are they also concerned about the proper physical development of their children? How parents motivate their children to do physical exercise for the proper physical development? In order to promote physical games, exercises, etc., more UEMs (73%) used 'explaining' as the most frequent technique while 'own initiative' was the most significant response in the case of EMs (66%), $\chi^2(4) = 114.11, p < .01$. In case of EMs' children, it was reported that they themselves take initiative in doing 'physical exercises' or 'playing'. UEMs are usually at home, therefore, they can explain the need for such activities to their children.

Independence to the Child Provision for independence to the child was measured in terms of freedom provided to them in going out and in expressing disapproval. The obtained responses are shown in Table 3.4.

1. Degree of freedom in going out independently : Whether children can go to nearby areas, (school, market, to a friend's house etc.) on their own or parents do not allow them? Freedom to the children in going out on their own was significantly greater in the group of UEMs (48%) as compared to EMs (28%). About 25 per cent of EMs in comparison to 7 per cent of UEMs did not allow their children to go out independently, $\chi^2(4)=15.79, p < .01$. It may be true that mothers only allow in their presence. In that case, EMs may be apprehensive of some mishappening with their children in their absence and, therefore, did not give freedom at all.

2. Degree of freedom in expressing disapproval : If parents are very strict, children have to agree with them. Today, parents also give some independence to children to express their disapproval. Results showed that in general UEMs (32%) allowed greater

Table 3.4 : Responses of Employed and Unemployed Mothers Regarding Children's Independence

Aspects of Independence	Unemployed Mothers (N=80) *f* (%)		Employed Mothers (N=120) *f* (%)		$(df)\chi^2$
Degree of Freedom in Going Out Independently					
Complete	2	(2)	2	(2)	
Mostly	38	(48)	34	(28)	
Sometimes	34	(43)	50	(42)	
Less	6	(7)	31	(25)	
Never	0	(0)	3	(3)	(4)=15.79**
Degree of Freedom in Expressing Disapproval					
Complete	26	(32)	27	(23)	
Mostly	12	(15)	18	(15)	
Sometimes	18	(23)	36	(30)	
Less	16	(20)	30	(25)	
Never	8	(10)	9	(8)	(4)=3.69

** $p < .01$

freedom to their children in this regard as compared to EMs (23%). On other response categories, a similar pattern was observed.

Interaction with Siblings Children at home have to spend most of their time with siblings while eating, studying, watching TV, reading comics or playing. For healthy development, children should have good relationship with their siblings. Therefore, it is also important to know as to how children interact with their younger or older siblings, how frequently they quarrel, help, share or play with each other? Table 3.5 presents the findings regarding this issue.

1. Incidence of quarrels with siblings : Children generally start fighting or arguing on very trivial matters. Although it is undesirable, but it is not considered as abnormal. It is observed

Table 3.5 : Responses of Employed and Unemployed Mothers regarding Child's Interaction with Siblings

Aspects of Interaction with Siblings	Unemployed Mothers (N=80) *f*	(%)	Employed Mothers (N=120) *f*	(%)	$(df)\chi^2$
Quarrel with Siblings $					
Frequently	2	(2)	12	(10)	
Sometimes	26	(32)	33	(28)	
Rarely	42	(53)	53	(44)	
Never	10	(13)	22	(18)	(3)=5.99
Sharing with Siblings					
Complete	40	(51)	55	(50)	
Mostly	12	(15)	22	(20)	
Sometimes	16	(21)	21	(19)	
Less	10	(13)	13	(11)	(3)=0.63
Helping the Siblings					
Complete	40	(50)	59	(49)	
Mostly	26	(33)	36	(30)	
Sometimes	10	(13)	19	(16)	
Rare	4	(4)	6	(5)	(3)=0.47

$ - Reverse the scoring

that children of same sex have more disputes than the opposite ones. Less incidence of such behaviours suggests that the child has smooth relationship. Mothers in both the groups reported less incidence of quarrel with siblings.

2. *Sharing with siblings :* Children have to share several things with their siblings, such as space, games, books and comics, and eatables. If the child has good relationship with siblings, there will be more sharing of things etc. Responses as reported by mothers in both the groups suggested that children usually shared with their siblings.

3. *Helping the siblings :* Is there any difference in the helping behaviour of children when their mothers are working or when they remain full-time at home? Results did not suggest any

difference across both groups. More than 50 per cent of mothers in both the groups reported that children help each other whenever required.

Interaction with Peers In school going children, peers play an important role in child's personality and social development. Cordial relationship with friends at school or in the neighbourhood leads to healthy development of children. Mothers were also asked about the relationship between the children and their peers, and responses were obtained on the following aspects (Table 3.6).

1. Friendship with neighbouring children : Children's social life is also very important in their proper personality development. Age group of children taken in this study had greater interaction with peers, and, therefore, it is necessary to know the relationship between them. With regard to interaction with peers, the responses revealed that about 50 per cent of mothers in both the groups perceived good relationship. As compared to EMs, more UEMs expressed better relationship with their peers.

2. Freedom in expressing anger towards friends : While playing with friends, children sometimes have disputes with them. Sometimes they express their anger towards friends in front of the family members also. What is the frequency of such behaviours? Regarding this aspect, 58 per cent of UEMs in comparison to 39 per cent of EMs reported that 'sometimes' children do express anger towards friends. 53 per cent of EMs, as compared to only 36 per cent of their counterparts, told that their children 'never' showed such behaviour, $\chi^2(1) = 5.06, p < .05$.

3. Sharing thoughts about friends with mothers : Children generally tell their good or bad ideas and attitudes towards their friends. On this aspect, 55 per cent of EMs and 40 per cent of UEMs reported that 'mostly' children shared thoughts related to friends. But 30 per cent of UEMs, as compared to only 8 per cent of EMs, reported rare incidence of such behaviour, $\chi^2(4) = 21.85, p < .01$.

Table 3.6 : Responses of Employed and Unemployed Mothers regarding Child's Interaction with Peers

Aspects of Interaction with Peers	Unemployed Mothers (N=80) f(%)		Employed Mothers (N=120) f(%)		$(df)\chi^2$
Friendship with Neighbouring Children $					
Less than average	6	(7)	2	(2)	
Average	16	(20)	39	(33)	
Good	40	(50)	57	(47)	
Very Good	18	(23)	22	(18)	(3)=7.29
Expressing Anger Towards Friends					
Does not tell	4	(5)	6	(5)	
Never	29	(36)	63	(53)	
Sometimes	46	(58)	47	(39)	
Frequently	1	(1)	4	(3)	(3)=3.65*
Sharing Thoughts about Friends with Mother					
Always	4	(5)	16	(13)	
Mostly	28	(35)	50	(42)	
Sometimes	24	(30)	45	(37)	
Rarely	16	(20)	3	(3)	
Never	8	(10)	6	(5)	(4)=21.85**
Reaction to Quarrel with Friends					
Restricting play	2	(2)	4	(3)	
Scolding	0	(0)	11	(9)	
Explaining	28	(35)	47	(39)	
Knowing the cause	40	(50)	53	(45)	
No interference	10	(13)	5	(4)	(4)=12.46*

* $p < .05$; ** $p < .01$.

$ - Reverse the scoring

4. Reaction to quarrels with friends : Disputes with friends are sometimes reported to parents also. In that case, what is the general reaction of the parents? Parents either 'restrict' their playing, 'scold' the child, 'explain' or try to 'know the cause' of such incidents. Sometimes parents think that let the child solve his/her own problem and they do not interfere in such matters. A considerable number of mothers in both the groups (50% and 45%) tried to 'know the cause' and 'explained' to live in harmony (35% and 39%). Only 9 per cent of EMs reported 'scolding', whereas 13 per cent of UEMs showed 'no interference', $\chi^2(4) = 12.46, p < .05$.

Perceived and Desired Characteristics of Children

Children have many desirable and undesirable characteristics and mothers usually have their own views about them. Also, mothers expect that some qualities must develop in their children. In the present study mothers were simply asked to perceive the most liked and disliked characteristics in children. The responses were obtained through a list of 15 attributes.

The analysis of 'liked characteristics' presented in Table 3.7 reveals that the two groups of mothers had different views. EMs perceived their children as sweet and polite, obedient, hard-working and responsible in that order. In contrast, UEMs considered their children obedient, hard-working, regular in studies, helping and systematic.

With respect to disliked characteristics in children, it was noted (Table 3.7) that a small section of mothers (18% in unemployed and 23% in employed groups) could not identify such characteristics. The unemployed group reported disobedience and stubbornness as most frequent disliked behaviours followed by quarrel, mischief and lack of interest in studies. The mothers in employed group, too viewed these as disliked characteristics. In addition, they indicated lying, being unsystematic and shyness as other disliked characteristics. On the whole, the responses of both groups of mothers were considerably similar.

Finally, mothers were asked to indicate their views regarding most desired characteristics in children on a checklist of 15 traits. The first preferences, thus obtained, are shown in Table 3.7. Most of UEMs (48%) considered 'hardworking' as the most desired characteristic followed by 'disciplined', 'honest', 'independent' and 'obedient'. 'Responsible' and 'couargeous' were least frequently reported. On the other hand, EMs reported 'hardworking' (52%) and 'honest' (26%) as most desired characteristics followed by 'independent'. Characteristics, such as, 'obedience', 'discipline', 'responsibility', 'organization', 'punctuality' were least frequently mentioned.

Discussion

Discipline plays an important role in the process of socialization and personality development through which parents and significant others guide their children in the direction of what is socially acceptable within a given culture. Discipline fulfils certain needs of children and thus adds to their happiness and attaining personal and social adjustment. Parents use various disciplinary techniques to reinforce and control behaviour of their children. These techniques have diversified effects on children's personality. Parents' use of disciplinary practices is affected by various factors, such as, gender, birthorder, and age of the child, family structure, employment status of parents etc.

In the present study, the responses of employed and unemployed mothers were compared on disciplinary practices related to child's day-to-day life. In this regard, various facets of discipline, parental involvement in child related activities and matters, family environment, interaction and relationship with siblings and peers were investigated. Whether mother's employment status shows any impact on these aspects? In the study three types of maternal employment, i.e. teaching, nursing and clerical were taken into account to study the impact of maternal employment on child rearing and disciplining practices. 36 variables related to various aspects of child-rearing and disciplining were selected and results showed that on 19 variables both the groups (employed and

Table 3.7 : Responses of Employed and Unemployed Mothers regarding Liked, Disliked and Desired Characteristics of Children

Children's Characteristics	Unemployed Mothers (N=80) *f*(%)		Employed Mothers (N=120) *f*(%)	
Liked Characteristics				
Obedient	24	(28)	27	(23)
Helping	8	(10)	6	(5)
Responsible	6	(8)	17	(14)
Systematic	8	(10)	5	(4)
Honest	6	(8)	6	(5)
Hard Working	14	(18)	19	(16)
Regular in Study	10	(13)	10	(8)
Polite	4	(5)	30	(25)
Disliked Characteristics				
Disinterested in Studies	8	(10)	14	(12)
Disobedient	18	(23)	16	(13)
Stubborn	18	(23)	22	(18)
Quarrelsome	10	(13)	12	(10)
Unsystematic	2	(3)	6	(5)
Irresponsible	0	(0)	3	(3)
Lier	2	(3)	6	(6)
Mischievous	10	(7)	12	(10)
Shy	0	(0)	1	(1)
No response	14	(18)	27	(22)
Most Desired Characteristics				
Hard Working	38	(48)	62	(52)
Punctual	4	(5)	1	(1)
Honest	8	(10)	31	(26)
Obedient	6	(8)	6	(5)
Careful	0	(0)	0	(0)
Independent	8	(10)	10	(8)
Social	0	(0)	0	(0)
Responsible	4	(5)	4	(3)
Cautious	0	(0)	0	(0)
Patient	0	(0)	1	(1)
Knowledgeable	0	(0)	0	(0)
Courageous	2	(2)	0	(0)
Disciplined	10	(12)	4	(3)
Organized	0	(0)	1	(1)
Enthusiastic	0	(0)	0	(0)

unemployed) differed significantly in their responses. It was observed that on some aspects unemployed mothers reported more use of 'scolding' and 'depriving'. It can be assumed that unemployed mothers are most of the time present when the child shows some negative behaviour, and can immediately react. On the other hand, EMs in some instances reported more use of physical punishment. In case of employed mothers such behaviours are executed in their absence, and sometimes they are not even reported to mothers. However, when a negative behaviour is executed in their presence it is treated with harsher techniques. Relatively larger number of employed mothers reported the use of 'explaining'. It was also observed that employed mothers reported a variety of disciplining techniques in comparison to their counterparts as in case of teaching cleanliness, reaction to disobedience and lying. On the other hand, employed mothers mostly reported the use of 'explaining', and a very few physical punishment also. Regarding 'degree of expected discipline' and 'operative level of discipline', employed mothers reported 'higher level' whereas unemployed mothers expressed an 'average level' in both the cases. Consistency in mothers' reactions to child's negative behaviour was observed more in case of employed mothers.

The quality of parent-child interaction and positive and negative reinforcements that growing children receive in the home setting determine, their behavioural and personality characteristics as well as their general orientation towards life. In the collectivist society of India, mother, father, siblings and other family members are involved in shaping the personality of children by rewarding, ignoring and punishing their behaviours. On the other hand, children also have power to influence family members by their actions. In recent past, psychologists have made efforts to identify and measure molar variables of child rearing and relating them to various characteristics of the developing child. The child-rearing practices of mothers have been most extensively studied because of their relatively greater accessibility and due to the fact that they spend maximum time with the child. Mothers usually have greater knowledge and understanding about the activities and behaviours of the child than fathers and other family members. Regarding parent-child relationship and involvement, it was observed that both the groups expressed almost similar pattern of responses. In the present study, only nuclear families were taken for study. It is understood that in such families parents and children have more opportunities to share thoughts, ideas, emotions etc. they have more understanding and interaction with each other. Such relationship helps in healthy development of child's personality and maintaining congenial family environment. Mothers in employed group expressed their dissatisfaction regarding the amount of spare time spent with their children. It is clear that working mothers have to observe many responsibilities, both at home and at work place. Therefore, except for important and urgent matters, they hardly have any time for children. However, they try to spare more time for children from their busy schedule and attend to their children's demands and needs.

Regarding relationship with siblings and peers, both groups reported good relationship. It was found that in employed mother's case, children shared more matters related to friendship and employed mothers expressed more concern regarding dispute related to peers. In working mothers' families, children have to maintain good relationship with friends and peers, and children usually solve their problems themselves, because most of the time parents are not available at home.

The results of the present study suggest that both groups showed their concern about healthy development of child's personality. They were quite aware about the impact of various disciplining techniques and expressed caution regarding using any particular technique. The groups of employed and unemployed mothers were mostly educated atleast up to matriculation. Many of them were post-graduate also. In urban areas, parents have more exposure to various media, therefore, they become cautious when they discipline their children. Children are also very sensitive. They know that their parents have very little time for fulfilling all their demands, therefore, they also help parents in solving problems and behave according to the need of the situation. They learn to go with the mood of their parents. It is also observed that children of employed mothers mature at early age and they become independent in many respects.

4

FAMILY BACKGROUND, DISCIPLINARY PRACTICES AND CHILDREN'S PERSONALITY

The growth and development of specific personality traits in children are shaped by many variables including employment status of mother's child-rearing and background variables. In this regard, age, education, marital and employment status of parents, number of children in the family, child's gender, age and ordinal position, family income, rural/urban background, locality, physical and entertainment facilities available at home, social support available in rearing the child etc. play important role. Similarly, what type of disciplinary techniques parents use in socializing their children also affects the personality development of these children. Studies in this regard show that as compared to maternal employment status, mother's education is a more influential factor in child rearing (Suseela, Devi & Devdas, 1970). Educated mothers permitted greater independence, encouraged vocalization in their children, were more strict and suppressed children's aggression more and indicated greater use of reward and punishment (Singh & Sharma, 1976; Seth & Saksena, 1978; and Rai, 1979). Mothers' interaction with their children did not show any impact of the rural/urban background (Singh & Kaur, 1981). Family background factors such as, family size, family pattern (extended/nuclear) and individual's birth order affected children's perception of maternal acceptance, and the incidence of perceived maternal acceptance was greater in small families than in larger ones (Sandhu & Bhargava, 1987). In a recent study by Punia, et al., (1995), it was found that the cultural and societal norms of a society affect the use of different disciplinary techniques.

When both parents are working outside for financial gains, many variables at home as well as in the surroundings affect the family environment. It is true that when children come home in parents, especially mother's, absence they need somebody or something to keep them busy. When they are kept busy in either entertainment or hobbies, or looked after by some one, they do not feel mother's absence too much. Therefore, entertainment facilities at home such as T.V., V.C.R., video games, comics, story books, music system etc. help them to spend their spare time meaningfully. If some family members such as grandparents or uncle and aunt are staying with them, then also they have somebody to talk to. Presence of part-time or full-time servant, good neighbourhood and some hobby club in the vicinity all directly or indirectly influence their personality development. Living in an independent house or flat can also have some impact. Similarly, parent's age, education and religion, child's age, ordinal position and number of siblings differentially influence child's personality. Therefore, to examine the relationship between background variables and disciplinary techniques with children's personality, the present study included various demographic variables also. It is known that children of this age group have more influence of media, peer group and schooling also.

It was hypothesized that adequacy of physical space available at home, entertainment facilities, social support, help available to mother in child-rearing and congenial environment in the neighbourhood would facilitate the development of personality positively. Similarly parent's age, education, occupation etc. will also have some impact on personality development of children. With this in view, the relationship between the family background variables and parental disciplinary practices with children's personality was investigated.

Measures

Background Information Schedule: To investigate the family background variables, an information schedule in Hindi was developed. This schedule consisted of two parts. Part-I dealt with the information about family and the child which included age, education, occupation, religion of parents, size of the family, age, sex, educational level and ordinal position of the child, and his/her siblings, and monthly family income. Part-II dealt with information about physical facilities available to the child, viz. presence of a servant, type of house, number of rooms, physical space available for different activities at home, entertainment facilities (e.g. Books, Games, TV, VCR), facilities available outside the home to use spare time, and any help in child-rearing from others.

Questionnaire for Parental Disciplinary Practices: The details of these measures have been given in chapter 3.

Measures of Personality Children's personality was studied with the help of following measures, the details about which are given in chapter 2.

Early School Personality Questionnaire (ESPQ)

Story-Pictorial Embedded Figure Test (SP-EFT)

Results

Background and Child-rearing Variables and Personality Traits

Tables 4.1 to 4.13 present the correlation coefficients describing relationships between family background and child-rearing variables with 13 personality factors on ESPQ. Although the study included a large number of variables, however, for want of clarity, only those relationships which were significant, atleast in one group of children, are reported in the presentations.

Factor-A : Outgoing/Reserved On this factor, the boys in UEMs' group showed positive relationship between reservedness and variables like parent's educational level, spending spare time in hobbies etc. by the child, positive reaction by the parents if the child loses something in the school, and understanding between mother and the child. Similarly, in the case of boys of EMs, father's educational level and understanding between mother and the child were positively related to reservedness. Girls in this group showed positive relationship between outgoingness and presence of social support (full– time servant) whereas mother's higher educational level and more entertainment facilities at home facilitated development of more reservedness in them. (Table 4.1)

Table 4.1 : Relationship between Background and Child-rearing Variables with Factor A: Outgoing *Vs* Reserved

Background and Child-rearing Variables	Unemployed Mothers		Employed Mothers	
	Boys (N=40)	Girls (N=40)	Boys (N=73)	Girls (N=47)
Mother's education	– 33*	09	– 06	– 43**
Father's education	– 34*	05	– 22*	– 17
Social support	00	– 18	02	35*
Entertainment facilities at home	– 23	13	01	– 31*
Spare time activity of the child (playing or hobbies)	– 32*	09	06	01
Explanation or Encouragement to keep things properly when child loses something in the school	– 35*	– 08	06	11
Understanding between mother and the child	02	09	– 34*	08

* $p < .05$; ** $p < .01$.
Note : Decimal points are omitted.

Factor-B : More Intelligent/Less Intelligent In case of UEMs, boys scoring high on this factor, were treated with appreciation and satisfaction regarding their abilities, interest etc. While girls in the same group, who were higher in ordinal position were found more intelligent and were treated with positive techniques to promote cleanliness and obedience, mothers paying equal attention to all matters than the studies only, and showing more satisfaction with their abilities. (Table 4.2)

Table 4.2 : Relationship of Background and Child-rearing Variables with Factor B : More Intelligent *Vs* Less Intelligent

Background and Child-rearing Variables	Unemployed Mothers		Employed Mothers	
	Boys (N=40)	Girls (N=40)	Boys (N=73)	Girls (N=47)
Child's Ordinal position	13	36*	13	– 23
Use of positive techniques to teach cleanliness	– 10	34*	13	03
Positive reaction to obedience	22	32*	16	09
Mother's maximum attention to child's all matters	06	18	– 27*	03
Appreciation of child's abilities	32*	– 03	– 01	15
Satisfaction with child's interests/habits etc.	31*	31*	– 04	16

* $p < .05$; ** $p < .01$

Note : Decimal points are omitted.

Factor-C : Ego Strength/General Emotionality In the present study, the boys of UEMs showed relatively more general emotionality when they were allowed to express disapproval, always helped their siblings and mothers enquired about the cause when they quarrelled with their peers or did not interfere. Ego strength was found positively related to mother's satisfaction with child's habits, interest etc. In case of girls, ego strength was found positively related with availability of space and entertainment facilities at home, positive reaction to obedience and appreciation of child's good performance. In the same group, more incidents of lying behaviour and quarrel with siblings were found related to more general emotionality. In EMs' group, boys higher in ordinal position, having relatively older mothers and who were allowed to express anger towards peers were found more emotional. In the same group, ego strength was found related positively with entertainment facilities at home, and positive techniques to keep things properly when child loses something in the school. In case of EMs, girls showed more ego strength when more entertainment facilities were available at home, parents used more positive techniques to promote cleanliness and obedience, showed satisfaction with their interest, habits etc. and tried to know the cause of quarrel with peers or did not interfere. (Table 4.3)

Table 4.3 : Relationship of Background and Child-rearing Variables with Factor C: Ego Strength *Vs* General Emotionality

Background and Child-rearing Variables	Unemployed Mothers		Employed Mothers	
	Boys (N=40)	Girls (N=40)	Boys (N=73)	Girls (N=47)
Child's ordinal position	25	– 14	– 22**	– 10
Mother's age	– 11	– 15	– 26*	– 01
Sufficiency of space at home	– 09	33*	10	– 03
Entertainment facilities at home	– 06	34*	22*	29*
Positive techniques to teach cleanliness	– 19	15	– 08	36**
Positive reaction to obedience	– 07	35*	18	27*
Incidents of lying	– 11	– 32*	13	– 08
Explanation or encouragement to keep things properly when child loses something in school	– 10	23	22*	09
Freedom in expressing disapproval	– 40**	03	13	02
Satisfaction with child's interests/habits etc.	41**	– 02	18	35**
Appreciation of child's good performance	– 01	43**	09	23
Quarrel with siblings	01	– 36*	– 05	06
Helping the siblings	31*	06	– 06	30*
Knowing the cause or no interference by mother as a reaction to child's quarrel with friends	– 52**	26	– 10	0
Freedom in expressing anger towards peers	03	– 08	– 24*	– 15

* $p < .05$; ** $p < .01$

Note : Decimal points are omitted.

Factor-D : Affected-By-Feelings/Emotionally Stable On this factor, positive relationship was observed in case of boys of UEMs between trait, like, affected-by-feelings and age of mothers, high expectation regarding obedience, more incidence of lying behaviour, and positive reaction to child's quarrels with peers. Girls in the same group showed positive relationship between affected-by-feelings and positive reaction to lying behaviour. They were found relatively more emotionally stable with father's higher educational level, higher level of expected discipline and more parental understanding regarding child's matters. In case of boys in the group of EMs, less incidence of quarrels with siblings was found related positively to emotional stability. In the same group, girls' emotional stability was found related positively with independent house, more understanding between mother and the child, more monitoring of child's activities by mothers and also when mothers paid equal attention to all the matters told by the child. (Table 4.4)

Factor-E : Assertive/Humble In case of UEMs, assertive boys showed relationship with more freedom in expressing disapproval and also when they were allowed to share their peer related thoughts with mothers. In the same group, humility was observed when parents appreciated child's hard work and reinforced or actively participated in promoting physical activities. Girls of UEMs were found assertive when they were allowed to express disapproval, and were asked to share with their siblings. The same group showed positive relationship with parents' reinforcement and active participation in promotion of physical activities, and more freedom in expressing anger towards peers. Positive relationship between assertiveness and positive techniques to teach cleanliness, consistency in mother's reaction to child's negative behaviour, explanation or encouragement to keep things properly when child loses something in school and positive reaction (no interference or knowing the cause) to child's quarrels with peers was found in the boys of EMs. Humility in boys of EMs was found related with the use of positive techniques by parents to inculcate good habits, and trust in child's abilities. Higher level of expected discipline led to humility in the group of girls of EMs. Assertiveness was related with parents' reinforcement and active participation in promoting physical activities. (Table 4.5)

Table 4.4 : Relationship of Background and Child-rearing Variables with Factor D : Affected-by-Feelings *Vs* Emotionally Stable

Background and Child-rearing Variables	Unemployed Mothers		Employed Mothers	
	Boys (N=40)	Girls (N=40)	Boys (N=73)	Girls (N=47)
Mother's age	36*	– 26	19	04
Father's educational level	16	– 38*	– 10	08
Type of house	– 03	16	– 12	– 47**
Degree of expected obedience	36*	– 10	– 02	– 02
Degree of expected discipline	– 01	– 31*	– 15	– 10
Incidents of lying	43**	03	08	06
Positive reaction to lying	– 13	38*	– 12	–22
Explanation or encouragement to keep things properly when child loses something in school	32*	27	– 19	12
Understanding between parents regarding child's matters	–10	–30*	–07	17
Freedom in expressing disapproval	32*	– 09	– 07	13
Mutual understanding between mother and the child	– 03	04	00	31*
Monitoring child's activities	– 27	– 23	– 13	– 28**
Mother's maximum attention related to child's all matters	– 06	– 20	03	– 36**
Incidents of quarrels with siblings	– 09	00	– 24*	– 05
Positive reaction to quarrel with friends	31*	03	05	02

* $p < .05$; ** $p < .01$.

Note : Decimal points are omitted.

Factor-F : Happy-Go-Lucky/Sober Boys in UEMs' group showed sobriety with variables like sufficient space at home for studies, play etc., parents' more use of positive techniques to teach cleanliness and considering child's wish to gratify the need of the

Table 4.5 : Relationship of Background and Child-rearing Variables with Factor E : Assertive *Vs* Humble

Background and Child-rearing Variables	Unemployed Mothers		Employed Mothers	
	Boys (N=40)	Girls (N=40)	Boys (N=73)	Girls (N=47)
Child's ordinal position	12	– 05	00	– 34*
Type of house	– 14	– 09	– 13	– 28*
Positive techniques to teach cleanliness	– 02	06	36**	– 05
Degree of expected discipline	– 09	– 03	– 01	– 36**
Positive techniques to promote positive habits	– 13	18	– 28*	– 08
Consistency in mother's reaction to child's negative behaviour	12	16	23*	– 10
Explanation or encouragement to keep things properly when child loses something in school	15	– 15	26*	04
Freedom in expressing disapproval	45**	30*	– 11	06
Trust in child's abilities	01	28	– 28*	02
Appreciation of child's hard work	– 36*	– 02	09	06
Reinforcement and active participation in promotion of physical activities	35*	– 35*	– 16	29*
Sharing with siblings	02	37*	– 15	– 09
Positive reaction to child's quarrels with friends	14	17	22*	19
Freedom in expressing anger toward peers	– 02	– 31	07	– 19
Sharing peer related thoughts with mothers	38*	– 10	– 01	12

$^{*}p < .05$; $^{**}p < .01$.

Note : Decimal points are omitted.

child inspite of insistence. In case of girls, father's higher educational level, availability of entertainment facilities at home, parents' use of positive techniques to teach cleanliness and promote good habits, rewarding child's hard work and judging child's abilities, interests (high as compared to others), make them more happy-go-lucky type. Boys in EMs' group were found sober with high level of expected discipline, parents' explanation or encouragement to keep things properly when child loses something in school, more understanding between mother and the child, more trust in child's activities and mother's reinforcement or active participation in promoting physical activities in the child. Girls in EMs' group showed negative relationship with mother's age and sobriety. (Table 4.6)

Table 4.6 : Relationship of Background and Child-rearing Variables with Factor F : Happy-Go-Lucky *Vs* Sober

Background and Child rearing Variables	Unemployed Mothers		Employed Mothers	
	Boys (N=40)	Girls (N=40)	Boys (N=73)	Girls (N=47)
Mother's age	– 21	20	– 03	– 34*
Father's educational level	– 23	36*	– 02	– 12
Sufficiency of space at home	– 46**	12	10	02
Entertainment facilities at home	– 06	49**	– 11	03
Positive techniques to teach cleanliness	– 32*	39**	01	00
Degree of expected discipline	11	– 12	– 22*	– 19
Positive techniques to promote positive habits	– 02	35*	– 16	– 25
Explanation or encouragement to keep things properly when child loses something in school	– 04	13	– 22*	01
Understanding between mother and the child	17	06	– 36**	– 25
Trust in child's activities	00	10	– 30**	04
Appreciation of child's hard work	– 01	30*	05	04
Judging child's abilities compared to others	17	45**	– 10	– 04
Reinforcement and mother's active participation in promotion of physical activities	13	– 06	– 26*	– 12
Friendship with other children	– 13	– 31*	– 03	– 15

*$p < .05$; **$p < .01$.

Note : Decimal points are omitted.

Factor-G : Conscientious/Expedient On this factor conscientious boys in UEMs' group showed relationship with positive techniques to keep things properly when child loses something in school, less persistence of negative behaviour and more independence in going out to nearby areas. Mother's higher educational level, and sufficient space available at home were positively related to conscientiousness in case of girls of UEMs. Expedience in the same group was found related with social support (full time servant). In boys of EMs, expedience was characterized by constant help in child-rearing by relatives and parents' use of positive techniques to teach cleanliness. Immediate gratification of child's demands and trust in child's activities were correlated positively with conscientiousness. (Table 4.7)

Table 4.7 : Relationship of Background and Child-rearing Variables with Factor G : Conscientious *Vs* Expedient

Background and Child-rearing Variables	Unemployed Mothers		Employed Mothers	
	Boys (N=40)	Girls (N=40)	Boys (N=73)	Girls (N=47)
Mother's educational level	24	40**	16	– 08
Social support	17	– 35*	– 02	– 09
Sufficiency of space at home	– 13	30*	06	– 07
Entertainment facilities at home	– 11	45**	– 08	01
Help in child rearing from others	02	10	– 35**	05
Positive techniques to promote positive habits	– 12	02	– 36**	22
Positive reaction to child's insistence	– 03	– 04	23*	– 17
Explanation or encouragement to keep things properly when child loses something in the school	37**	18	17	– 02
Degree of persistence of negative behaviour	45**	27	– 11	– 06
Freedom in going out independently	38*	04	01	10
Trust in child's activities	– 18	– 12	35**	21

*$p < .05$; **$p < .01$

Note : Decimal points are omitted.

Factor-H : Venturesome/Shy Looking at the obtained correlations between factor H and the background and child-rearing variables, it is clear that the boys in UEMs' group, characterized by trait like venturesome, showed positive correlations with child's higher ordinal position, high level of expected discipline, more parental understanding in child's matters, mothers paying equal attention to child's all matters, and showing satisfaction with child's interests, habits etc. Availability of sufficient space and entertainment facilities at home and parents' use of positive techniques to teach cleanliness facilitate development of venturesomeness in girls of UEMs. In case of boys of EMs, venturesomeness was positively related to availability of sufficient space at home, whereas shyness showed positive relationship with help in child-rearing by others and rare occurrence of negative behaviour. (Table 4.8)

Table 4.8: Relationship of Background and Child-rearing Variables with Factor H : Venturesome *Vs* Shy

Background and Child-rearing Variables	Unemployed Mothers		Employed Mothers	
	Boys (N=40)	Girls (N=40)	Boys (N=73)	Girls (N=47)
Child's ordinal position	39**	– 03	16	15
Sufficiency of space in the house	01	48**	24*	– 02
Entertainment facilities at home	– 03	53**	– 06	– 08
Help in child rearing from others	07	12	– 25*	– 06
Positive techniques to teach cleanliness	– 11	47**	07	09
Degree of expected discipline	32*	– 19	12	– 13
Degree of persistence of negative behaviour	23	– 15	– 23*	12
Parental understanding regarding child's matters	30*	– 15	06	01
Mother's maximum attention to child's all matters	36*	14	11	– 12
Satisfaction with child's interests, habits etc.	38*	21	03	– 01

$*p < .05$; $**p < .01$.

Note : Decimal points are omitted.

Factor-I : Tenderminded/Toughminded Girls in the group of UEMs, showed positive relationship between tendermindedness and less incidence of quarrel with siblings. In case of EMs, boys showed positive relationship between tendermindedness and father's higher level of education and parents' explanation or encouragement to keep things properly when child loses something in the school. Mother's consistent behaviour towards child's negative behaviours helps in developing toughmindedness in the boys of EMs. Girls in this group showed positive relationship between tendermindedness and father's higher educational level. (Table 4.9)

Table 4.9: Relationship of Background and Child-rearing Variables with Factor I : Tenderminded *Vs* Toughminded

Background and Child-rearing Variables	Unemployed Mothers		Employed Mothers	
	Boys (N=40)	Girls (N=40)	Boys (N=73)	Girls (N=47)
Father's education	15	14	22*	36**
Consistency in mother's reaction to child's negative behaviour	10	– 02	– 39**	08
Explanation or encouragement to keep things properly when child loses something in the school	19	23	24*	25
Incidents of quarrels with siblings	– 07	34*	17	10

* $p < .05$; **$p < .01$.
Note : Decimal points are omitted.

FACTOR–J : Restrained/Vigorous Boys in the group of UEMs showed positive relationship between restrainedness and parents' use of positive techniques to teach cleanliness, and girls, in the same group with parents' use of explanation or encouragement to keep things properly when child loses something in school, and reaction to child's good performance depending upon the situation. Restrainedness was observed in case of boys of EMs, with relatively older mothers and presence of a full-time servant at home. Vigorousness in the same group was positively related with parents' educational level, availability of entertainment facilities at home, high level of expected obedience and actual discipline, parents' use of positive techniques to inculcate positive habits, monitoring child's activities regularly, and reaction to child's good performance depending upon the situation. Girls showed restrainedness when social support was available, and their hard work was appreciated by the parents. In their case, father's educational level, family income, spending spare time by engaging in hobbies etc., freedom in expressing disapproval and reaction to child's good performance according to the situation were positively related to vigorousness. (Table 4.10)

Table 4.10: Relationship of Background and Child– rearing Variables with Factor J : Restrained *Vs* Vigorous

Background and Child rearing Variables	Unemployed Mothers		Employed Mothers	
	Boys (N=40)	Girls (N=40)	Boys (N=73)	Girls (N=47)
Mother's age	– 01	– 01	23*	21
Mother's educational level	03	– 01	– 29*	– 20
Father's educational level	– 01	– 27	– 24*	– 28*
Family income	04	17	– 17	– 29*
Social support	– 26	15	25*	31*
Entertainment facilities at home	– 11	– 26	– 22*	– 04
Spare time activity of the child	– 21	– 08	– 01	– 36*
Positive techniques to teach cleanliness	32*	04	05	14
Degree of expected obedience	01	00	– 35**	01
Level of actual discipline	20	– 04	– 51**	– 05
Use of explanation and reward to promote positive habits	15	– 11	– 31**	– 06
Explanation or encouragement to keep things properly when child loses something in school	01	36*	– 10	– 24
Freedom in expressing disapproval	– 05	– 26	– 07	– 30*
Monitoring child's activities	20	19	– 33**	07
Appreciation of child's hard work	12	05	12	36**
Reaction to child's good performance according to the situation	18	31*	– 24*	– 30*
Promotion of physical activities	22	27	– 25*	– 04
Friendship with other children	03	21	– 31**	– 01
Knowing the cause and no interference as the reactions to quarrels with friends	26	05	– 23*	– 10
Freedom in expressing anger towards peers	– 11	00	– 04	37**

* $p < .05$; ** $p < .01$.

Note : Decimal points are omitted.

Factor-N : Shrewd/Forthright Boys in case of UEMs showing forthrightness evinced positive relationship with variables like sufficiency of space at home, spending spare time in hobbies etc. and immediate or conditional fulfilment of child's insistence. Shrewdness in case of girls in UEMs' group was related with appreciation of child's hard work and parents' satisfaction with child's interests, habits etc. Boys in EMs' group showed positive relationship between shrewdness and parents' reaction to child's disobedience according to the situation, whereas forthrightness was found related with child's use of spare time in hobbies and parents' positive reaction to child's losing something in school. In girls, forthrightness was positively related with parents' use of positive techniques to teach cleanliness. (Table 4.11)

Table 4.11 : Relationship of Background and Child-rearing Variables with Factor N : Shrewd *Vs* Forthright

Background and Child-rearing Variables	Unemployed Mothers		Employed Mothers	
	Boys (N=40)	Girls (N=40)	Boys (N=73)	Girls (N=47)
Sufficiency of space at home	– 40**	– 09	06	– 04
Spare time activity of the child	– 29*	– 17	– 27*	13
Positive techniques to teach cleanliness	– 24	17	– 12	– 29*
Reaction to disobedience according to the situation	– 18	04	22*	– 10
Immediate fulfilment or on condition to child's insistence	– 38*	– 15	– 09	– 09
Explanation or encouragement to keep things properly when child loses something in the school	– 21	16	– 34**	04
Appreciation of child's hard work	– 06	40**	09	08
Satisfaction with child's interests, habits etc.	– 13	36*	– 07	19

* $p < .05$; ** $p < .01$

Note : Decimal points are omitted.

Factor-O : Apprehensive/Placid Table 4.12 shows positive correlation between apprehensiveness and rare incidence of lying behaviour and mother's knowing the cause or no interference in child's quarrel with peers, in case of boys in UEMs' group. Girls in the same group showed positive relationship between placidity and mother's educational level, entertainment facilities available at home and mother's knowing the cause or no interference in child's quarrel with peers. Apprehensiveness was related with social support available at home. Boys in EMs' group showed positive relationship between apprehensiveness and mother's age, help in child rearing from relatives and high operational level of discipline. Independent house and entertainment facilities at home were found positively related with placidity in case of girls of EMs. (Table 4.12)

Table 4.12 : Relationship of Background and Child-rearing Variables with Factor O : Apprehensive *Vs* Placid

Background and Child-rearing Variables	Unemployed Mothers		Employed Mothers	
	Boys (N=40)	Girls (N=40)	Boys (N=73)	Girls (N=47)
Mother's age	04	– 17	24*	02
Mother's educational level	09	– 36*	– 07	11
Social support	02	35*	05	24
Type of house	– 03	19	– 22**	– 41**
Entertainment facilities at home	– 10	– 45**	– 24*	– 39**
Help in child rearing from others	– 06	– 01	24*	05
Operative level of discipline	– 09	09	23*	07
Incidence of lying	35*	– 13	11	00
Positive reaction to lying	– 09	11	– 24*	– 05
Knowing the cause or no interference as reactions to quarrels with friends	34*	– 37*	11	00

* $p < .05$; ** $p < .01$.
Note : Decimal points are omitted.

Factor-Q-4 : Tense/Relaxed In boys of UEMs' group, this factor was positively related to consistent behaviour of mothers regarding negative behaviour of children, whereas it was negatively related to mother's equal attention paid to all matters told by the child, appreciation of child's hard work, parents' satisfaction with child's interests, habits etc., thus, showing more relaxedness in these children. Girls in UEMs' group showed positive relationship between spending spare time in hobbies etc., less incident of lying behaviour and child's need gratification on the basis of the situation. Relaxedness was found positively related with high level of expected discipline. A positive relationship was found in case of boys of EMs between relaxedness and positive reaction to lying, explanation and encouragement to keep things properly, less occurrence of negative behaviour, reinforcement or active participation of parents in promoting physical activities and greater sharing of peer related thoughts by mothers. In case of girls of EMs, mothers' educational level was positively related to tension and reaction to child's performance according to situation was positively related to relaxedness. (Table 4.13)

Relationship of Background and Child-rearing Variables with Psychological Differentiation

Table 4.14 indicates the value and direction of significant correlations between the disembedding scores (DS) on Story–Pictorial EFT with background and child rearing variables. It is clear that in case of boys of UEMs, child's age, mother's age and educational level, and 'reaction to losing something in the school' were significantly positively related to DS. However, mother's judgement about child's abilities was negatively related to it. Boys of EMs showed positive relationship between DS and child's age and the techniques used to teach cleanliness, promotion of physical games. In the case of girls of EMs, child's age and techniques used to promote good habits were related positively with DS.

Table 4.15 reports the relationship between variables of family background and disciplinary methods with time scores (TS) on the SP-EFT. It may be noted that in this case, negative correlation means greater differentiation. Mother's level of education and quarrel with siblings were positively related to TS whereas child's age was negatively related to it in the case of boys of UEMs. With regard to girls of the same group a positive relationship between monitoring

Table 4.13: Relationship of Background and Child-rearing Variables with Factor Q-4 : Tense *Vs* Relaxed

Background and Child-rearing Variables	Unemployed Mothers		Employed Mothers	
	Boys (N=40)	Girls (N=40)	Boys (N=73)	Girls (N=47)
Mother's educational level	28	19	– 05	28*
Spare time activity of the child	10	39**	– 05	14
Degree of expected discipline	00	– 30*	– 17	02
Incident of Lying	01	39**	– 18	13
Positive reaction to lying	– 13	– 03	– 28*	06
Consistency in mother's reaction to child's negative behaviour	32*	10	– 06	– 05
Explanation or encouragement to keep things properly when child loses something in school	– 04	– 12	– 28*	– 11
Degree of persistence of negative behaviour	– 28	17	– 27*	– 06
Mother's maximum attention to child's all matters	– 33*	04	– 11	00
Appreciation of child's hard work	– 31*	– 16	10	17
Satisfaction with child's interests, habits etc.	– 34*	– 20	– 21	06
Reaction to child's performance according to situation	– 11	– 20	– 03	– 34*
Reinforcement and mother's active participation to promote physical activities	06	06	– 22*	10
Sharing peer related thoughts with mother	01	– 25	– 35**	04

* $p < .05$; ** $p < .01$.
Note : Decimal points are omitted.

the child's activities and TS was found. Negative relationship was obtained with child's age, facility of servant, and mother's satisfaction with child's abilities, habits and interests. The boys of employed mothers showed positive relationship between TS and less incidence of quarrel with siblings, while mother's age was negatively related to it. In case of girls of EMs, help received in child rearing from others, and freedom to express anger towards friends were positively related to TS. Child's age, family income, consistency in mother's reactions to child's negative behaviour, reaction to child's quarrel with friends, freedom in expressing disapproval toward parents, and parent's faith in child's activities were negatively related with TS.

Table 4.14 : Relationship of Background and Child-rearing Variables with Disembedding Scores on SP-EFT

Background and Child-rearing Variables	Unemployed Mothers		Employed Mothers	
	Boys (N=40)	Girls (N=40)	Boys (N=73)	Girls (N=47)
Child's age	59**	24	26*	54**
Mother's age	34*	03	12	22
Mother's education	43**	04	05	23
Positive techniques to teach cleanliness	03	– 11	23*	– 02
Reinforcement to promote positive habits	– 10	28	12	27*
Positive reaction to losing something in school	40**	29	– 04	04
Appreciation of child's hard work	– 31*	05	08	– 12
Mother's involvement to promote physical exercise	16	04	24*	– 03

* $p < .05$; ** $p < .01$.
Note : Decimal points are omitted.

Findings of the present study suggest that family background factors and the parental practices to control and modify children's behaviours play an important role in the development of personality of children. In this regard, child's age, parents' age and educational level, family income, social support and positive and negative techniques to shape the behaviour of the child, appear to have differentially influenced the personality development of children of working and non-working mothers. It is obvious that child's age and gender are important factors in determining parents' treatment of the child. Although all parents know that use of positive techniques to discipline the child leads to development of positive personality traits in children, but the situation, and parents' mood also decide the use of disciplinary techniques.

Table 4.15 : Relationship of Background and Child-rearing variables with Time Scores on SP-EFT

Background and Child-rearing Variables	Unemployed Mothers		Employed Mothers	
	Boys (N=40)	Girls (N=40)	Boys (N=73)	Girls (N=47)
Child's age	– 52**	– 36*	– 20	– 55**
Mother's age	– 22	– 11	– 23*	– 17
Mother's educational level	41**	13	– 05	12
Family income	– 28	21	06	– 29*
Social support	08	– 41**	08	06
Help in child-rearing from in-laws	09	– 18	– 03	30*
Consistency in mother's reactions to negative behaviour	25	03	– 02	– 41**
Freedom to express disapproval towards parents	09	– 14	09	– 31*
Trust in child's activities	– 02	– 16	– 07	– 28*
Monitoring child's activities	29	36*	– 10	– 18
Mother's satisfaction with child's abilities, interest, etc.	– 07	– 35*	– 14	– 09
Less incidence of quarrels with siblings	33*	13	26*	– 02
Freedom to express anger towards peers	09	00	– 14	36**

*$p < .05$; ** $p < .01$

Note : Decimal points are omitted.

Discussion

The present study included a variety of background variables and disciplining aspects to investigate their relationship with the development of personality traits and psychological differentiation as measured by ESPQ and SP-EFT in the groups of children of EMs and UEMs. The values of correlation coefficients as depicted in Tables 4.1 to 4.15 suggest mixed type of relationship with various personality factors. Analysis of these relationships does not suggest any uniform pattern of relationship between the background variables and children's personality factors in the children (boys and girls) of EMs and UEMs. A few relationships showed a relatively consistent pattern, such as mother's age, parents' educational status, availability of entertainment facilities at home etc.

The findings revealed that with increasing age of mothers, children showed traits like general emotionality, restrainedness, apprehensiveness, affected-by-feelings and sobriety. Mother's age showed a negative relationship with personality factors in case of boys. Parent's higher educational status helps in developing positive personality characteristics in their children because education and exposure to a wider world enable them to look at things with a broader perspective. Educated parents try to make the environment highly informative, organized and maintain discipline. They make family environment well structured and parent-child interactions qualitatively richer in terms of experiential background. In the present study, mother's higher education showed positive relationship with traits like being vigorous, relaxed, conscientious, placid, and reserved. Several studies in this area suggest that educated mothers permitted greater independence to children and encouraged more verbalization. They seemed strict, suppressed children's aggression more and indicated greater use of reward and punishment (Rai, 1979; Singh & Sharma, 1976; Seth & Saksena, 1978). Educated mothers either in rural or in urban areas, enjoy greater interaction with their children (Singh & Kaur, 1981). Suseela, Devi and Devdas (1970) also found similar trends. In case of father's educational level, children in both groups were found relatively more emotionally stable, tenderminded, vigorous, sober and happy-go-lucky when fathers were highly educated. It was also observed that boys of EMs showed a stronger relationship as compared to other groups.

Other background variables included type of social support available (no servant/part-time/full-time servant), living in an independent house or in a flat, entertainment facilities available at home and outside the home etc. Social support in terms of servant's presence could be advantageous in two ways, i.e. help in household activities and also a feeling of safety and relaxedness on the part of mother. Also, the parents feel that children are not alone at home in their absence, they are safe from any mishappening. Mothers are less anxious and worried about their children, if a good servant is there to look after their children. In the present study, presence of a full time servant was found more beneficial for children's personality development. Generally, EMs keep a maid or a part–time servant for household purposes and a very few employ somebody to look after the child. Keeping a full time servant in big cities is not safe nowadays.

If a child is living in a multi-storied building and the family members have good relationship with neighbours it can inculcate a feeling of security in child as well as parents. The child may have good friends to spend his/her spare time with them. The child may also be helped by the neighbours in case of any problem. Although living in an independent house inculcates such personality traits as emotional stability, placidity, humility and vigorousness, children are safer in multi-storied buildings, where there is somebody always next door to help them when needed. The child can learn a few good things from others also, because (s)he has more opportunity to interact with many.

It is very important to know how children spend their spare time and how much entertainment facilities are available at home. When the children are alone at home, after doing their home work, they can spend their time either watching TV or reading books, magazines etc., or playing indoor or outdoor games. Thus, entertainment facilities available at home, keep the child busy and child does not feel mother's absence too much. If some hobby centres or clubs are available in the vicinity, the child can spend his/her spare time more fruitfully and meaningfully. It is very important for the parents to know about child's interests. If parents do not supervise children's spare time activities, and children are engaged in some wrong doing, it can have an adverse influence on children's personality development. Children should watch informative and entertaining programmes on TV. Same is the case with magazines and other comics and children's literature. In recent studies conducted in India regarding child development and effects of mass media, it has been reported that atleast one of the parents should spare some time and watch good programmes with their children and also know about child's peer group at school and in neighbourhood.

In Indian context, a nuclear family does not mean that no other family members are living with the family. Generally relatives from both sides do visit from time to time. Especially, at the time of child's birth and after sometime mothers usually get help from some family members. It not only relieves them from extra burden of child-rearing, but also helps in household chores. Thus, mothers can continue their job after the birth of the child. They need not unnecessarily be anxious about the child being alone at home with a servant/maid servant or if available, in a creche.

Besides maternal employment, child's age, ordinal position and gender, parents' mood and many other factors also determine parents' behaviour with the child. Parents may react differentially to the same behaviour in different situations. Sometimes presence of others also determines severity of parents' reaction towards child's undesirable behaviour. We know that parents generally do not react harshly in front of others, however, if the child exhibits the same undesired behaviour in front of the parents the reaction may be altogether different. Although in the present findings mothers had reported consistency in the responses to such behaviours, practically it is not possible because several other variables influence parents' behaviour towards the child.

In the present work, the age group under study was between 7 to 12 years. At this stage, the main emphasis is on disciplinary process. To become a good citizen and a successful and satisfied individual the child should develop some behavioural characteristics such as being disciplined, obedient, systematic, organized, cautious, punctual, independent and also developing good and healthy relationship with siblings and friends. To inculcate good habits, parents use positive techniques to reinforce the child to repeat such behaviours, and punitive techniques to check the recurrence of undesired and socially disapproved behaviours.

Regarding relationship between parental disciplinary practices and children's personality characteristics, it was observed that when parents use positive disciplinary practices such as, reinforcement (reward, explaining) instead of punitive ones (scolding, spanking, depriving from something, no talking etc.), development of positive personality traits is facilitated, irrespective of their mothers' employment status. In every day life, children do exhibit many undesired behaviours such as lying, disobeying, insisting for something in the market, losing something in school etc. Parents use different techniques to regulate such behaviours, depending upon the situation. In the present study mixed relationships were observed between personality factors in children and mothers' reporting about the use of different disciplining practices.

5

MANAGING CHILDREN IN PROBLEMATIC SITUATIONS

The disciplinary demands become more important and complex in some than in other circumstances, particularly when the child engages in behaviours which are socially non-conforming. In a day-to-day life situation, children exhibit a variety of behaviours which are problematic in nature, such as telling a lie, stealing something, showing hostile behaviour toward siblings or peers etc. Parents react to such behaviours in different ways depending upon the situation. Sometimes they react mildly and sometimes very harshly for the same behaviour. It is also observed that when children show an undesired behaviour for the first time, parents take recourse to induction, scolding or spanking. When children show such behaviours repeatedly then parents use harsh or punitive techniques. Sometimes parents simply threaten the child to check the occurrence of his/her undesired behaviour and do not punish.

In the present study, an attempt was made to study the congruence between the responses of parents and children regarding parents' reactions to children's problematic behaviours. Parents usually report socially desirable responses. They know that children should be made to understand what is wrong and what is right. They should not be punished with harsh techniques like spanking or scolding. However, if children show undesired behaviour repeatedly parents use harsh techniques also. Once the behaviour of the child and reaction of parents is over, parents generally forget the whole episode. If we wish to study actual behaviour of parents for a particular problematic behaviour of a child, we should cross check it with children's perception of parents' responses. With this purpose 13 problematic situations were identified and by using semi-projective technique, mothers and children both were asked to give their responses imagining those situations.

Measures

Semi-Projective Measure of Parental Practices : In this technique, a set of 13 situations depicting children's problematic behaviours was developed in Hindi in a story/event-telling form. These situations described a few day-to-day events, depicting children's undesired behaviours. Both mothers and children were asked about the possible reaction of parents. Basically three types of responses were obtained.

(i) Mother's responses and children's perception of these responses when child executes undesirable behaviour for first 2-3 times.

(ii) Perception of mothers and children regarding father's responses for child's problematic behaviours.

(iii) Responses of mothers and their perception by children regarding persistent problematic behaviours of the child.

The reactions of parents included the categories of 'physical punishment', 'spanking', 'scolding', 'no talking', 'depriving from something' and 'explaining'. Events showing undesirable behaviours included coming late from play, insisting for something in market, stealing something in school, disrespect to elders, misbehaviour with friend, damaging neighbours' belongings during play, telling lie, beating the younger sibling, not keeping the belongings properly, complaining about the friends, not helping the friends, disobeying and damaging something at home and damaging friend's belongings.

Results

Mother's Responses and Children's Perception of Problematic Behaviours

The responses of mothers and children obtained through the semi-projective technique are depicted in Table 5.1. This Table reports the responses as well as chi-square values computed to designate the differences between the responses of unemployed mothers and employed mothers (AB) and children of UEMs and EMs (CD). The analysis of responses indicated the following trends in relation to different problem situations.

1. Coming late from play : Children in the age group of 7 to 12 are more interested in play activities and are least bothered about studies and other things. Although, parents see to it that children should not play more than the prescribed time limit, yet, children tend to break the rule and generally want to play more. It is not necessary that the playing is always outside the home, sometimes at home also they are involved in playing indoor games. The response pattern of mothers showed significant difference when they were asked to express their views regarding this situation. About 58 per cent of UEMs as compared to 37 per cent of EMs reported use of 'scolding' and 'depriving'. On the other hand, a large number of EMs (60%) as compared to only 40 per cent of UEMs responded to by 'explaining', $\chi^2 (2) = 8.60, p < .01$. It suggests that UEMs are more particular about maintaining discipline. It can be assumed that UEMs, most of the time, remain at home, and they can monitor child's activities. Therefore, they reported 'scolding' if the child comes late. On the other hand, EMs may not be able to monitor child's each and every activity and take such situation lightly.

Regarding children's perception of mothers' reaction to the above situation, about 50 per cent of children in both the groups reported use of 'explaining'. About 35 per cent and 43 per cent of children in unemployed and employed mothers' group reported 'scolding' and 'depriving'. A very few of them reported 'spanking' also.

2. Insistence to buy something in market: When children accompany their parents to market, inspite of telling them not to insist for anything, children insist to buy something in the market. In such a situation, parents react differently depending upon the situation. Either children are explained not to insist in the market or they are

Table 5.1 : Responses of Mothers and their Perception by Children regarding Problematic Behaviours of Children

Situations and Response Categories	Mothers' Responses UEMs (N=80) f(%) A	EMs (N=120) f(%) B	Children's Perception UEMs (N=80) f(%) C	EMs (N=120) f(%) D	$(df)\chi^2$ AB AC	$(df)\chi^2$ CD BD
Coming Late from Play						
Spanking	2(2)	3(2)	8(10)	7(6)		
Scolding/Depriving	46(58)	44(37)	28(35)	52(43)	(2)=8.60**	(2)=2.10
Explaining	32(40)	73(61)	44(55)	61(51)	(2)=9.87**	(2)=3.34
Insistence to buy Something in the Market						
Spanking	0(0)	3(2)	8(10)	10(8)		
Scolding	8(10)	12(10)	6(8)	19(16)		
Depriving	4(5)	0(0)	2(2)	3(3)	(5)=18.53**	(5)=10.93*
Explaining	40(50)	84(70)	52(65)	53(44)	(5)=17.45**	(5)=19.14**
Negative incentive	20(25)	18(15)	10(12)	28(23)		
Fulfil the wish	8(10)	3(3)	2(3)	7(6)		
Stealing Something in the School						
Spanking	0(0)	4(3)	4(5)	14(12)		
Scolding	2(3)	12(10)	12(15)	21(17)		
Depriving	5(6)	1(1)	0(0)	20(17)	(4)=14.68**	(4)=27.51**
Explaining	71(89)	93(78)	58(73)	65(54)	(4)=19.45**	(4)=40.16**
Reinforcement for not to repeat	2(2)	10(8)	6(7)	0(0)		

(Contd.)

Table 5.1: *(Contd.)*

Situations and Response Categories	Mothers' Responses		Children's Perception			
	UEMs (N=80) f(%) A	EMs (N=120) f(%) B	UEMs (N=80) f(%) C	EMs (N=120) f(%) D	$(df)\chi^2$ AB AC	$(df)\chi^2$ CD BD
Disrespect to Elders						
Spanking	0(0)	1(1)	2(3)	3(2)		
Scolding	12(15)	22(18)	20(25)	26(22)	(3)=2.51	(3)=0.30
Depriving	0(0)	2(2)	2(2)	3(3)	(3)=7.16	(3)=1.80
Explaining	68(85)	95(79)	56(70)	88(73)		
Misbehaviour with Friend						
Spanking	2(3)	6(5)	4(5)	11(9)		
Scolding	24(30)	15(13)	12(15)	17(14)		
Depriving	2(2)	3(2)	6(7)	9(8)	(4)=9.86*	(4)=8.36
Explaining	34(43)	60(50)	46(58)	48(40)	(4)=9.67*	(4)=5.94
Reconciling	18(22)	36(30)	12(15)	35(29)		
Damaging Neighbours' Things During Play						
Spanking	2(2)	0(0)	8(10)	10(8)		
Scolding/Depriving	4(5)	17(14)	4(5)	21(17)	(3)=12.94**	(3)=7.41
Explaining	68(85)	102(85)	64(80)	81(68)	(3)=4.12	(3)=18.28**
Reconciling	6(8)	1(1)	4(5)	8(7)		

Table 5.1: *(Contd.)*

Situations and Response Categories	Mothers' Responses		Children's Perception			
	UEMs (N=80) f(%) A	EMs (N=120) f(%) B	UEMs (N=80) f(%) C	EMs (N=120) f(%) D	$(df)\chi^2$ AB AC	$(df)\chi^2$ CD BD
Telling Lie						
Spanking/Scolding	2(2)	9(7)	14(17)	35(29)	(1)=1.44	(1)=2.93
Explaining	78(98)	111(93)	66(83)	85(71)	(1)=8.40**	(1)=17.39**
Beating The Younger Siblings						
Spanking	0(0)	1(1)	4(5)	11(10)		
Scolding	18(22)	14(12)	10(12)	24(20)		
Depriving	0(0)	1(1)	2(2)	4(3)	(3)=5.34	(3)=4.23
Explaining	62(78)	104(86)	66(81)	81(67)	(3)=8.39*	(3)=15.62**
Not Keeping The Belongings at proper place						
Spanking	0(0)	6(5)	4(5)	4(3)		
Scolding	20(25)	16(13)	10(12)	36(30)		
Depriving	0(0)	2(2)	4(5)	5(4)	(3)=9.12*	(3)=8.38*
Explaining	60(75)	96(80)	62(78)	75(63)	(3)=11.37**	(3)=11.96**
Complaining About Friends						
Showing indifference	2(2)	6(5)	8(10)	16(13)		
Spanking	10(13)	0(0)	0(0)	7(6)		
Scolding	0(0)	2(2)	6(8)	8(7)	(3)=17.45**	(3)=5.59
Explaining	68(85)	112(93)	66(82)	89(74)	(3)=19.63**	(3)=17.78**

(Contd.)

Table 5.1: *(Contd.)*

Situations and Response Categories	Mothers' Responses UEMs (N=80) f(%) A	EMs (N=120) f(%) B	Children's Perception UEMs (N=80) f(%) C	EMs (N=120) f(%) D	$(df)\chi^2$ AB AC	$(df)\chi^2$ CD BD
Not Helping the Friends						
Spanking/Scolding	2(2)	5(4)	12(15)	23(19)		
Explaining	44(55)	61(51)	40(50)	53(44)	(2)=0.61	(2)=0.86
Explaining the need	34(43)	54(45)	28(35)	44(37)	(2)=7.91**	(2)=13.15
Disobeying and Damaging Something at home						
Spanking/Scolding	14(16)	28(23)	16(20)	28(23)		
Depriving	2(3)	2(2)	6(7)	8(7)	(3)=12.78**	(3)=.53
Explaining to obey	20(28)	40(33)	36(45)	49(41)	(3)=14.04**	(3)=7.16
Explaining	44(63)	50(42)	22(28)	35(29)		
Damaging Friend's Belongings						
Spanking/Scolding	46(58)	7(6)	6(7)	21(18)		
Explaining	32(80)	53(44)	46(58)	46(38)	(2)=26.03**	(2)=8.38**
Compensation/Reconciling	2(2)	60(50)	28(35)	53(44)	(2)=13.18**	(2)=7.93**

* $p < .05$; ** $p < .01$

scolded. Sometimes they are warned that if they insist like this, next time they will be asked to remain at home. Some parents gratify child's wish. When children show such a behaviour outside the home, a substantial number of EMs (70%) said that the child is generally 'explained'. In contrast, only 50 per cent of the UEMs used 'explaining' as a technique. A small number of UEMs also reported the use of 'negative incentive' (25%) and 'gratification' (10%). In case of EMs, about 15 per cent of them reported the use of 'negative incentive' and a very few (3%) used 'gratification'. The response pattern showed significant difference, $\chi^2(5)=18.53$, $p<.01$

Children's responses showed significant differences. About 65 per cent of children in UEMs' group as against 44 per cent in EMs' group, reported 'explaining' generally used by mothers. 'Negative incentive' was reported by 23 per cent of children in EMs' group as compared to 13 per cent in UEMs' group. A small number of children reported the use of 'spanking' and 'scolding', $\chi^2(5)=10.93$, $p<.05$.

3. *Stealing something in school:* Children at this age level are generally fascinated by fancy things like pen, pencil, eraser, sharpener, etc. Sometimes they steal their friends' belongings in the school. Parents either use harsh techniques (spanking, scolding, etc.) or simply explain the consequences of such behaviour. Sometimes children are told that they can tell about such things to the parents, and if possible they will also be given the same. A significant difference was found among the responses of mothers of the two groups. When child shows such behaviour, a fairly large number of UEMs (88%) as against 78 per cent of EMs, reported that mothers usually 'explain' the consequences of such behaviour. A very small number of EMs mentioned 'scolding' (10%) and 'reinforcement for not repeating' (8%), $\chi^2(4)=14.68$, $p<.01$.

In children's groups, 'explaining' was the dominant response in case of UEMs' group. About 73 per cent of children in this group reported 'explaining' as a reaction to such behaviour. On the other hand, 54 per cent of children in EMs' group reported 'explaining'. In addition to 'explaining', the children in this group also reported the use of 'spanking' (12%), 'scolding' (17%) and 'depriving' (16%). A significant difference was observed in the response pattern of children, $\chi^2(4) = 27.51, p < .01$.

4. Disrespect to elders : While disciplining the child, showing respect to elders, at home as well as in the society, is considered an important aspect. What do parents do if the child does not show such a behaviour ? Both the groups reported almost similar response pattern. Occurrence of such an incident is usually responded to by 'explaining' by a considerably large number of mothers in both the groups (85%; 79%). A small number of mothers reported 'scolding' (15%; 18%).

A similar pattern of responses was observed in children's sample also, where about 70 per cent of them in UEMs group and 73 per cent in EMs' group reported 'explaining' followed by 'scolding' (25% and 22%).

5. Misbehaviour with friends : This type of behaviour is very common in the age group of children included in the present study. When children show incidence of such behaviour, what are the responses of mothers and do mothers differ in their responses according to their employment status? In regard to this question, mothers in both groups reported a variety of responses. 'Explaining' was mentioned by more mothers (UEMs, 43% ; EMs, 50%), followed by 'scolding' (30%) and 'reconciling' (23%) in UEMs' group. In EMs' group, 'reconciling' was reported by 30 per cent of mothers and 'scolding' by 12 per cent of mothers.

Children also perceived similar pattern of responses in this situation. 'Explaining' was reported by more children in UEMs' group (58%) than in EMs' group (40%). 'Reconciling' was reported by more children in EMs' group (29%) than in UEMs' group (15%). 'Scolding' was reported by equal number of children in both the groups.

6. Damaging neighbour's things during play : Such incidents happen frequently and regularly when children play outside the house. In this situation, a considerably large number of mothers

(85%) in both groups reported 'explaining' followed by 'scolding' in case of EMs (14%) and 'reconciling' (8%) by UEMs, $\chi^2(3)=12.94, p<.01$.

In children's sample, a slightly different pattern was observed although the dominant response was 'explaining' in both groups (80%, 68%), children in UEMs' group reported 'spanking' (10%) and in EMs' group 'scolding' (17%) and 'spanking' (8%). 'Reconciling' was reported by a very small number of children in both groups (5% and 7%).

7. *Telling a lie:* To avoid punishment or reprimand from parents, children do not report if they damage something at home or do something wrong. They generally lie when it is noticed by the parents. In such situations, almost all mothers in both groups reported the use of 'explaining'. About 97 per cent of UEMs and 92 per cent of EMs reported 'explaining' when children lie. 'Scolding' and 'spanking' were reported by a very small number of mothers in both the groups (2% and 9%).

'Explaining' was also reported by a considerably large number of children in both the groups (83% and 71%) followed by 'spanking' and 'scolding' (18% and 29%).

8. *Beating the younger sibling:* Such incidents are very common in almost all families. When children show such behaviour, the most frequent response given by mothers in both the groups reported 'explaining' (78% and 86%). 'Scolding' was observed more in UEMs' group (22%) as compared to their counterparts (12%).

The pattern of responses was found similar in children's group also. However, more children in UEMs' group reported 'explaining' (81%) than in EMs' group (67%). 'Scolding' (20%) and 'spanking' (10%) were reported by more EMs' children than UEMs' children (12% and 5%). It can be assumed that housewives generally remain at home during the occurrence of such an incident and they can react immediately, whereas in EMs' case, the intensity of reaction decreases when the incident has occurred in the past.

9. *Not keeping the belongings at proper place:* Keeping things at

proper place is an important aspect to make the child systematic and organized. In this situation about 75 per cent to 80 per cent of mothers reported 'explaining'. 'Scolding' was reported more in case of UEMs (25%) than EMs (13%). Only 5 per cent of EMs reported 'spanking' and 2 per cent 'depriving'. It seems that UEMs are more particular about it. The response pattern showed significant differences, $\chi^2(3)=9.12, p<.05$.

Children in their reporting perceived 'explaining' as the common response (78% and 63%) for showing such behaviour. The difference in the response pattern is observed in case of 'scolding' where more children in EMs' group (30%) as compared to UEMs' group (12%) reported 'scolding'. Other responses, although by a very few children, included 'spanking', and 'depriving', $\chi^2(3) = 8.38, p < .05$.

10. Complaining about friends: Children usually complain about their disputes, quarrels, etc., with friends in school as well as in the neighbourhood. Parents sometimes allow them to express and explain the matter, sometimes 'scold' if they frequently report such things, and sometimes do not pay heed to such matters. A common parental response to it was 'explaining'. Both employed and unemployed mothers responded to by 'explaining' (85%, 93%) when child complains about a friend. More UEMs (13%) reported 'spanking' as compared to none of EMs. Significant differences were found in the responses of UEMs and EMs, $\chi^2(3)=17.45, p < .01$.

As regards children's perception, a considerably large number of children in both groups reported 'explaining' (82% and 74%). In EMs' group, 13 per cent of children as compared to 10 per cent of children in UEMs' group, reported that mothers do not pay attention to such behaviours. 'Scolding' was reported by a very small number of children.

11. Not helping friends: To have good relationship with friends, children should always help the friend in need. Parents also tell the children to help their friends. Sometimes they simply tell the children to help friends, and sometimes explain the need of helping friends. In this regard more than 50 per cent of mothers in both groups reported 'explaining', and 'explaining the need' of helping friends (43% and 45%).

The children also reported 'explaining' (50% and 44%) and 'explaining the need' (35% and 37%) by their mothers if they do not help their friends. Besides these responses, children in both groups, though a very small number, reported 'scolding' also. However significant difference was not observed in the response patterns of children in UEMs and EMs groups.

12. Disobeying and damaging something at home: Sometimes children during play or while doing some mischief, damage something at home. If the child shows such behaviour, parents respond in a variety of ways. Mothers in both the groups simply 'explain' (63% and 42%). About 28 per cent of UEMs and 33 per cent of EMs 'explained to obey' when child damages something at home. 'Scolding' was reported by more number of EMs (23%) as in comparison to only 6 per cent of UEMs, $\chi^2(3)=12.78, p < .01$.

Children reported that mothers usually 'explain to obey' (45% and 40%) rather than simply 'explaining' (28% and 30%). 'Scolding' (15% and 21%) and 'depriving from something' (7%) were also observed in their reportings. Mother's employment status did not show much influence in this respect.

13. Damaging friend's belongings: Due to carelessness children sometimes damage friends' possessions in school. If it happens with their children, both UEMs and EMs showed significant differences in their responses. In UEMs' group, about 80 per cent of mothers reported the use of 'explaining' and 15 per cent 'spanking' and 'scolding'. In contrast, more EMs (44%) reported 'compensation' for the loss to the friend and 'explaining' (50%), $\chi^2(2) = 26.03, p < .01$.

Children in the groups of employed and unemployed mothers differed significantly in their responses. More children in UEMs' group (58%) in comparison to 38 per cent in EMs' group reported 'explaining' whereas more children of EMs reported 'compensation and reconciling' (44%) and 'spanking' and 'scolding' (18%), $\chi^2(2)=8.38, p < .01$.

In children's sample, children and mothers in unemployed group differed in their reportings. Children in UEMs' group, unlike their mothers, reported 'explaining' (58%) and 'compensation' (30%). In EMs' group, more children, like their mothers reported 'compensation' (43%) and 'explaining' (38%). 'Scolding' was also reported by 16 per cent of children in EMs' group. Significant difference was observed in their perception of mothers' responses $\chi^2(2) = 10.51, p < .01$.

A close perusal of results given in Table 5.1 suggests that UEMs and EMs showed significant differences in their response pattern in the situations like 'coming late from play', 'stealing something in the school', and 'damaging friend's belongings'. In similar situations, children of UEMs and EMs reported significant differences in their perceptions regarding situations like, 'insistence to buy something in the market', 'stealing something in the school', 'not keeping the belongings properly' and 'damaging friends' belongings'. The results suggest that employment status of mothers did not show much impact on mothers' use of disciplinary practices. Children's groups also did not differ much in their perceptions. However, when mother's responses and children's reporting regarding same problematic behaviours were compared it was observed that in UEMs' group, except two situations, i.e. 'disrespect to elders' and 'damaging neighbour's things during play', responses of mothers and children differed significantly. In EMs' group also almost similar differences were observed in the reportings of mothers and their children.

Perception of Mothers and Children regarding Father's Responses for Children's Problematic Behaviours

An attempt was also made to know the responses of fathers regarding same problematic behaviours as perceived by mothers and their children. The results are presented in Table 5.2 and the description of these responses is given below:

1. *Coming late from play :* When mothers were asked about reaction of father, the main response categories included 'explaining' and

'scolding'. About 60 per cent of UEMs and 55 per cent of EMs reported 'explaining' and 'scolding' by 33 per cent of UEMs and 35 per cent of EMs.

As regards children's views, 'explaining' was reported by 30 per cent to 40 per cent of children in both groups respectively. In comparison to mothers, more children in both groups reported about other techniques. In EMs' group, children reported use of 'scolding' (27%), 'spanking' (22%), and 'depriving' (18%) in that order. In UEMs' group, children reported the use of 'scolding' (32%), 'spanking' (15%), and 'depriving' (12%) by their father.

2. *Insistence to buy something in the market* : Mothers in both groups (50%, 59%) reported that father would also 'explain', if the child shows such behaviour. About 23 per cent of mothers in both groups suggested that sometimes 'negative incentive' is also used. 'Spanking' and 'scolding' were reported by a very small number of mothers in both groups (15% and 12%).

Almost equal number of children in both groups reported the use of 'negative incentive' (32% and 35%) and 'explaining' (33% and 27%) by their fathers. Children in both the groups reported 'spanking' and 'scolding' (23%, 27%).

3. *Stealing something in school* : Regarding fathers' responses a considerably large number of UEMs (95%) reported the use of 'explaining' as against only 78 per cent of EMs. 'Scolding' and 'depriving' (11%), 'reinforcement for not repeating' (8%) and 'spanking' (3%) were reported by EMs. The pattern of responses showed significant differences, $\chi^2(1) = 9.43, p < .01$.

Children in both the groups reported similar pattern of responses regarding fathers' responses to such behaviour. Children also perceived their fathers using 'explaining' (50%, 39%) and 'reinforcement for not repeating' (27%, 25%). Relatively more children as compared to their mothers, in both the groups reported 'spanking' (8% and 11%) and 'scolding' and 'depriving' (15%, 25%) by fathers.

4. *Disrespect to elders* : In mothers' sample, a large number of UEMs (87%) and EMs (80%) reported 'explaining' by father when

Table 5.2 : Perception of Mothers and Children regarding Father's Responses for Children's Problematic Behaviours

Situation and Response Categories	Mothers' Responses		Children's Perception			
	UEMs (N=80) f(%) A	EMs (N=120) f(%) B	UEMs (N=80) f(%) C	EMs (N=120) f(%) D	$(df)\chi^2$ AB AC	$(df)\chi^2$ CD BD
Coming Late from Play						
Spanking	2(2)	4(3)	12(15)	26(22)		
Scolding	26(33)	42(35)	26(33)	33(27)	(3)=0.63	(3)=2.90
Depriving	4(5)	8(7)	10(12)	21(18)	(3)=12.91**	(3)=29.42**
Explaining	48(60)	66(55)	32(40)	40(33)		
Insistence to buy Something in the Market						
Spanking/Scolding	12(15)	14(12)	18(23)	32(27)		
Depriving	4(5)	0(0)	4(5)	6(5)		
Negative incentive	18(22)	28(23)	26(32)	42(35)	(4)=7.36	(4)=1.031
Explaining	40(50)	71(59)	26(33)	32(27)	(4)=5.62	(4)=30.68**
Fulfil the wish	6(8)	7(6)	6(7)	8(6)		
Stealing something in School						
Spanking	0(0)	4(3)	6(8)	18(16)		
Scolding/Depriving	2(3)	13(11)	12(15)	29(23)	(3)=11.57**	(3)=4.23
Explaining	76(95)	93(78)	40(50)	45(38)	(3)=40.98**	(3)35.19**
Reinforcement for not to repeat	2(2)	10(8)	22(27)	28(23)		

(Contd.)

Table 5.2 : *(Contd...)*

Situation and Response Categories	Mothers' Responses UEMs (N=80) f(%) A	Mothers' Responses EMs (N=120) f(%) B	Children's Perception UEMs (N=80) f(%) C	Children's Perception EMs (N=120) f(%) D	$(df)\chi^2$ AB AC	$(df)\chi^2$ CD BD
Disrespect to Elders						
Spanking	0(0)	1(1)	6(8)	12(10)		
Scolding	10(13)	18(15)	24(30)	42(35)		
Depriving	0(0)	2(2)	10(12)	12(10)	(4)=4.54	(4)=2.35
Explaining	70(87)	96(80)	38(48)	48(40)	(4)=33.25**	(4)=43.05**
Showing indifference	0(0)	3(2)	2(2)	6(5)		
Misbehaviour with Friend						
Spanking	0(0)	2(2)	8(10)	27(22)		
Scolding	14(18)	12(10)	14(18)	18(15)		
Depriving	0(0)	3(2)	6(7)	12(10)	(4)=7.88	(4)=6.24
Explaining	42(52)	53(44)	28(35)	36(30)	(4)=16.80**	(4)=38.27**
Reconciling	24(30)	50(42)	24(30)	27(23)		
Damaging Neighbours' Things during Play						
Spanking/Scolding	4(5)	15(12)	24(30)	53(44)		
Depriving	4(5)	12(10)	10(12)	16(13)	(3)=7.55*	(3)=5.85
Explaining	66(83)	90(75)	42(53)	43(36)	(3)=23.38**	(3)=40.69**
Reconciling	6(7)	3(3)	4(5)	8(7)		

(Contd.)

Table 5.2 : *(Contd...)*

Situation and Response Categories	Mothers' Responses UEMs (N=80) f(%) A	Mothers' Responses EMs (N=120) f(%) B	Children's Perception UEMs (N=80) f(%) C	Children's Perception EMs (N=120) f(%) D	$(df)\chi^2$ AB AC	$(df)\chi^2$ CD BD
Telling Lie						
Spanking	0(0)	5(4)	8(10)	37(31)		
Scolding	10(13)	19(16)	20(25)	39(32)	(3)=10.25**	(3)=32.02**
Depriving	0(0)	8(7)	4(5)	17(14)	(3)=19.44**	(3)=66.87**
Explaining	70(87)	88(73)	48(60)	27(23)		
Beating the Younger Siblings						
Spanking	0(0)	2(2)	8(10)	35(29)		
Scolding	18(23)	19(16)	30(37)	44(37)	(3)=3.26	(3)=23.76**
Depriving	0(0)	1(1)	4(5)	17(14)	(3)=20.76**	(3)=98.46**
Explaining	62(77)	98(81)	38(48)	24(20)		
Not Keeping the Belongings at proper place						
Spanking	0(0)	6(5)	4(5)	27(23)		
Scolding	12(15)	17(14)	18(23)	37(31)	(3)=5.55	(3)=24.36
Depriving	0(0)	2(2)	6(7)	17(14)	(3)=13.33	(3)=57.04**
Explaining	68(85)	95(79)	52(65)	38(32)		

(Contd.)

Table 5.2 : *(Contd...)*

Situation and Response Categories	Mothers' Responses UEMs (N=80) f(%) A	EMs (N=120) f(%) B	Children's Perception UEMs (N=80) f(%) C	EMs (N=120) f(%) D	$(df)\chi^2$ AB AC	$(df)\chi^2$ CD BD
Complaining about Friends						
Showing indifference	16(18)	13(12)	8(10)	28(23)		
Spanking	6(7)	0(0)	8(10)	17(14)	(3)=15.80**	(3)=9.51*
Scolding	0(0)	9(7)	20(25)	32(27)	(3)=27.60**	(3)=56.84**
Explaining	58(75)	98(81)	44(55)	43(36)		
Not Helping the Friends						
Spanking/Scolding	2(3)	5(4)	20(25)	45(38)		
Explaining	44(55)	61(51)	24(30)	36(30)	(2)=0.61	(2)=4.31
Explaining the need	34(42)	54(45)	36(45)	39(32)	(2)=20.67**	(2)=40.86**
Disobeying and Damaging Something at Home						
Spanking	0(0)	2(2)	4(5)	25(21)		
Scolding/Depriving	24(30)	28(23)	30(38)	50(42)		
Explaining to obey	22(27)	28(23)	20(25)	23(19)	(3)=3.33	(3)=13.28**
Explaining	34(43)	62(52)	26(32)	22(18)	(3)=5.83	(3)=45.34**

(Contd.)

Table 5.2 : *(Contd...)*

Situation and Response Categories	Mothers' Responses		Children's Perception			
	UEMs (N=80) f(%) A	EMs (N=120) f(%) B	UEMs (N=80) f(%) C	EMs (N=120) f(%) D	$(df)\chi^2$ AB AC	$(df)\chi^2$ CD BD
Damaging Friend's Belongings						
Spanking/Scolding	30(38)	11(9)	14(18)	53(44)		
Explaining	48(60)	53(44)	40(50)	35(29)	(2)=53.47**	(2)=16.31**
Compensation/ Reconciling	2(2)	56(47)	26(32)	32(27)	(2)=27.12**	(2)=37.80**

* $p < .05$; ** $p < .01$

children show disrespect to elders. 'Scolding' was reported by a very small number of mothers (13% and 15%) in both the groups.

About 48 per cent of children in UEMs' group and 40 per cent in EMs' group, reported 'explaining' and 'scolding' (30% and 35%) 'Spanking' was reported by a very few children (7% and 10%).

5. *Misbehaviour with friends :* Both groups of mothers reported 'explaining' (52% and 44%) and 'reconciling' (30% and 42%). 'Scolding' was reported by a very small number of mothers in both groups (18% and 10%).

In children's groups, the response pattern was almost similar. More children in case of EMs (22%) reported 'spanking' as compared to children of UEMs (10%). Maternal employment did not show any significant impact on other response categories.

6. *Damaging neighbour's things during play :* Regarding this situation, larger number of mothers in both groups perceived their husbands using 'explaining' (83% and 75%). 'Spanking' and 'scolding' were reported in case of EMs more (14%), $\chi^2(3) = 7.55$, $p < .05$.

More children in UEMs' group (53%) than EMs' group (36%) reported 'explaining'. Children in EMs' group (44%) reported more about 'spanking' and 'scolding' than in UEMs' group (30%). Similar pattern was observed for other response categories. About 19 per cent of children in EMs' group reported 'spanking' by their father as compared to 7 per cent of children in UEMs' group.

7. *Telling lie :* Statistically significant difference was observed regarding this aspect. Both UEMs (87%) and EMs (73%) reported 'explaining' by their husband. However, in case of EMs 'spanking', 'scolding' and 'depriving' were also reported more than their UEMs, $\chi^2(3) = 10.25, p < .01$.

Mothers' employment status showed significant differences on the response pattern of children also. More children in UEMs' group (60%) reported 'explaining' than children in EMs' group (23%). Children in EMs' group reported more 'spanking' (31%) and 'scolding' (32%), as compared to the children of UEMs' (10% and 25%). The group of children differed significantly in their responses, $\chi^2(3) = 32.02, p < .01$.

8. Beating younger siblings : As regards fathers' reaction to this situation, mothers in both groups reported 'explaining' (77% and 82%) followed by 'scolding' (23% and 16%).

Children regarding this situation showed significant differences. Larger number of children in UEMs' group reported 'explaining' (48%). On the other hand, only 20 per cent of children in EMs' group reported 'explaining'. Equal number of children in both the groups reported 'scolding' (37%). 'Spanking' was mentioned by more children of EMs (29%), χ^2 (3) = 23.76, $p< .01$.

9. Not keeping the belongings properly : Mothers did not differ regarding fathers' reaction to this situation. Almost all mothers in both groups reported 'explaining' (85% and 79%) and a very few 'scolding' (15% and 14%).

In children's group, UEMs' children mainly reported 'explaining' (65%) and 'scolding' (23%), whereas the children in EMs' group reported 'explaining' (32%), 'scolding' (31%) and 'spanking' (23%). The responses in these groups differed significantly, $\chi^2(3) = 24.36, p < .01$.

10. Complaining about friends: Generally, children report to their mothers about such incidents and hardly go to father. In case of reporting to father, mothers in both the groups reported 'explaining' as the dominant response by father followed by 'showing indifference' (18%, 22%). The responses of UEMs and EMs showed significant difference, $\chi^2(3)=15.80, p < .01$.

Regarding children's perception of fathers' reaction, about 55 per cent of children in UEMs' group, reported use of 'explaining' whereas in EMs' group only 36 per cent of children did so. A fairly large number of children in both groups (25% and 27%) reported 'scolding'. In EMs' group 23 per cent of children reported that fathers would 'show indifference'. 'Spanking' was also reported in children's group (10% and 14%), $\chi^2(3) = 9.51, p<.01$.

11. Not helping friends : Mothers in both groups reported that if such behaviour is reported to fathers, they would also 'explain' (55% and 51%) or 'explain the need' (42% and 45%).

Children in UEMs' group (45%) as compared to EMs' group (32%) reported that father would 'explain the need'. 'Explaining' was equally reported by both groups (30%). Children in both groups also reported 'scolding' and 'spanking' (25%, 38%).

12. Disobeying and damaging something at home : Similar pattern of responses was observed in this situation. The main response of fathers reported by mothers regarding this situation was 'explaining' (43%, 52%). Almost equal number of mothers in both groups reported the use of 'explaining to obey' (27%, 23%) and 'scolding' (30% and 23%).

As regards children's responses, 'scolding' was reported by more children in both groups (38%, 42%). 'Explaining' and 'explaining to obey' were reported by more children in UEMs' group (32% and 25%) than their counterparts (18% and 19%) from EMs' group. Children in EMs' group reported 'spanking' also (21%). The difference in the response pattern of children in both groups is statistically significant, $\chi^2(2) = 13.28, p < .01$.

13. Damaging friend's belongings : On this aspect, both UEMs and EMs differed significantly regarding their responses. Regarding fathers' responses, more UEMs reported 'explaining' (60%) and 'scolding' and 'spanking' (38%) whereas EMs reported 'explaining' (44%) and 'compensation' (47%), $\chi^2(2) = 53.47, p < .01$.

Children's groups also differed significantly regarding fathers' responses. More children in UEMs' group reported 'explaining' (50%), followed by 'compensation' (32%). In EMs' group, more number of children reported 'scolding' and 'spanking' (44%) followed by 'explaining' (29%) and 'compensation' (27%), $\chi^2(2) = 16.31, p < .01$. Comparison of mothers' and children's responses shows that in UEMs' group, more mothers reported 'scolding' whereas more children reported 'compensation'. In EMs' group, 'explaining' and 'compensation' were reported by more mothers and children reported more 'scolding'.

A close perusal of fathers' responses as perceived and reported by mothers and children shows that out of 13 situations, mothers in both groups showed significant differences regarding 5 situations whereas, children showed on 6 situations. Further, the children in both groups, as compared to mothers, reported use of more punitive techniques by fathers. Regarding father's responses to these problematic situations, mother's employment status did not show much influence. However, almost in all situations significant differences were found in the responses of fathers as perceived by mothers and children regarding these situations.

Responses of Mothers and their Perception by Children regarding Persistent Problematic Behaviour of Children

In the present study, three types of responses from each participant (mothers and children) were obtained regarding mothers' and fathers' reactions to undesired behaviour shown by the child persistently. Responses thus obtained for the persistent behaviour are presented in Table 5.3 and interpretation of the responses is as follows:

1. Coming late from play: If the child persistently comes late from play mothers in both the groups reacted by 'spanking' (25%, 39%) and 'scolding' (38%, 28%), followed by 'depriving from something' and 'explaining the need' of being in time. The pattern of responses showed significant differences, $\chi^2(3)=32.19, p < .01$.

With regard to children's perception of mothers' responses, about 50 per cent of children in both groups reported 'spanking' as the most frequent response, followed by 'scolding' (38%, 25%) and in case of EMs, 'depriving' (21%) also. The difference in the responses was statistically significant, $\chi^2(3)=8.89, p < .05$.

2. Insisting for something in the market: When child shows such behaviour, 'spanking' (25%, 24%) and 'scolding' (35%, 32%) were reported by most of the UEMs and EMs. Also, 15 per cent of UEMs and EMs used 'explaining'. About 18 per cent of UEMs and 21 per cent of EMs used 'negative incentive', telling the child that they will not bring the child next time if (s)he insists in the market. The pattern of responses was found similar across both the

Table 5.3 : Responses of Mothers and their Perception by Children regarding Persistent Problematic Behaviour of the Children

Situation and Response Categories	Mother's Responses		Children's Perception			
	UEMs (N=80) *f*(%) A	EMs (N=120) *f*(%) B	UEMs (N=80) *f*(%) C	EMs (N=120) *f*(%) D	*(df)*χ^2 AB AC	*(df)*χ^2 CD BD
Coming Late from Play						
Spanking	20(25)	47(39)	40(50)	62(52)		
Scolding	30(38)	33(28)	30(38)	30(25)	(3)=32.19**	(3)=8.89*
Depriving	18(22)	23(19)	6(7)	25(21)	(3)=16.67**	(3)=12.09**
Explaining	12(15)	17(14)	4(5)	3(2)		
Insistence to buy Something in the Market						
Spanking	20(25)	29(24)	36(45)	48(40)		
Scolding	28(35)	38(32)	20(25)	25(21)		
Depriving	4(5)	2(2)	2(2)	24(20)		
Negative incentive	14(18)	26(21)	12(15)	16(13)	(5)=3.55	(5)=31.91**
Explaining	12(15)	18(15)	2(2)	5(4)	(5)=26.17**	(5)=38.49**
Fulfil the wish	2(2)	7(6)	8(11)	2(2)		
Stealing something in School						
Spanking	0(0)	6(5)	30(38)	60(50)		
Scolding/Depriving	8(10)	11(9)	44(55)	43(36)		
Explaining	48(60)	75(63)	4(5)	12(10)	(3)=4.90	(3)=7.53
Reinforcement for not to repeat	24(30)	28(23)	2(2)	5(4)	(3)=110.77**	(3)=123.16**

(Contd.)

Table 5.3: *(Contd.)*

Situation and Response Categories	Mother's Responses UEMs (N=80) *f*(%) A	Mother's Responses EMs (N=120) *f*(%) B	Children's Perception UEMs (N=80) *f*(%) C	Children's Perception EMs (N=120) *f*(%) D	$(df)\chi^2$ AB AC	$(df)\chi^2$ CD BD
Disrespect to Elders						
Spanking	10(12)	29(24)	42(52)	63(52)		
Scolding	46(58)	62(52)	24(30)	33(28)	(3)=6.53	(3)=2.51
Depriving	14(18)	11(9)	12(15)	15(12)	(3)=32.09**	(3)=21.70**
Explaining	10(12)	18(15)	2(3)	9(8)		
Misbehaviour with Friend						
Spanking	16(20)	38(32)	46(58)	51(42)		
Scolding	32(40)	36(30)	26(33)	16(13)		
Depriving	16(20)	31(26)	4(5)	26(22)	(4)=6.33	(4)=30.82**
Explaining	10(13)	10(8)	2(2)	24(20)	(4)=29.67**	(4)=16.29**
Reconciling	6(7)	5(4)	2(2)	3(3)		
Damaging Neighbours' Things during Play						
Spanking	12(15)	38(32)	34(42)	50(42)		
Scolding	34(43)	29(24)	24(30)	24(20)		
Depriving	22(27)	37(31)	18(23)	16(13)	(3)=10.73**	(3)=15.68**
Explaining	12(15)	16(13)	4(5)	30(25)	(3)=16.65**	(3)=14.69**

(Contd.)

Table 5.3: *(Contd.)*

Situation and Response Categories	Mother's Responses		Children's Perception			
	UEMs (N=80) *f*(%) A	EMs (N=120) *f*(%) B	UEMs (N=80) *f*(%) C	EMs (N=120) *f*(%) D	$(df)\chi^2$ AB AC	$(df)\chi^2$ CD BD
Telling Lie						
Spanking	20(25)	55(46)	36(45)	61(51)		
Scolding	44(55)	41(34)	30(38)	17(14)	(3)=11.63**	(3)=9.49*
Depriving	4(5)	10(8)	12(15)	11(9)	(3)=18.36**	(3)=13.95**
Explaining	12(15)	14(12)	2(2)	31(26)		
Beating the Younger Siblings						
Spanking	34(43)	47(39)	44(55)	58(50)		
Scolding	28(35)	37(31)	24(30)	21(18)	(3)=3.93	(3)=13.18**
Depriving	8(10)	17(14)	8(10)	11(9)	(3)=6.45	(3)=8.21
Explaining	10(12)	19(16)	4(5)	27(23)		
Not Keeping the Belongings at proper place						
Spanking	18(22)	32(27)	38(48)	49(41)		
Scolding	38(48)	63(53)	32(40)	25(21)	(3)=8.60*	(3)=25.93**
Depriving	6(7)	15(12)	8(10)	10(8)	(3)=20.74**	(3)=35.67**
Explaining	18(23)	10(8)	2(2)	36(30)		

(Contd.)

Table 5.3: *(Contd.)*

Situation and Response Categories	Mother's Responses UEMs (N=80) f(%) A	EMs (N=120) f(%) B	Children's Perception UEMs (N=80) f(%) C	EMs (N=120) f(%) D	$(df)\chi^2$ AB AC	$(df)\chi^2$ CD BD
Complaining about Friends						
Showing indifference	2(2)	6(5)	10(12)	20(17)		
Spanking	10(13)	0(0)	20(25)	21(17)	(3)=16.86**	(3)=10.59**
Scolding	0(0)	1(1)	40(50)	43(36)	(3)=91.80**	(3)=108.42**
Explaining	68(85)	113(94)	10(13)	36(30)		
Not Helping Friends						
Spanking	0(0)	7(6)	22(27)	37(31)		
Scolding	42(52)	61(51)	40(50)	40(33)		
Depriving	4(5)	5(4)	8(10)	7(6)	(4)=8.12	(4)=13.42**
Explaining	12(15)	26(22)	2(3)	19(16)	(4)=37.06**	(4)=26.66**
Explaining the need	22(28)	21(17)	8(10)	17(14)		
Disobeying and Damaging Something at Home						
Spanking	16(20)	45(37)	50(62)	63(52)		
Scolding	44(55)	36(30)	20(25)	12(10)	(3)=13.91**	(3)=18.53**

(Contd.)

Table 5.3: *(Contd.)*

Situation and Response Categories	Mother's Responses		Children's Perception			
	UEMs (N=80) *f*(%) A	EMs (N=120) *f*(%) B	UEMs (N=80) *f*(%) C	EMs (N=120) *f*(%) D	$(df)\chi^2$ AB ACρμα	$(df)\chi^2$ CD BDρμα
Depriving	14(17)	26(21)	8(10)	37(31)	(3)=31.21**	(3)=19.04**
Explaining to obey	6(8)	15(12)	2(3)	8(7)		
Damaging Friend's Belongings						
Spanking	8(10)	14(12)	30(37)	33(27)		
Scolding	54(68)	75(62)	40(50)	60(50)	(3)=1.55	(3)=11.38**
Explaining	12(15)	16(13)	2(3)	20(17)	(3)=23.77**	(3)=12.70**
Compensation	6(7)	15(13)	8(10)	7(6)		

* $p < .05$; ** $p < .01$.

groups of mothers.

A significant difference in the responses of children was observed regarding this situation. About 40 per cent of children in both groups reported use of 'spanking'. Other response categories included 'scolding' (22%, 21%) and 'negative incentive' (13%). In case of children of UEMs, 20 per cent of them reported 'fulfilment of wish', whereas children in EMs' group reported 'depriving' (20%), $\chi^2(3) = 15.68, p < .01$.

3. *Stealing something in the school :* Mothers in both groups shared almost similar pattern in regard to their responses to such behaviour. In addition to 'explaining' (60% and 63%) a large number of mothers in both groups reported 'reinforcement for not repeating' (30% and 23%). A very small number of UEMs and EMs (10%, 9%) reported 'scolding' and 'depriving'.

In case of children's perception, more children of UEMs (55%) reported 'scolding' and 'depriving' followed by 'spanking' (38%), whereas, more children in EMs' group reported use of 'spanking' (50%), followed by 'scolding' and 'depriving' (36%).

4. *Disrespect to elders :* Responses of mothers revealed that more than 50 per cent of them would use 'scolding' if the child persistently exhibits such behaviour. 'Spanking' was also reported, by mothers in both groups (12% and 24%). Other response categories included 'depriving' by UEMs (18%) and 'explaining' by UEMs and EMs (12% and 15%).

Children's responses in both the groups showed similar pattern. More than 50 per cent of children in both groups reported use of 'spanking' (52% by both) followed by 'scolding' (30%, 28%) and 'depriving' (15% and 12%).

5. *Misbehaviour with friend :* When children show incidents of such behaviour persistently, mothers in both the groups reported the use of 'scolding' (40% and 30%) and 'spanking' (20% and 32%). More EMs (26%) used 'depriving from something' as compared to UEMs (20%) who reported 'explaining' (13 %) also.

The children in UEMs' group reported 'spanking' more (58%)

followed by 'scolding' (33%). On the other hand, children in EMs' group reported more use of 'spanking' (42%), followed by 'explaining' (20%), 'depriving' and (20%) 'scolding' (13%) by their mothers, $\chi^2(4) = 30.82, p < .01$.

6. Damaging neighbours' things during play: Regarding this situation, the responses of UEMs and EMs showed significant differences, $\chi^2(3) = 10.73\ p < .05$. UEMs reported 'scolding' more (43%) as compared to their counterparts (24%) who reported more use of 'spanking' (32%) for showing such behaviour. 'Depriving' (27% and 31%) and 'explaining' (15% and 13%) were equally mentioned by both the groups.

Difference in the pattern of responses was found statistically significant in case of children's groups, $\chi^2(3) = 15.68\ p < .01$. Children in their responses told that mothers would use 'spanking' (42%, 42%) and 'scolding' (30%, 20%). However, children of UEMs reported greater use of 'depriving from play' (23%) by their mothers whereas 'explaining' was reported by more children in EMs' group.

7. Telling lie: In persistence of this behaviour, more UEMs (55%) reported use of 'scolding' as compared to their counterparts (34%), who used 'spanking' (46%) more than UEMs (25%). 'Explaining' was also reported by a very small number of mothers in both groups (15% and 12%), $\chi^2(3) = 11.63$, $\underline{p} < .01$.

Children in both the groups perceived more use of 'spanking' (45%, 51%). In case of UEMs' children, 'scolding' was the second most frequent response (38%), whereas in case of EMs, 'explaining' was reported by more children (26%). A small number of children in UEMs' group also reported 'depriving' (15%), $\chi^2(3) = 9.49$, $p<.05$.

8. Beating younger siblings: Such incidents are common in almost all families. In such a situation, 'spanking' was reported by more mothers (43% and 39%) followed by 'scolding' (35% and 31%). 'Explaining' was reported by a very few mothers in both the groups (12% and 16%).

The children showed significant differences regarding their responses. In UEMs' group, about 55 per cent of children reported 'spanking' and 30 per cent 'scolding', whereas children in EMs' group reported 'spanking' (48%) followed by 'explaining' (23%) and 'scolding' (18%), $\chi^2(3) = 13.18, p < .01$.

9. Not keeping the belongings at a proper place: If the child does not keep things properly, in spite of 'explaining', 'scolding' as a reaction was used by a greater number of mothers in both the groups (48% and 53%). Almost equal number of UEMs reported 'spanking' (22%) and 'explaining' (23%). About 27 per cent of EMs reported 'spanking' and 'depriving' (12%) and 'explaining' (8%). A significant difference in the responses of mothers was found, $\chi^2(3)=8.60, p < .05$.

In children's perception of mothers' responses, 'spanking' was reported by both the groups (48% and 41%). A considerable number of children in UEMs' group reported 'scolding' (40%) as compared to only 21 per cent in EMs' group. 'Explaining' was reported by a significantly large number of children in EMs' group (30%), as compared to only 2 per cent of children in UEMs' group. The difference in the responses was significant, $\chi^2(3) = 25.93, p < .01$.

10. Complaining about friends : Almost all mothers (85%, 94%) reported 'explaining', if the child persistently complains about the friends. A very small number of UEMs also expressed 'spanking' (13%). Mothers understand that children do have disputes with friends. Even after having complaints about the friends, children still have good relationship with them. Therefore, they might have thought that only 'explaining' could help their children to overcome such trivial matters.

Children reported a variety of responses in case they exhibit such behaviour repeatedly. About 50 per cent of children in UEMs' group and 36 per cent in EMs' group reported 'scolding' by parents. 'Spanking' was reported by 25 per cent of children in UEMs' group as compared to 17 per cent of their counterparts. More children in EMs' group (30%) reported 'explaining'. 'Showing indifference' was also reported by both groups (12% and 17%), $\chi^2(3)= 10.59, p < .05$.

11. Not Helping friends : Inspite of 'explaining the need' of helping friends, if the child does not help friends, mothers reported a similar response pattern. About 50 per cent of mothers in both groups reported 'scolding' as the response, followed by 'explaining the need of helping' in case of UEMs (28%) and 'explaining' in case of EMs (22%).

In comparison to mothers, children reported a different response pattern. Although a considerable number of children in case of UEMs (50%) and EMs (33%) reported 'scolding' by mothers if they do not help a friend, 27 per cent of children in UEMs' group and 31 per cent in EMs' group reported 'spanking'. A small number of children in both the groups reported 'explaining the need' (10%,14%) and 'explaining' in EMs' group (16%), $\chi^2(4) = 13.42, p < .01$.

12. Disobeying and damaging something at home : If the child persistently disobeys and damages the things at home, mothers in both the groups differed in their responses. Employment status of mothers showed a significant impact. In case of UEMs, more mothers reported 'scolding' (55%) and less about 'spanking' (20%). On the other hand, a considerable number of EMs (37%) reported the use of 'spanking' and 'scolding' (30%). 'Depriving from something' as a reaction was reported by both the groups (17%, 21%), $\chi^2(3)=13.91, p < .01$.

More than 60 per cent of children in UEMs' group and 50 per cent in EMs' group reported 'spanking' as the response if they damage something at home. 'Scolding' was reported by 25 per cent of children in UEMs' group, whereas 'depriving' (31%) and 'scolding' (10%) were also reported in case of EMs, $\chi^2(3)=18.53, p< .01$.

13. Damaging friend's belongings: If it happens with their children persistently, 68 per cent of UEMs and 62 per cent of EMs reported 'scolding' as the response to such behaviour. A small number of mothers in UEMs' group also reported 'explaining' (15%) and 'spanking' (10%). In EMs' group, 13 per cent of them reported 'compensation' to the friends and 'explaining' and 12 per cent of them used 'spanking' also.

In children's group, 50 per cent of children in both the groups reported 'scolding' for damaging friend's things, and 37 per cent in UEMs' and 27 per cent in EMs' group reported 'spanking'. A small number of children in EMs' group reported 'explaining', $\chi^2(3)=11.38, p< .01$.

Perception of Problematic Behaviours : Congruence between Mothers and Children

With a view to examine the extent of congruence between mothers' responses and children's perception of these responses to problematic behaviours of the child, the obtained data from these two sources were analyzed. A close perusal of the results presented in Tables 5.1 to 5.3 reveals some interesting trends.

A comparative analysis of the findings suggests that maternal employment alone did not have critical impact on disciplinary practices. It was observed that mothers in both the groups reported almost similar response towards undesired behaviour exhibited by their children, either showing it for the first 2-3 times or persistently. More mothers, in both the groups, reported the use of 'explaining', 'scolding', 'depriving from something' and 'no talking' in that order. Sometimes they threaten their children and if they repeat such behaviour, they are treated harshly. There are a few behaviours, although undesired, such as coming late from play, insisting for something in the market, disrespect to elders, etc., where mothers think that making them understand (explaining) or use of mild disciplinary techniques can help. However, for some behaviours, such as, damaging neighbour's things, telling lie, not keeping the belongings properly, disobeying and damaging something at home etc., need stricter disciplinary practices. Moreover, mothers in both the groups, may vary in their perception of severity of desired and undesired behaviours. In some families, a particular behaviour may be considered very undesired and in some families, it may not be so. Besides other things, sociocultural aspects also play an important role in what is socially acceptable and what is not? Every family has its own morals, standards, rules and regulations. Another factor in the treatment of child by the parents is child's age. Younger children are usually treated with mild disciplinary practices and there are comparatively less expectations from them by the parents and elders.

Children, in comparison to their mothers, reported more punitive practices, such as 'spanking', 'scolding', and to a lesser extent, 'no talking' and 'depriving from something' for exhibiting a persistently undesired behaviour. When a child shows such behaviours, parents usually warn him/her for not repeating the act. But, barring a few behaviours, children often repeat such behaviours. Children think that because parents had warned them, in the past, for not repeating the act, now if they show such behaviour they will be punished with harsh techniques. They become more apprehensive.

Sometimes, the parental treatment for a particular behaviour, may depend upon the mood of the parents and the circumstances also. An undesired act may be severely punished in one situation but may not even be noticed in another situation. These factors affect parents' behaviour with children. Maternal employment influences the home environment and interaction among the family members. It may lead to differential treatment of the child by the parents while disciplining him/her.

The above analysis of responses given by mothers and their children suggests that as compared to their mothers, children perceived their fathers using more harsh techniques for the negative behaviour of their children. Thus, degree of congruence in the use of disciplinary techniques used by mothers and their perception by children was limited.

6

MARITAL ADJUSTMENT AND CHILDREN'S PERSONALITY

Maternal employment influences family environment on account of rearrangements and adjustments to accommodate the job demands. Its effect on marital relationship and adjustment is also partly due to the role conflicts and tensions emerging out of employment. If it is felt that the primary duties of housewife and mother are not performed adequately, it might lead to guilt feelings on the part of mother and cause conflict between wife and husband. It may yield disharmony in the family. Marital relationship is an important factor influencing home environment and shaping the personality of children. Marital relationship involves the most intimate type of emotional relationship, mutual acceptance, cooperation, understanding, trust, self-sacrificing and sharing of role-responsibilities. The middle class people generally hold the view that employment of married women breeds marital discord and disharmony, and adversely influences the health and development of children. It is also held that when the mother is working, children are neglected and not properly looked after. In Indian society, household responsibility and child-rearing are considered to be women's responsibility. When mother is working she gets lesser time for her spouse and offsprings. For mothers, children get priority in comparison to their spouse and they try to spend maximum spare time with their children. Husband generally wants that his wife should not only complete her housewife's job but should also take care of him. Sometimes at work place, women have to work with male colleagues and there may be more interaction with them. Occasionally women have to stay after the scheduled working time to complete some urgent work. All these factors directly or indirectly influence their family and marital life.

Marriage is the most intimate type of all human interactions. Although it is an intensely private affair, but it is public as well. In our society, the family is legally, a married pair, i.e. a man and a woman lawfully wed. Sociologically, a family is a primary group made up of parents and their immediate offsprings. Social scientists have tried to ascertain the characteristics that might best assure marital adjustment and marital happiness. In married life it is both interpersonal and intrapersonal interaction that is liable to affect marital adjustment. Kapur (1971) considered it "...... as the state of relationship, in marriage there is an overall feeling in husband and wife of happiness and satisfaction with their marriage and with each other." Thus, the emphasis is upon the harmonious relations of husband and wife. Satisfaction in marital relationship is the most important ingredient of marital adjustment. As changes take place in family cycle, perceived satisfaction of couples also changes. The adjustment problems in marital relationship may arise over factors such as sex, social life, religion, economic problems, relationship with in-laws, friends, recreation and the working status of women.

When a woman works outside the home for economic gains, she has to make some adjustment with her spouse. The couple needs lot of understanding and sharing. Saksena, Agarwal and Singh (1977) found that working mothers were more susceptible to marital conflict. Gupta and Ganguli (1982) observed that working mothers expressed maximum conflict in relation to mother's role and there was negative effect of work on marital relationship. In a study by Barar and Barar (1990), it was found that marital conflict leads to high separation anxiety in pre-schoolers. As regards employment it has been found that dual career couples are more likely to contemplate divorce. They often have difficulty resolving their desire to be successful both at work and at home. It is stated that, being employed, a working woman has to face two fronts, the home and the occupation. So there are more demands, stresses, conflicts, problem situations in her case than in case of her unemployed counterpart who has to perform singular role of a housewife only. Her employment status may influence, to some extent, her marital adjustment.

In the present study, Cattell's trait approach of personality was adopted. Cattell contemplates that any trait may represent the outcome of the operations of environmental factors, hereditary factors, or some mixture of the two. Cattell further suggests that surface traits represent the outcome of both environmental as well as hereditary factors. Source traits may be divided into those that reflect hereditary or constitutional factors and those derived from environmental factors. He argues that 'environmental-mould' traits spring from the moulding effects of social institutions and physical realities which constitute the cultural pattern. Thus, it is clear that traits are susceptible to environmental influences particularly during younger age.

Maternal employment in the present work constitutes an important source of environmental influence through stages in the quality of parental interaction with children which influences the personality of children. It is contended that maternal employment influences the family environment and marital relationship of husband and wife, which in turn, may influence parental treatment with children. All these directly or indirectly influence the personality of children. It was hypothesized that there will not be any significant difference in the level of marital adjustment of employed and unemployed mothers and better marital adjustment of parents facilitates development of positive personality traits in their children.

Measures

Marital Adjustment Inventory: The inventory developed by Kumar and Rohatgi (1976) was used to measure marital adjustment of parents. It contains 27 'Yes/No' type items. A 'Yes' response is assigned a score of 1 except for three items (4, 18, 21) in which reverse is applicable. The higher the score, the higher would be the marital adjustment. The split-half reliability of the inventory is estimated at .49 and retest reliability is estimated at .47. The validity of the inventory has been estimated at .71.

After obtaining the consent, Marital Adjustment Inventory was given to employed and unemployed mothers to be filled by themselves. The investigator checked the inventory before collecting it to ensure that all the items have been responded to. To study the relationship between parental marital adjustment and children's personality, ESPQ and SP-EFT scores discussed in Chapter 2 were used.

Results

The mean scores on the marital adjustments inventory are shown in Table 6.1. These scores indicate that there is no appreciable difference in the mean scores of marital adjustment of mothers in both the groups. However, the ranges of scores showed that marital adjustment was slightly better in mothers of girls in the unemployed mothers' group.

Table 6.1 : Marital Adjustment Scores for the Four Groups of Mothers

Groups	N	Ranges of Scores	Mean	SD
UEMs in Boys' Group	40	13 to 27	22.81	3.58
UEMs in Girls' Group	40	22 to 27	23.84	1.35
EMs in Boys' Group	73	17 to 27	23.19	2.72
EMs in Girls' Group	47	10 to 27	22.79	3.11
UEMs (Total)	80	13 to 27	23.30	2.80
EMs (Total)	120	10 to 27	23.03	2.89

Table 6.2 represents marital adjustment categories and number and percentage of UEMs and EMs in each category. It shows that about 4 per cent of mothers in unemployed group and 4 per cent in employed group showed 'very poor' or 'poor' adjustment, about 3 per cent mothers in UEMs' group and 19 per cent in EMs' group had reported 'average' level of adjustment. About 12 per cent of UEMs and 19 per cent of EMs showed 'good' marital relationship. Main difference in marital relationship is seen in the category of 'very good' adjustment, where about 78 per cent of UEMs and only 58 per cent of EMs expressed this level of adjustment. $\chi^2(4) = 12.75, p < .05$.

Table 6.2: Responses of Unemployed and Employed Mothers on Marital Adjustment Inventory

Scores	Caregories	Unemployed Mother's (N=80)		Employed Mothers (N = 120)		
		f	%	*f*	%	χ^2
23-27	Very good	62	(78)	70	(58)	
21-22	Good	10	(12)	23	(19)	
18-20	Average	2	(3)	23	(19)	
16-17	Poor	4	(5)	3	(3)	
10-15	Very Poor	2	(2)	1	(1)	df (4)=12.75*

Parental marital relationship influences the behaviour of parents toward the child which in turn affects personality development of the child. The correlation coefficients between parents' level of marital adjustment and children's personality traits are shown in Table 6.3. It was found that marital adjustment showed negative relationship with factor A in case of boys in both the groups, showing 'reservedness' growing with high level of marital adjustment. factor C, evinced negative relationship with marital adjustment, especially, in case of girls of EMs. It suggested that with increase in marital adjustment, general emotionality also increases. Highly significant relationship with factor D, was found in case of boys of UEMs. This indicates relatively greater emotional stability in this group. The boys of UEMs also showed negative but marginally significant relationship with factor E, which suggests that boys of UEMs, with high level of parental marital adjustment, are more humble. The boys of EMs showed negative relationship with factor F, whereas girls of UEMs and EMs showed low positive relationship with it. Thus, boys of EMs were found more sober while girls, in both groups were more happy-go-lucky with high level of parental marital adjustment.

Boys in UEMs' group showed negative relationship, whereas children of EMs showed positive relationship between marital adjustment and factor I. Better marital relationship in case of UEMs, led to toughmindedness in boys. Factor J (Restrained *Vs* Vigorous) was positively related to marital adjustment in case of

Table 6.3 : Relationship of Marital Adjustment of Parents and Children's Scores on ESPQ.

Personality Factors	Unemployed Mothers		Employed Mothers	
	Boys (N=40)	Girls (N=40)	Boys (N=73)	Girls (N=47)
A Outgoing *Vs* Reserved	– 16	08	– 12	09
B More Intelligent *Vs* Less Intelligent	– 05	– 04	10	08
C Ego Strength *Vs* Gen. Emotionality	– 12	– 04	11	– 23
D Affected by Feelings *Vs* Emotionally Stable	– 39**	– 11	09	– 15
E Assertive *Vs* Humble	– 29	15	15	– 02
F Happy-Go-Lucky *Vs* Sober	– 08	22	– 22*	21
G Conscientious *Vs* Expedient	– 01	04	06	– 06
H Venturesome *Vs* Shy	0	– 12	03	08
I Tender *Vs* Toughminded	– 25	– 07	19	14
J Restrained *Vs* Vigorous	26	– 01	– 09	06
N Shrewd *Vs* Forthright	– 16	05	– 19	13
O Apprehensive *Vs* Placid	– 28	02	– 03	– 19
Q-4 Tense *Vs* Relaxed	– 21	– 09	– 26*	11

* $p < .05$; ** $p < .01$

boys of UEMs, showing relatively greater restrainedness with better adjustment of parents. With factor N (Shrewd *Vs* Forthright) in case of boys in EMs' group showed a weak negative relationship. This revealed that boys of EMs are more forthright with better parental marital relationship. Boys of UEMs evinced negative correlation between parental marital relationship and factor O. It shows that boys of UEMs are more placid when parents have better marital relationship. Similarly, in case of the boys of EMs negative relationship between factor Q-4 and marital adjustment was obtained. Parents' marital adjustment was found positively associated with 'relaxedness' in boys in case of EMs. Boys of UEMs were found more relaxed with better parental marital adjustment (Factor Q-4, Tense *Vs* Relaxed).

Discussion

Marital relationship is a very important factor influencing home environment and shaping the personality of children. It involves the most intimate type of emotional relationship, mutual acceptance, cooperation, understanding, trust, self-sacrificing and sharing of role-responsibilities. For better marital adjustment, both husband and wife must learn to live together, to share, to compromise, to accommodate, to adjust and to plan together. Parental marital adjustment influences treatment of parents with their children thus shaping the personality development of children.

In the present study, the level of marital adjustment was found higher in case of UEMs as compared to the EMs. Due to the nature of job, office timings and other job obligations, husband and wife may get less opportunity to understand each other. EMs not only have to observe the household chores but also try to give more time to their children. When children are young, mothers have to provide maximum care. Thus, they may have less time to think about their relationship with their husband. This might have also been expressed in the responses of EMs about marital adjustment. Their greater concern for children is shown in the relationship between marital adjustment and 13 personality factors on ESPQ.

A close perusal of results suggests that out of 13 factors, only 3 factors (D, F & Q-4) were significantly related to marital adjustment of parents. The study also revealed that the relationship between marital adjustment and child's personality traits was found significant in the case of boys. Boys in UEMs' group showed relationship between parental marital adjustment and personality factors like emotional stability, humility, toughmindedness, vigorousness and placidity. As level of marital adjustment was relatively higher in UEMs' group, it may suggest that cordial relationship between parents leads to healthy family environment which might have facilitated the development of such traits in their children. Although the mean score was highest in case of girls in UEMs group, no significant relationship was observed. Similarly, marital adjustment of parents showed negative relationship with factor Q-4 in case of boys in EMs' group, suggesting more sobriety and relaxedness with higher level of marital adjustment of parents. It appears that parents' marital relationship is a more salient factor in the personality development of boys as compared to girls. It is notable that almost all the traits become stronger with increase in the degree of marital adjustment. Educated parents are more aware about the effect of family environment on children's personality development. Therefore, they try to maintain good and healthy interaction with their children, and try to check the repercussions of marital dissatisfaction on child-rearing. As Juneja (1979) has argued, though EMs provide less care to their children, they seem to have relatively greater degree of concern and attachment. These findings suggest that high level of marital adjustment of parents facilitates healthy personality development in children.

Present study shows that marital relationship of parents was positive in both the groups. However, a significant difference in the degree of marital adjustment of employed and unemployed mothers was observed showing relatively higher level of marital adjustment in case of UEMs. Marital adjustment of parents showed relationship with almost all personality factors on ESPQ except B, G and H. Marital relationship of parents was moderately related with some personality traits in children. Its relationships with factor D, F and Q-4 were statistically significant in different groups of children. In case of boys of UEMs, factor D (Affected by feelings *Vs* Emotionally stable) was negatively correlated with marital relationship showing greater emotional stability with better marital adjustment of parents. In boys of EMs, marital relationship showed significant negative relationship with factors F and Q-4, suggesting sobriety and relaxedness in children with parents' better marital relationship.

Marital adjustment of parents importantly influences the family environment, and determines treatment given by the parents to their children. It is important to remember that parents have a relationship with each other as well as with their children. They serve as a source of mutual emotional and physical support, and comfort to their children. Working mothers have dual task load and constant demands are placed upon them in their caretaking role. These mental and physical stresses can be reduced by the mutual support and appreciation of the spouse. It was observed that when fathers are supportive of mothers, high mother-child involvement and sensitive, competent and affectionate mother-infant relationships are found. Therefore, it is very important that husband and wife have cordial relationship with each other. This provides sense of security and loving environment in the family context. Children feel that they are living in a family where parents have good relationship and are loving. Such feeling helps in the healthy development of personality. It is also true that husband and wife may have some disputes or disagreements regarding various aspects of their role as husband or wife and as parents, but they can resolve such problems by discussing with each other. They need to have complete understanding to have a healthy relationship and adjustment. Working parents should be extra cautious about their relationship because it affects the personality development of their children. Working parents are mostly away from home due to their job demands and when they are at home and do not have cordial relationship, children may be the sufferers.

7

FAMILY AND JOB DEMANDS

It is true that work affects life profoundly, although not always in ways that are simple or straight forward. Job determines daily schedules, which in turn affect how much time parents have at their disposal for their children. Job determines family income and, therefore, affects the resources available at home. At a subtler level, work affects parent's self-esteem and thus, their happiness as human beings as well as parents. Working mothers' job demands play an important role in their lives. There are several aspects which directly or indirectly affect their family life. Support by family members at home and in job related matters, especially by their husbands, make them feel satisfied. If working mothers do not get support from their children and husband in performing household chores, it makes them exhausted and they cannot work effectively both at home and at their work place. It is observed that when women work for financial reasons, they get some support from their family members. But when they work for their self-satisfaction or for utilizing their time or abilities fruitfully, less adjustments are made by the family members. If the working hours are fixed, mothers can adjust their time for household chores and interaction with children and husband. They try to maintain social relations also and can spare time for some entertainment.

It is also very important as to how children, husband and working mothers themselves perceive their working outside the home. Expression of 'importance' by family members provides self- pride to the working mothers. Similarly satisfaction with the time spent with family members also affects their functioning positively. Very few jobs are perceived as 'women's jobs', such as nursing, teaching, clerical etc. Majority of women themselves prefer to choose teaching and clerical jobs because of less work pressure and better work environment. These jobs generally do not disturb their family, personal and social life, but job of nursing is generally not opted or preferred by females. Somehow they are forced to enter into such type of job. Reddy (1986) in his study reported that the sex-linked statuses peculiar to females are respected much more by the society than their other statuses, but these vocations have specific problems of their own. Most of the nurses in his study reported that the timings for their duties seem to be too erratic and difficult to cope up with. In the present study, an attempt was also made to know about working mothers' views on different aspects related to family matters and job.

Measures

Questionnaire for Working Mothers: To obtain information about how employment influences the family and marital life of employed mothers, a questionnaire measure was developed in Hindi language. A detailed description of various aspects covered in it is given below:

(i) *Aspects Related to Family Experiences :* Items such as reasons for taking up a job, perception of maternal employment by family members, pressure on family members, effect of mother's job on daily routine, feeling of not spending time with family members, effects on child-related activities and supervision of children were included in this part. All these items were rated on 3-point scale ranging from "negative" to "positive" and " less" to " mostly or much". Other categories of responses were according to the content of the item.

(ii) *Job Demands :* It consisted of 12 items such as feeling of responsibility in job, job related preparation, leave facility, working on holidays, over time, extra work in colleague's absence, length of service, working hours and mode of transport. For some items, actual number or score was noted.

(iii) *Sharing* : It consisted of 2 items, namely, sharing in decision making, in household activities by husband and by children. In these items 'never' to 'always' categories were used for obtaining the responses.

Results

Working mother's specific life conditions vary with the type of job, and play an important role in the parent-child interaction and family environment. With this in view, additional data regarding mother's job conditions were obtained. They were asked to indicate their perception and reactions to job and household problems. The detailed description of the responses thus obtained are shown in Table 7.1.

Reasons for taking a job : It was observed that with regard to the reason for taking up a job outside the home, family's financial condition was most crucial in the case of clerks (60%) and nurses (92%). Clerks also reported that because they had learnt stenography and typing, therefore, they took up the job (20%). About 10 per cent of the clerks told that because they were working before marriage, and after marriage there was no problem in continuing, hence, they continued working. On the other hand, teachers also reported 'working before marriage' (37%). They said that as their working did not have any adverse effect on their married life and household activities, therefore, they continued working after marriage also. About 30 per cent of the teachers also reported 'use of time' and 'use of ability' as the reasons for taking a job. They reported that when their children started going to school, they were left with sufficient spare time, and because they were qualified, they started teaching either in their children's school or in some other school. Their job timings coincided with their children's school timings and therefore, the children did not feel their absence from home.

Perception of maternal employment by the family members : Mothers were asked to tell about how they themselves, their husband and their children perceived their working outside the

Table 7.1: Types of Occupation and Employed Mothers' Job and Home related Experiences

Job and Home related Variables	Clerks (N=40)		Teachers (N=40)		Nurses (N=40)		Total (N=120)	
	f	%	*f*	%	*f*	%	*f*	%
Reasons for Taking a Job								
Financial condition	24	(60)	2	(5)	37	(92)	63	(53)
Use of spare time	2	(5)	12	(30)	1	(2)	15	(13)
Use of abilities	8	(20)	11	(28)	1	(3)	20	(16)
Working before marriage also	6	(15)	15	(37)	1	(3)	22	(18)
Perception of Maternal Employment								
By Husband								
Important	22	(55)	1	(2)	34	(85)	57	(48)
Indifferent	11	(28)	23	(58)	5	(13)	39	(32)
Unimportant	7	(17)	16	(40)	1	(2)	24	(20)
By Self								
Important	32	(80)	35	(88)	35	(88)	102	(85)
Indifferent	5	(13)	4	(10)	2	(5)	11	(9)
Unimportant	3	(7)	1	(2)	3	(7)	7	(6)
By Children								
Important	23	(57)	35	(88)	30	(75)	88	(73)
Indifferent	4	(10)	3	(8)	4	(10)	11	(9)
Unimportant	13	(33)	2	(4)	6	(15)	21	(18)
Pressure of Household Work								
On Husband								
Much	14	(35)	6	(15)	23	(57)	43	(35)
Average	13	(33)	10	(25)	12	(30)	35	(30)
Less	13	(32)	24	(60)	5	(13)	42	(35)
On Self								
Much	23	(58)	5	(12)	32	(80)	60	(50)
Average	10	(25)	18	(45)	7	(18)	35	(29)
Less	7	(17)	17	(43)	1	(2)	25	(21)
On Children								
Much	23	(58)	27	(68)	32	(80)	82	(68)
Average	11	(28)	7	(17)	7	(18)	25	(21)
Less	6	(14)	6	(15)	1	(2)	13	(11)

(Contd.)

Table 7.1: *(Contd.)*

Job and Home related Variables	Clerks (N=40)		Teachers (N=40)		Nurses (N=40)		Total (N=120)	
	f	%	*f*	%	*f*	%	*f*	%
Effect of Maternal Employment on Different Activities of the Family								
Positive	0	(0)	07	(17)	1	(2)	8	(7)
Indifferent	7	(18)	15	(38)	5	(13)	27	(22)
Negative	33	(82)	18	(45)	34	(85)	85	(71)
On Children								
Positive	0	(0)	1	(2)	1	(2)	2	(2)
Indifferent	7	(18)	13	(33)	2	(5)	22	(18)
Negative	33	(82)	26	(65)	37	(93)	96	(80)
Feeling of not Spending Time With Husband								
Mostly	16	(40)	19	(47)	27	(68)	62	(51)
Sometimes	17	(43)	14	(35)	4	(10)	35	(29)
Less	7	(17)	7	(18)	9	(22)	23	(20)
With the Children								
Mostly	24	(60)	18	(45)	29	(73)	71	(59)
Sometimes	8	(20)	8	(20)	2	(5)	18	(15)
Less	8	(20)	14	(35)	9	(22)	31	(26)
Supervision of Children By								
Creche	5	(12)	2	(5)	4	(10)	11	(9)
Servant	8	(20)	15	(38)	1	(2)	24	(20)
Family members	12	(30)	12	(30)	0	(0)	24	(20)
Children themselves	13	(33)	2	(5)	34	(86)	49	(40)
Parents	2	(5)	9	(22)	1	(2)	12	(11)
Sharing in Decision Making								
More	30	(75)	0	(0)	25	(62)	55	(46)
Sometimes	9	(23)	24	(60)	9	(23)	42	(35)
Rare	1	(2)	16	(40)	6	(15)	13	(19)
Sharing Household Responsibilities By Husband								
More	18	(45)	2	(5)	24	(60)	44	(37)
Sometimes	18	(45)	14	(35)	9	(23)	41	(34)
Rare	4	(10)	19	(47)	7	(17)	30	(25)
Not required	0	(0)	5	(12)	0	(0)	5	(4)

(Contd.)

Table 7.1: *(Contd.)*

Job and Home related Variables	Clerks (N=40)		Teachers (N=40)		Nurses (N=40)		Total (N=120)	
	f	%	*f*	%	*f*	%	*f*	%
By Children								
More	8	(20)	0	(0)	16	(40)	24	(20)
Sometimes	21	(53)	5	(12)	11	(28)	37	(31)
Rare	11	(27)	29	(73)	13	(32)	53	(44)
Not required	0	(0)	6	(15)	0	(0)	6	(5)
Help from Husband in Job related Matters								
Always	28	(70)	28	(70)	33	(83)	89	(74)
Sometimes	12	(30)	12	(30)	7	(17)	31	(26)
Feeling of Job Responsibility								
Yes	29	(72)	25	(62)	32	(90)	90	(75)
No	11	(28)	15	(38)	4	(10)	30	(25)
Any Job related Work at Home								
Yes	10	(25)	21	(52)	0	(0)	31	(26)
No	30	(75)	19	(48)	40	(100)	89	(74)
Availability of leave								
Mostly	4	(11)	25	(63)	21	(52)	50	(42)
Sometimes	11	(27)	6	(15)	6	(15)	23	(19)
Less	25	(62)	9	(22)	13	(33)	47	(39)
Working on Holidays								
Mostly	8	(20)	20	(50)	15	(38)	43	(34)
Rarely	32	(80)	20	(50)	25	(62)	77	(66)
Over time/Extra Work								
Mostly	4	(10)	10	(25)	25	(63)	39	(32)
Sometimes	10	(25)	2	(5)	5	(12)	17	(14)
Less	26	(65)	28	(70)	10	(25)	64	(54)
Extra Work in Colleague's Absence								
Mostly	26	(65)	20	(50)	35	(87)	81	(68)
Less	14	(35)	20	(50)	5	(13)	39	(32)
Mode of Transport								
Own Vehicle	13	(32)	19	(48)	1	(2)	33	(27)
With Husband	12	(30)	0	(0)	1	(2)	13	(11)
Public Transport	9	(23)	5	(12)	1	(2)	15	(13)
Official	6	(15)	12	(30)	18	(46)	36	(30)
On Foot	0	(0)	4	(10)	19	(48)	23	(19)

home. Mothers in nursing group (88%) reported that their husband considered it 'very important' for their family compared to 55 per cent of clerks and only 2 per cent of teachers. In case of teachers, a sizeable number of mothers reported that their husband showed 'indifference' (58%) or considered it 'unimportant' (40%). In our society women's job is considered important only when it caters to the financial need of the family. However, it is also very important for a woman to work for self-satisfaction.

As regards their self-perception about working outside the home, almost all mothers (about 85%) considered it very 'important', reason being financial or self-satisfaction. Mothers in all the groups reported that children also considered their mother's job 'important' (75%). Nowadays maternal employment has become a status symbol and children feel pride in having mothers working.

Pressure of household work : When mothers work outside the home, family members also have to share the burden of household chores. This has dual effect on the family life. Although it increases the burden on the part of the family members, at the same time, it provides comfort to mothers in the family setting. In this regard, nurses as compared to other groups reported 'much pressure' (57%) whereas teachers (60%) reported 'less pressure' of household work on husband. Almost equal number of mothers in clerical group reported in all categories. Similarly nurses and clerks reported 'much pressure' on 'self' (80%, 58%) whereas teachers (68%) reported 'maximum' pressure on children. It was noted that sharing of so called mothers' responsibilities created heavy work pressure on 'self' and children.

Effect on different activities of the family : In day-to-day life, a family has various types of activities such as entertainment, social gatherings, playing indoor or outdoor games etc. In a nuclear family, there is more interaction among the family members. When mother starts working, the type of job may influence various activities of the family differentially. Nurses and clerks reported (85% and 82%) 'negative effect' on overall activities of the family. Teachers have also reported the 'negative effect' (45%). However, a comparatively small number of teachers have mentioned 'neutral effect' (38%). Similarly, regarding activities related to children showed more 'negative effect' in almost all the three groups, however, maximum by nurses (93%) and less by teachers (65%). It seems that almost all mothers expressed negative effect of maternal employment on their household and other activities except the fact that better financial condition owing to maternal employment enhanced the need gratification in children.

Feeling of not spending time with family members : Working women generally feel dissatisfied with the time spent with their husbands and children, as they have to perform various household chores after returning from the job. In this regard, more 'nurses' (68%) reported 'dissatisfaction' in comparison to clerks and teachers (40%, 47%). In addition, teachers and clerks also reported 'sometimes' and 'less' dissatisfaction. Similarly more number of nurses (73%) showed dissatisfaction with the amount of time spent with the children. About 60 per cent of clerks and 47 per cent of teachers 'mostly' felt dissatisfied. As teachers reported usually their working hours coincided with children's school timings, so they felt 'less' dissatisfaction (35%) with the time spent with their children.

Supervision of children during mother's absence : In mother's absence due to the employment, children are to be looked after by either creche, servant/maid, family members, parents or a little older children look after themselves. Mostly mothers in clerical and teaching jobs reported that children were looked after by servant and family members (husband, siblings, in-laws or grandparents).

A large section of mothers from nursing profession (86%) reported that children looked after themselves as there was no creche facilities available, and sometimes due to odd duty hours it was not possible. Nurses also reported that during night duty, children themselves took care of them. It may be noted that the mode of child's supervision varies with the age of children.

Sharing in decision making : Generally, in our society decisions are taken by the males. As women are also sharing the financial burden of the family, the question arises whether they have some sharing in decision making or not? Responses to this issue showed that a comparatively large number of clerks (75%) in comparison to nurses (62%) showed greater participation in decision making. As regards teachers, 60 per cent of them reported that in some cases they were asked to give their opinion, whereas in most of the cases they did not participate in decision making.

Sharing household responsibilities by the family members: In modern times, the family structure is usually nuclear and family size is also small, and if mother is working then the family members have to share the burden of household chores. When asked about this, 'more' sharing by husband was reported by nurses and clerks (60%, 45%) as compared to only 5 per cent of teachers. About 47 per cent of teachers reported that their husband rarely shared the household responsibility. It suggests that the type of job and duty hours determine the extent of help required from husband. Almost similar pattern was observed in case of getting help from children. 73 per cent of teachers reported that their children rarely shared the household responsibility as compared to only 27 per cent of clerks and 32 per cent of nurses.

Help from husband in job related matters : Almost all mothers reported that their husbands rendered assistance to them in sorting out their 'professional problems' or related matters.

Feeling of job responsibility: If a job requires high degree of responsibility, it affects a working woman's family life also. As it is clear from the type of jobs taken in this study, nurses' job requires greater commitment and sincerity. More nurses (90%) reported greater job responsibility as compared to clerks (42%) and teachers (62%).

Any job related work at home : Some professions require prior preparation or working at home also. If it requires such type of work, then it may interfere with household chores as well as with family interaction. When teachers were asked about this aspect, about 50 per cent of them reported that they did need to prepare for the next day if they are engaged with higher classes. They have to check home work and examination copies generally at home. On the other hand nurses (100%) did not need to do such work at home. They have to perform efficiently at their work place only. About 25 per cent of clerks reported that 'sometimes' they have to bring incomplete work at home.

Availability of leave: Working mothers were also asked about any problem in getting leave whenever required. About 63 per cent of teachers and 52 per cent of nurses did not report any problem in getting leave. Clerks reported that they have less availability of leave due to more pressure of work.

Working on holidays : As compared to clerks, teachers (50%) and nurses (38%) reported working on holidays, whereas clerks said that they rarely had to work on holidays. If a woman gets full time for family and household chores, it gives more time for family interaction and there is greater satisfaction in life.

Overtime/Extra work: If there is some extra work or need to work after the scheduled working hours, women have to stay back at work place for some time. Nurses (63%) reported that in situations of an emergency or a colleague not turning up at the scheduled duty hours, they cannot leave the place of duty and have to work extra time. 90 per cent of clerks hardly face such situation whereas about 25 per cent of teachers reported that due to some programme or meeting they had to remain in the school after scheduled timings.

Extra work in colleague's absence: When a colleague is on leave, or busy in some other work, others have to share his/her duties. About 50 per cent of teachers, 65 per cent of clerks and 87 per cent of nurses reported that they had to work extra if a colleague is absent.

Mode of transport: If the work place is in the vicinity and convenient transport facilities are available, it saves a lot of time and energy.

About 30 per cent of clerks either had their own vehicle or they accompanied their husband. 23 per cent of them used public transport. Most of the teachers (48%) had their own vehicles and 30 per cent of them used school bus. Nurses either used public transport or in case of nearby area they also used to go on foot. Nurses reported their dissatisfaction regarding public transport.

Discussion

In the present study, the impact of type of job (clerical, teaching and nursing) on various aspects of family functioning were analyzed. The main reason why mothers opted for taking job outside the home, a large number of teachers reported 'utilizing spare time' whereas clerks and nurses reported 'due to financial reason'. Nurses reported maximum dissatisfaction in family affairs, especially regarding caring for children. Sharing of responsibility was reported by clerks and nurses but teachers reported that they hardly needed any help. Nurses reported that they usually had to lock their children at home because they could not leave their children and home in neighbour's care and responsibility. Length of service in all the groups revealed that usually teachers started their job after the children were grown up whereas clerks and nurses continued their work after marriage. Educational level of clerks and nurses was lower as compared to teachers.

In an informal discussion with the participating mothers, it was found that nurses appeared to be the most dissatisfied and frustrated group. They reported that they have to work very hard, but their job is not considered a respectable one (as they perceive it). According to the reporting of nurses, most of them started working before marriage. They continued even after the birth of their children, and faced a lot of problems, because they could not get much help from their family members. They had flexible duty hours which certainly affected the child-care and family functioning. Their duty hours kept changing and hence they could not follow a set routine. They expressed unhappiness about not devoting adequate attention to home and children. Although their responses regarding disciplinary techniques were almost similar, their behaviours showed that they could not devote as much attention to children's behaviour as they would have liked to. After returning from duty, they were so pre-occupied with household activities and children's studies that at the end of the day they were totally exhausted. Most of the nurses reported that they did not get much help from husband and children in the household activities. Regarding entertainment and social visits, they reported that due to the nature of their duty, they could hardly get any chance for such activities.

Most of the nurses reported that they had to lock up their children during their duty hours. They were worried that their children, being young, may go out leaving the house open. They were hesitant to seek help from neighbours as it was a daily affair. Those whose husbands were in private jobs had more problems because they used to go to work early and returned late in the evening. The educational level of these couples was lower as compared to other groups. The mothers could not pay adequate attention to children's studies. Most of the children were going for coaching classes as husbands were also not well-educated.

Teachers' group showed maximum satisfaction regarding their family life and about children. They did not report any problem regarding children as their duty hours and children's school timings usually coincided. They were satisfied that children did not require to remain alone at home for a long period of time. Most of the teachers told that their children had to do their work themselves, because the mothers, although at home, were usually busy doing household chores. These mothers laid lot of emphasis on studies as they wanted their children to do well academically and face the challenges of growing competitive world successfully. Being teachers themselves, they felt that their children should not lag behind in studies. As compared to other two groups, the socio-economic status and educational status of teachers and their spouse were high. They could provide better facilities to their children and also had entertainment and good social life. They reported sharing in decision making as well as sharing household responsibilities by husband and children. However, teachers complained that they had to carry correction work at home and teachers teaching higher classes needed some preparation at home.

Because of such work they sometimes could not participate in social gatherings and family affairs. On the other hand they expressed happiness about having vacational job. Thus they could compensate their busy time schedule during school days with spending full-time with their family. Mothers in this group also showed satisfaction regarding utilizing their capabilities and attaining financial gains.

Mothers in clerical group were moderately satisfied with their working and household matters. Most of them were previously staying in a joint family, but later on due to space problems, separated into nuclear family. Because of this reason they did not face problems in child-rearing. When children were very young, they were left with their grandparents. As they grew up they did not need to go there daily, but only on weekends. A very few mothers in this group reported that long working hours exhaust them and during evening hours they did not feel like doing anything except necessary household work. Children were made to study. They used to receive some help from their husband and older children. Older children used to help the younger ones in doing homework and other household chores. Entertainment was not a regular feature in the family. It all depended on the availability of time during the weekends. If they had to observe social obligations, then the entertainment would shift to next weekend. Children understood their problems and did not complain much about anything and also did not demand anything.

In the present study, comparison of all groups in employed mother's group reveals that almost all mothers yielded similar responses. Teachers and clerks reported satisfaction regarding their roles as mothers, wives and working women, whereas nurses shared some frustration and dissatisfaction regarding the type of job and support available at home. It suggests that type of job and physical and psychological support available at home determine women's feeling of satisfaction. Bhopal being a comparatively small place, working women generally do not face hassles of work place and home. Children can also move without any problem or risk. It provides a sense of relief to working parents.

8

CONCLUSIONS

In the Indian society mothers play a vital role in the rearing of children, particularly during the early years of development. If mothers are employed they get relatively less time for disciplining the child. It is generally held that such a condition would influence the development of personality of the child adversely. But working mothers also try to spend maximum time in caring for and fulfilling the demands and requirements of children. Whenever they get time, children receive priority in mothers' schedule, as compared to other household chores. They often plan and adjust their schedule of daily activities accordingly. As they are in a better financial position, they can afford to compensate for their absence by other means too. On the other hand, housewives try to derive satisfaction through other mechanisms. Since they stay mostly at home, they can save more money and plan their schedule in such a way that they derive satisfaction through developing various hobbies etc.

The present study demonstrates linkages across maternal employment, child-rearing and disciplinary practices and personality characteristics of children. These linkages, however, cannot allow to determine decisively the directions of relationship as the data were collected at one time point. With a view to determine the functional relationship among these sets of variables, we need longitudinal studies in which data are collected at many time points. Nevertheless, the findings do point to certain trends which have already been hinted at .

Taken as a whole, present findings clearly indicate the salient role of maternal employment in the growth and development of child's personality. However, maternal employment seems to influence child's personality through various moderator and process variables, such as, characteristics of family and home environment, marital adjustment of parents, parental treatment of the child, age and sex of the child, child's perception of parents and their disciplinary practices and other variables. These factors differently influence and shape the dispositions of child's personality. The interrelationship of these variables has been schematically represented in Figure 8.1, which shows the relationship of maternal employment status with home environment and background factors. Mothers opt for an employment out of the home because of some specific conditions, such as, the problem of utilization of time, utilization and expression of personal abilities or some economic reasons. At the same time, maternal employment status is linked directly to home environment and family functioning. Although, marital adjustment of parents emerged as an important factor in the present study determining the nature and extent of disciplining practices used by parents, it was not found to be directly related to maternal employment. Rather, maternal employment status was found to be determined by certain environmental and demographic characteristics of the family. Figure 8.1 clearly represents this relationship. Figure also shows that pattern of disciplining or treatment method of the child as adopted by parents is determined jointly by the level of marital adjustment of parents and characteristics of family and home environment. However, under certain circumstances, marital adjustment of parents may be directly linked to the nature and severity of the methods of child treatment. Although employed and unemployed mothers seem to discipline their children differently, it is largely determined by the characteristics of home environment and family functioning as well as nature and extent of marital adjustment of parents.

Treatment along with various combinations of age and sex differentially influences the child's perceptions of both discipline as well as disciplinarian (parents) which, in turn, shapes the personality of the child. However, child's perception of discipline and disciplinarian is also related to his or her own personality characteristics. Also, personality characteristics of the child, to some extent, influence the home and family environment as well as level

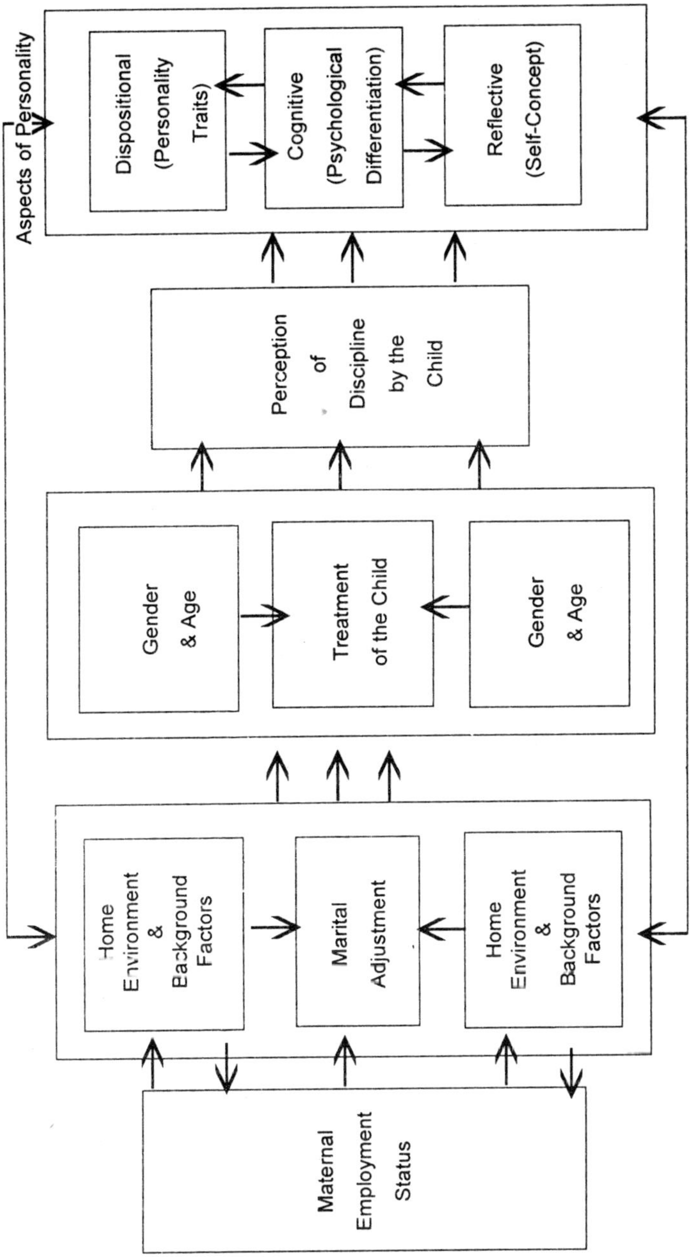

Fig. 8.1 : A Schematic representation of Interrelationships of Different Variables with Aspects of Child's Personality

of marital adjustment of parents.

The findings revealed that the personality traits and psychological differentiation in children of employed and unemployed mothers showed several differences and similarities. Mothers in both the groups differed to some extent in the adoption of child-rearing and disciplinary practices. The findings of the study show that maternal employment is importantly related to development of different aspects of personality in children. Owing to the demands faced by dual career women, the performance of mother's role assumes a complex form. Perhaps the developmental ecology of children consists of many constraints and affordances. While present findings did not indicate that the experiential worlds of children in families with employed and unemployed mothers are uniquely structured, they did indicate that the arrangement of different activities and parent-child interactions varied in important ways. They present different types of developmental conditions. It was observed that the relationship between age and personality traits varied in the groups of children of UEMs and EMs. Some of the traits were invariant across age groups while others showed increase in their strength with advancing age. The study also indicated that parenting styles of UEMs and EMs and their perception by children showed some commonalities as well as differences. Perhaps the broader context and higher level of variables add common effects while some of the features were conditioned by the peculiarities of family setting.

As background data reveal, most of the children (70%) in both the groups lived either in multi-storied or block type buildings. In independent type of houses, children do not receive immediate attention from anybody, whereas in other types of houses, neighbours' presence may bring certain degree of feeling of security. Regarding entertainment facilities, children in both the groups received similar facilities. Sinha (1982) has contended that the relationships with peers and physical facilities play an important role in the socialization of children. As mother's employment brings changes in the immediate environment of the family, other aspects shared by children in both the groups start converging.

Results of the study suggest that barring a few situations,

mothers in both the groups took recourse to almost similar disciplinary techniques in dealing with children. The results suggest that UEMs and EMs differed only in reaction to disobedience, techniques to promote good habits, reaction to losing something in the school and helping the child in spite of being busy in some task. However, mothers in general used mild disciplinary techniques and mild punishment for the undesired behaviour. In day-to-day life, parents come across many problematic situations related to child's behaviour. Some parents react with harsh and strict techniques whereas others take it easy and use only mild disciplinary techniques. Because maternal employment influences the family environment, it may also influence the way parents react to different problematic situations.

The findings indicate that out of 13 situations, EMs used 'explaining' most frequently, whereas UEMs reported the use of 'explaining' in five situations only. The frequency of 'scolding' as a response was equal in both the groups whereas the use of 'spanking' was slightly higher in the group of EMs. Surprisingly, 'depriving' and 'no talking' were least frequent responses in both the groups. A similar pattern of father's responses regarding children's problematic behaviours was perceived by mothers in both the groups. When children showed undesired behaviour for the first few occasions, parents' reaction was usually 'explaining', or sometimes 'scolding' depending upon the nature of undesired behaviour. But when children persistently demonstrated undesired behaviour in spite of 'explaining' the parents reported to adopt harsh punitive techniques like 'spanking' or 'depriving'.

It appears that when children continue to show undesired behaviour, more EMs responded harshly using greater amount of physical punishment, whereas UEMs dealt with children by 'scolding'. It can be assumed that EMs usually have scarcity of time and, therefore, when children persistently show undesired behaviour, they perhaps think that children can be made to understand only by physical punishment. 'Scolding' as compared to 'spanking', usually does not have much painful effect. However, in showing first few incidents of problematic behaviours by the child, EMs may be extra careful in treating with harsh methods, because their children do not enjoy their company for a longer period and if they scold or spank the child, it would make the child feel deprived of affection. The persistent problematic behaviour is harshly and strictly dealt by EMs. UEMs are generally at home all day, so whenever a child shows such behaviours they can stop the child by simple 'scolding' or 'explaining'.

It was observed that employed mothers are relatively more careful and cautious about their children. Several studies in this area reveal differential effects of different methods as well as relationship of maternal employment with different aspects of discipline. Now-a-days, a large number of mothers are engaged in some gainful employment. Their children as well as husbands understand the problems of mothers and, therefore, share household burden. Children receive the first priority from all parents and thus, obtain maximum attention in the family.

In the present study, the sample of mothers differed only in one respect, i.e. the employment status (full-time housewives/ employed mothers), and shared similar background in terms of family structure (nuclear family), minimum number of children (atleast two children), urban atmosphere and age of children (7 to 12 years). Thus, except ME, other characteristics of both the groups were almost similar. The immediate environment of children in family (especially mother's presence) was varied whereas the broader social context was equally shared by both the groups. The age group taken in the present study was more susceptible to the influences of peers, school, other adult models and mass media. Now-a-days, children increasingly spend their time in diverse activities. The growing child gradually moves towards independence and for him or her the people in broader environment (e.g. peers, adult role models) become significant, thus, the children of UEMs and EMs grow in environment or ecology which is partly shared and partly distinct. The same is depicted in Figure 8.2.

According to Bronfenbrenner (1977), the understanding of human behaviours on the part of one or two persons in the same place requires examination of multiperson systems of interaction, not limited to a single setting and must take into account aspects of the environment beyond the immediate situation containing the

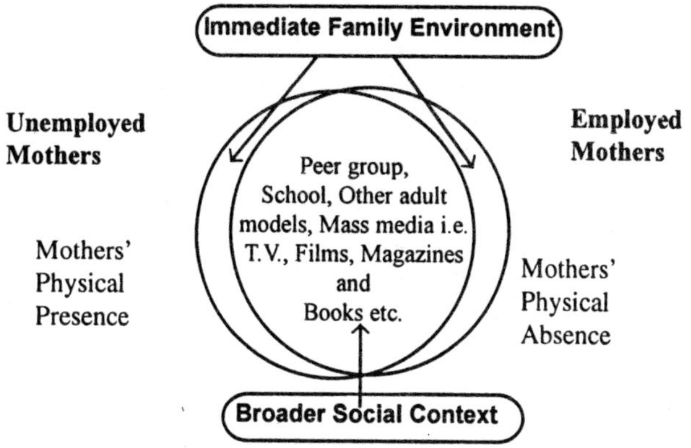

Fig . 8.2 : Common and Distinct Aspects of Ecology in the Groups of Unemployed and Employed Mothers

child. He viewed "ecology of human development" as "the scientific study of progressive mutual accommodation, throughout the life span, between growing human organism and the changing immediate environments in which it lives, as this process is affected by relations obtaining within and between these immediate settings, as well as the larger social contexts, formal and informal, in which the settings are embedded." As Sinha (1978) has noted, "three factors, namely the home, school and peer groups with physical facilities, nature of social interactions and activities common in each constitute the most important ecological influences on the psychological development of the child and these influences are relatively easier to discern or examine" (p.29).

On the whole, the present findings suggest that the role of mother is predominantly culture bound and the employed and unemployed mothers share more commonalities than differences. The professional role did not emerge as primary as the role of mother. This, however, should not be taken as an indicator of identity between the two. The employment status of mother has important influences on the patterning of family life, particularly, in social and affective climate which in turn, make the parent-child interaction distinct.

It appears that children whose mothers are employed develop

certain personality characteristics more strongly than others. Children of EMs were relatively more outgoing. In contrast, the children of UEMs were relatively more reserved, placid, egoistically strong, conscientious and vigorous. On the other hand, the high level of psychological differentiation observed in the children of EMs makes them equipped with a different behaviour potential. This may influence their capacity to cope up with momentary demands as well as meeting the challenges in life.

Some Implications

This effort has been directed towards mapping the contours of human development in the changing context of Indian family. The traditional Indian family, which still happens to be the prototypical image held by the majority, consists of an earning father, mother, who takes care of the responsibilities of the family and children within the four walls of home. The presence of grandparents may add other dimensions to this image. This prevalent view is challenged by the entry of woman/mother to the world of work outside the family. This change is often achieved at the cost of many other changes demanding reorganization or rearrangement on physical, social and psychological planes depending upon the age configuration and health status of family members. The routine of the family will have to be rearranged. The division of labour within the family and role definition may need to undergo important change. This will largely be social. The psychological change is mainly related to self and identity and situating them in the new context.

As not much work has been done in this area, the study did not verify any specific hypothesis but it did formulate some broad guiding assumptions and expectations. In the preceding section, the results of the study have been discussed keeping in view those assumptions. Keeping in mind the kind of study it is and the kind of data we have at our disposal, coupled with field experiences gained, the study appears to have the following implications.

1. Maternal employment is a significant event in the family

context with implication for child rearing. This works as a stressor for the family having mixed results. In order to capitalize its gains, one needs to create an environment of openness and sharing. It is only through informed and rational decision making that parents must conduct themselves in relation to themselves as well as children.

2. Parenting is a context bound phenomenon and the situational, contextual factors need to be attended to. Many of the apparent inconsistencies in parenting and parent-child interactions appear to be systematically related to situational demands. Parenting, therefore, should not be taken to be stereotypical, predeterminded and undirectional process. The presence of media, and other agents of socialization, particularly peers, also play their role and this should be recognised by the parents and their inputs should be adequately responded to. It is believed that exposure to mass media (particularly T.V.) and surroundings influence children's behaviour adversely. However, they should realize that their treatment with children is the more influential factor. The child should be treated as an individual. It is very important to know about the friends of their children, with whom children mix in the school, neighbourhood, etc. Parents generally do not know that their children are attending school regularly or not. In big cities, it is very difficult to know about the whereabouts of their children. It was reported during one of the visits to a school by the author that many children during the school timings are away from home but they do not come to school. Principal told that these children go to video parlours, and for getting money for such games they steal the same from their homes. Mothers, whether employed or unemployed, should spare time and watch their children.

3. Parenting in today's world cannot be considered as a spontaneous process dealt within an adhoc fashion. As joint and extended families are on decline and marriageable age is going up, there is no scope for parental modelling within the family so far as the new parents are concerned. The social mobility is also creating many discontinuities in family life.

This scenario demands sincere parental education. To this end, psychologists and other social scientists must join hands and take necessary steps. Many research findings have reported that parents need training in parenting practices, because children are facing many problems due to various reasons. Parental treatment with their children plays a vital role in this regard. Guidelines and literature should be made available to parents. Today, many psychologists opine that the parents and also the teachers in schools need counselling rather than children themselves.

4. Children are susceptible to experiential influences. Their attitudes, values, personality and other behavioural dispositions are shaped significantly by their personal experiences. Parents, therefore, are expected to play a critical role in arranging the environment and experiences for children. The present study indicated that the status of maternal employment is correlated with certain personality traits in children and there are variations in the field of discipline and rearing experiences to which these children are exposed to. These trends point to the possible mediating role of parental behaviour in shaping children's personality. If this is so, then parents should be made aware of this and facilitated to equip themselves with the role of active shapers of the personality of children.

5. The present study has also hinted at the fact that maternal employment is increasing day-by-day. Women's presence at work place and absence from home has implications for adjustments and arrangements so that the stresses emanating from women's work outside the home may be adequately coped. This is important for personal as well as societal growth and development of the child. It is no more a personal or individual problem. It is a social issue and solutions should be worked out at the level of society. This means that organizations employing women have to accommodate this fact as a part of reality and make necessary provisions for effective utilization of this important human resource. This will demand certain degree of restructuring and development of a new mind set that will allow

women as equal partners.

6. An issue related to the preceding one relates to the development of empathy and understanding among the family members. This is necessary if one wishes to capitalize on the gains of maternal employment for the family. In practice, this will mean reallocating household chores and responsibilities across family members. At present very few families consider mother's job important, may be due to any reason, and have sympathetic attitude towards them. Women generally have complaints that their husbands still think that household and child-rearing responsibilities should be observed by mothers only in spite of their sharing of economic burden of the family. Both husband and children should not only hold positive attitude and empathy towards mothers, but also share the household chores. This will make mothers satisfied and strong to perform their roles efficiently at home as well as at the work place.

Suggestions

A close perusal of the details of present investigation indicates that there is considerable scope for improvement and further investigation. Some of the salient issues which may be taken for further investigation are as follows:

1. With a view to decipher the influence of maternal employment, a more context sensitive and longitudinal design is warranted. Also, maternal employment cannot be considered as a unitary variable. The nature and extent of its effect on child and family also depend on the economic condition, age, family structure and type of job. A detailed analysis of maternal employment along with these variables would be useful for evolving strategies to manage the problem in work and family life.
2. The investigator's experience in the present investigation has indicated that maternal employment is linked with daily hassles and stresses which influence family life and adjustment in significant ways. This aspect has implications for child

development and needs detailed study.

3. Family can be approached in a number of ways and its functioning and consequences depend largely on availability of the support system. In Indian context, where social orientation is largely collectivist and environment is relatively less stable and predictable, support system warrants detailed analysis particularly in the case of employed mothers with younger children.

4. The present study has explored the dispositional, cognitive and reflective aspects of personality. It would be fruitful to look into other aspects of self and personality such as self-esteem, self-efficacy and other personality dimensions.

5. The home-work interface and the reciprocal influence of the two need detailed analysis.

BIBLIOGRAPHY

Agarwal, G., & Saksena, N. K. (1977). Emotional development of the child and role of the parents: An overview. *Child Psychiatry Quarterly, 10,* 1-7.

Allport, G.W. (1937). *Personality: A psychological interpretation.* New York: Holt.

Anandalakshmy, S. (1986). Children: Childhood, families, and the larger world. *Social Change, 16,* 79-87.

Anandalakshmy, S., & Bajaj, M. (1981). Childhood in the weaver's community in Varanasi: Socialization for adult roles. In D. Sinha, (Ed), *Socialization of the Indian child.* New Delhi: Concept.

Baldwin, A. L. (1948). Socialization and the parent-child relationship. *Child Development, 19,* 127-136.

Baldwin, A. L. (1949). The effect of home environment on nursery school behaviour. *Child Development, 20,* 49-62.

Bandura, A. (1962). Influence of model's reinforcement contingencies on the acquisition of imitative responses. *Journal of Personality and Social Psychology, 1,* 585-589.

Bandura, A. (1977). *Social learning theory.* Englewood Cliffs, N.J.: Prentice Hall.

Barar, S., & Barar, S. S. (1990). Separation anxiety in pre-school children. *Journal of Personality and Clinical Studies, 6,* 13-17.

Barglow, V. E., & Molitor, N. (1987). Effects of maternal absence due to employment on the quality of infant-mother attachment in a low-risk sample. *Child Development, 58,* 945-954.

Bassa, D. M. (1978). From the traditional to the modern: Some observations in changes in Indian child-rearing and parental attitudes with special reference to identity formation. In E.S. Anthony and C. Childand (Eds.), *The child and his family in a changing world.* New York: John Wiley.

Baumrind, D. (1967). Child care practices antecedating patterns of pre-school behavior. *Genetic Psychology Monographs, 75,* 43-88.

Baumrind, D. (1971). Current patterns of parental authority. *Developmental Psychology Monograph, 4,* (1 -2).

Baydar, N., & Brooks-Gunn, J. (1991). Effects of maternal employment and child-care arrangements on pre-schoolers cognitive and behavioral outcomes: Evidence from the children of the national longitudinal survey of youth. *Developmental Psychology, 27,* 932-945.

Beals, A.R. (1967). *Gopalpur: A south Indian village.* New York: Holt, Rinehart & Winston.

Begum, N. (1975). *Influence of educational qualification of parents, SES and size of family on the social participation of pre-schoolers.* Unpublished master's dissertation, Madras University, Madras.

Belsky, J.(1993). Etiology of child maltreatment: A developmental ecological analysis. *Psychological Bulleten,* 114 (3).

Berry, J.W. (1966). Temne and Eskimo perceptual skills. *International Journal of Psychology, 1,* 207-229.

Berry, J.W. (1976). *Human ecology and cognitive style: Comparative studies in cultural and psychological adaptation.* Toronto: Sage Publications.

Bhagat, A. (1997). Views expressed and cited in Sushma Chadha's article entitled *'Ma's not waiting at home'*, Pioneer, April 15, 1997.

Bhagat, A. (1998). *"Parents can make or mar child's personality"* In an article by Sudha Passi, *Times of India,* New Delhi (Daily)1998.

Bharat, S. (1992). The two pay cheque couples : An analysis of their housework, decision making, sex-role perceptions and attitudes, Bombay : TISS (Mimeo).

Bhargava, M., & Sadhu, R. (1989). Family size and family pattern as determinants of child's personality under condition of maternal acceptance - rejection. *Praachi Journal of Psycho-Cultural Dimensions, 5,* 1989.

Bhogle, S. (1978). Child rearing practices among three cultures. *Social Change, 8,* 5-13.

Bhogle, S. (1981). Socialization: Family and psychological differentiation. In D. Sinha (Ed.), *Socialization of the Indian child*, New Delhi: Concept.

Birnbaum, T. A. (1975). Life patterns and self-esteem in gifted family oriented and career committed women. In M.S. Mednick, S.S. Tongri, & L.W. Hoffman (Eds.), *Women and achievement*. Washington, D.C.: Hemisphere.

Bisht, S., & Sinha, D. (1981). Socialization: family and psychological differentiation. In D. Sinha (Ed.), *Socialization of the Indian child*, New Delhi: Concept.

Bornstein, M.H. & Lamb , M.E (Ed.) (1992). *Developmental Psychology*, 3rd Edition, New Jersey, Lawrence Erlbaum Assosiates.

Bowd, A.D. (1974). Retest reliability of the children's embedded figures test for young children. *Perceptual and Motor Skills, 39*, 442.

Bronfenbrenner, U. (1977). Towards an experimental ecology of human development. *American Psychologist, 32*, 513-531.

Bronfenbrenner, U., Alvarez, W. F., & Henderson, C. R. (1984). Working and watching: Maternal employment status and parents' perceptions of their three-year-old children. *Child Development, 55*, 1362-1378.

Brown, S.W. (1970). *A comparative study of maternal employment and nonemployment*. Unpublished doctoral dissertation, Mississippi State University.

Busse, T. V. (1968). Establishment of the flexible thinking factor in fifth grade boys. *Journal of Psychology, 69*, 93-100.

Busse, T.V. (1969). Child-rearing antecedents of flexible thinking.

Developmental Psychology, 1, 584-591.

Chadha, (1997). *'Ma's not waiting at home'*, Pioneer, New Delhi, April 15.

Chandra, S. (1974). *Cognitive development : Indians and Fijians*. Paper presented at the Second International Conference of International Association of Cross-Cultural Psychology, Kingston, Ontario, Canada.

Chatterjee, T. K., & Shah, V. (1981). A study of relationship between adjustment and perceived parental behaviour among male and female college students. *Our Education, 2*, 45-49.

Claeys, W., & De Boeck, P. (1976). The influence of some parental characteristics on children's primary abilities and field independence: A study of adopted children. *Child Development, 47*, 842-845.

Coats, S., Lord, M., & Jakabovics, E. (1975). Field dependence-independence, social-non-social play and sex differences in pre-school children. *Perceptual and Motor Skills, 40*, 195-202.

Colengelo, N., Rosenthal, D. M., & Dettmann, D. F. (1984). Maternal employment and job-satisfaction and their relationship to children's perceptions and behaviour. *Sex Roles, 10*, 9-10.

Comstock, M. L. C. (1973). Effects of perceived parental behavior on self-esteem and adjustment. *Dissertation Abstracts International (B), 34*, 465.

Cooley, C. H. (1902). *Human nature and the social order*. New York: Charles Schribner's Sons.

Coopersmith, S. (1967). *The antecedents of self-esteem*. San Francisco: W.H. Freeman.

Crandall, V. J., & Sinkeldam, C. (1964). Children's dependent and achievement behaviors in social situations and their perceptual field dependence. *Journal of Personality, 32*, 1-22.

Dani, V. (1995). Female stereotypes of adolescents as a function of gender, co-education and mother's employment. *Praachi Journal of Psycho-cultural Dimensions*, 2, 23-26.

Das, V. C., & Panda, K. C. (1977). *Effects of certain non-intellective variables on cognitive performance*. Unpublished research report. Regional College of Education, Bhubaneshwar.

Dawson, J. L. (1967). Cultural and psychological influences upon spatial-perceptual processes in West Africa: Part I. *International Journal of Psychology, 2,* 115-128.

Dekovic, M., & Janssens, J. M. (1992). Parents' child-rearing style and child's sociometric status. *Developmental Psychology, 28,* 925-932.

Devall, E., Stoneman, Z., & Brody, G. (1983). The impact of divorce and maternal employment on pre-adolescent children. *Journal of Applied Family and Child Studies, 35,* 153-159.

Dixit, R. C., & Vishnoi, P. L. (1980). Employment of the mothers as a determinant of mother-daughter relationship and the development of masculinity-feminity among young girls. *Psychologia, 23,* 167-172.

Dollard, J., & Miller, N. E. (1950). *Personality and psychotherapy*. New York: McGraw Hill.

Douvan, E., & Adelson, J. (1966). *The adolescent experience*. New York: Wiley.

Dreyer, A.S. (1975). *Family interaction and cognitive style: Situation and cross-sex effects*. In H.B. Biller (Chair). Beyond father absence: Conceptualization of father effects. Symposium presented at the meeting of the Society for Research in Child Development.

Dyk, R. B. (1969). An exploratory study of mother-child interaction in infancy in relation to the development of differentiation. *Journal of the American Academy of Child Psychiatry,* 8, 657-691.

Dyk, R. B., & Witkin, H. A. (1965). Family experiences related to the development of differentiation in children. *Child Development, 36,* 21-55.

Eastburg, M. & Johnson, W.B. (1991). Shyness and perception of parental benaviour. *Psychological Reports,* 66, 915-921.

Easterbrooks, M. A., & Goldbery, W. A. C. (1985). Effects of early maternal employment on toddlers, mothers and fathers. *Developmental Psychology, 21,* 774-784.

Edgerton, N. E. (1976). The relationship of cognitive style of young children to maternal child-rearing practices. *Dissertation Abstracts International, 36,* 5135 (A).

Efoghe, G.B. (1988). The effects of maternal employment and family size on Nigerian children's perception of maternal disciplinary tone. *International Journal of Behavioral Development, 12,* 12-22.

Egeland, B., & Sroufe, L. A. (1981a). Attachment and early maltreatment. *Child Development, 52,* 44-52.

Egeland, B., & Sroufe, L. A. (1981b). Developmental sequelae of maltreatment in infancy. *New Directions for Child Development, 11,* 77-92.

Eiduson, B., Cohen, J., & Alexander, J. (1973). Alternatives in child-rearing in 1970s. *American Journal of Orthopsychiatry, 43,* 721-731.

Eisenstadt, T.H., Eyeberg, S.,McNeil, C.B. & Newcomb, C. (1993) Parent child interaction therapy with behaviour problem children. Relative effect of two stages and overall treatment outcome. *Journal of Clinical Child Psychology*, 22 (1), 42-51.

Elliott, R. (1961). Inter-relationships among measures of field dependence, ability and personality traits. *Journal of Abnormal and Social Psychology, 63,* 27-36.

Erikson, E. H. (1968) *Identity, youth and crisis*. New York: Norton.

Eysenck, H. J. (1959). *The scientific study of personality*. London: Routledge & Kegan Paul.

Fisher, J. L., & Crawford, D.W. (1992). Co-dependency and parenting style. *Journal of Adolescent Research, 7,* 352-363.

Fleck, J. R. (1972) Cognitive styles in children and performance on Piagetian conservation task. *Perceptual and Motor Skills, 35,* 747-756.

Forgus, R. H., & Melamed, L. E. (1976). *Perception: A cognitive*

Forgus, R. H., & Melamed, L. E. (1976). *Perception: A cognitive State Approach*, New York: McGraw-Hill.

Forgus, R. H, & Shulman, B. H. (1979). *Personality: A cognitive view.* Englewood Cliffs, N.J.: Prentice-Hall.

Freud, S. (1949). *An outline of psychoanalysis* (Translated and newly edited by J. Strachey). New York: W.W. Norton.

Fromm, M. E. (1941). *Escape from freedom.* New York : Holt.

Ghadially, R., & Kazi, K. A. (1979). Attitude towards sex roles. *Indian Journal of Social Work, 40*, 65-71.

Ghosh, E. S. K., & Massey, R. R. K. (1979). *Cognitive differentiation: Effects of social class and type of schooling.* Unpublished research report, Department of psychology, Allahabad University, Allahabad.

Gold, D., & Andres, D. (1978a). Developmental comparisons between adolescent children with employed and non-employed mothers. *Merrill-Palmer Quarterly, 24*, 243-254.

Gold, D., & Andres, D. (1978b). Developmental comparisons between 10 year old children with employed and non-employed mothers. *Child Development, 49*, 75-84.

Gold, D., & Andres, D. (1978c). Relations between maternal employment and development of nursery school children. *Canadian Journal of Behavioural Science, 10*, 116-129.

Gopalan, S. (1995). *Women and employment in India.* New Delhi. Har-Anand Publications.

Gore, M. S. (1968). *Urbanization and family change.* Bombay: Popular Prakashan.

Gore, M. S. (1978). Changes in the family and the process of socialization in India. In A.E. James & C. Colette (Eds.) *The child in his family. (Vol.5).* New York: Wiley.

Gupta, M. P. (1990). Effects of parental machiavellianism on personally perceived self-esteem. *Indian Journal of Current Psychological Research, 5,* 104-108.

Gupta, G. R., & Ganguly, H. C. (1982). Marriage - work interaction: A study on Indian women. *Indian Journal of Clinical*

Psychology, 9, 113-123.

Hall, C., & Lindzey, G., (1957). *Theories of personality.* New York: Wiley.

Hamilton, J. L. (1982). A psychological study of perceived parental caregiving behaviours of elementary school children from working and non-working mothers' families. *Dissertation Abstract International (B), 43*, No. 09.

Harrell, J. E., & Ridley, C.A. (1975). Childcare, maternal employment and the quality of mother-child interaction. *Journal of Marriage and the Family care, 37*, 556-564.

Hart, C. H., Dewolf, D., Michele, W. P., & Burt, D. C. (1992). Maternal and paternal disciplinary styles: Relation with pre-schoolers playground behavioral orientation and peer status. *Child Development, 63*, 879-892.

Harter, S. (1985a). *The self-perception profile for children: Revision of the perceived competence scale for children, Manual.* University of Denver.

Harter, S. (1985b). *The social support scale for children.* Manual. University of Denver.

Hartley, R. E. (1966). *Sex roles from a child's viewpoint.* Paper presented at the annual meeting of the American Orthopsychiatric Association, San Fransisco.

Hassan, M. K., Enayatullaha, & Khalique, A. (1977). A study of anxiety in school children as related to child-rearing attitudes and some personality traits of parents. *Indian Journal of Psychiatric Social Work, 6*, 1-7.

Herzog, A. R., & Bachman, J.G. (1982). *Sex role attitudes among high school seniors : Views about work and family roles.* Ann Arbor Survey Research Centre, Institute for Social Research, University of Michigan.

Hock, E. (1978). Working and non-working mothers with infants: Perceptions of their careers, their infants' needs, and satisfaction with mothering. *Developmental Psychology, 4*, 37-43.

Hock, E. (1980). Working and non-working mothers and their infants: A comparative study of maternal caregiving characteristics and infant social behavior. *Merrill-Palmer Quarterly, 26*, 70-101.

Hoffman, L.W. (1961a). Mother's enjoyment of work and effects on the child. *Child Development, 32*, 187-197.

Hoffman, L.W. (1961b). Effects of maternal employment on the child. *Child Development, 32*, 181-199.

Hoffman, L.W. (1974). Effects of maternal employment on the child: A review of the research. *Developmental Psychology, 10*, 204-228.

Hoffman, L.W. (1978). Effects of maternal employment on the child: A review of the research. In H. Bee (Ed.), *Social issues in developmental psychology* (pp. 130-171). New York: Harper & Row.

Hoffman, L.W. (1979). Maternal employment. *American Psychologist, 34*, 859-865.

Hoffman, L.W. (1984). Maternal employment and the young child. In M. Perlmutter (Ed.), *Internation and parent-child relations in child development: The Minnesota symposia on child psychology* (vol.17). Hillsdale, NJ: Lawrence Erlbaum Associates.

Hoffman, L. W. (1989). Effects of maternal employment in the two-parent family. *American Psychologist, 44*, 283-292.

Hoffman, M. L. (1984). Parent discipline, moral internalization and development of prosocial motivation. In E. Staub. D. Bartal, J. Karlowsky, & J. Reykowsky (Eds.), *Development and maintenance of prosocial behavior* (pp. 117-137). New York: Plenum Press.

Hoffman, M. L., & Saltzstein, H. D. (1967). Parent discipline and child's moral development. *Journal of Personality and Social Psychology, 5*, 45-57.

Holtzman, W. H., Diaz-Guerrero, R., & Swartz, J.D. (1975). *Personality development in two cultures*. Austin, Texas:

University of Texas Press.

Hurlock, E. B. (1978). *Child development* (5th edition), New York: McGraw-Hill.

James, W. (1892). *Psychology: The briefer courses*. New York: Henry Holt.

Jenson, L., & Borges, M. (1986). The effects of maternal employment on adolescent daughters. *Adolescence, 21*, 659-666.

Johnson, M. K. (1996). *Effect of maternal employment in different stages of child's life.* Paper presented at the American Sociological Association Annual Meeting, August 15-20. University of Minnesota.

Joshi, M. C., & Daharwal, A. (1977). Child-rearing practices and personality of Satnamee children. *Indian Psychological Review, 15*, 7-12.

Joshi, M.C., & Tiwari, J. (1977). Personality development of children in relation to child-rearing practices among socio-economic classes. *Indian Psychological Review, 14*, 5-16.

Juneja, R. (1979). A comparative study of working and non-working mothers with respect to practices and problems of rearing children. *Indian Psychological Review, 18*, 1-4.

Kakar, S. (1978). *The inner world : A psychoanalytic study of child and society in India.* Delhi : Oxford University Press.

Kakar, S. (1981). *The inner world.* (2nd ed.). Delhi: Oxford University Press.

Kakkar, S. B. (1970). Family conflicts and scholastic achievement. *Indian Journal of Psychology, 45*, 159-164.

Kalra, S. K. (1979). Some aspects of childhood socialization of high achievers. In K. Srinivasan, P.C. Saxena & T. Kantikar (Eds.), *Demographic and socio-economic aspects of the child in India*. New Delhi: Himalaya.

Kapur, P. (1971). *Married and working women in India.* Delhi : Vikas Publishing House.

Kapur, R., & Gill, S. (1986). Relationship between parental acceptance-rejection and self-esteem. *Indian Psychological Review, 30*, 15-21.

Kelly, G.A. (1955). *The psychology of personal constructs*. New York: Norton.

Keith, P. M. (1988). The relationship of self-esteem, maternal employment, and work family plans to sex role orientations of late adolescents. *Adolescence, 23*, 959-966.

Kuhn, M. H., & McPartland, T. S. (1954). An empirical investigation of self-attitudes. *American Sociological Review, 19*, 68-76.

Kumar, K. (1993). Study of childhood and family. In T.S. Saraswathi & B. Kaur (Eds.), *Human development and family studies: An agenda for research and policy* (pp. 67-76). New Delhi: Sage.

Kumar, P., & Rohatgi, K. (1985). *Revised manual for marital adjustment questionnaire*. Department of Psychology, Sardar Patel University, Vallabh Vidyanagar.

Lal, J. N. (1968). *A study of development of certain personality factors among the elementary school going children*. Unpublished Ph.D. Thesis, University of Gorakhpur, Gorakhpur.

Lal, J. N. (1987). *Manual for early school personality questionnaire*. Department of Psychology, Gorakhpur University, Gorakhpur.

Lamb, J. N. (1982). *Maternal employment and child development*. Hillsdale, N. J.: Lawrence Erlbaum.

Lamberth, J., Rappaport, H., & Rappaport, N. (1978). *Personality: An introduction*. New York: Alfred A. Knopf.

Lavakare, N. A. (1994). A comparative study of problem and Non-problem children and their mothers. *Bombay Psychologists*, 11(1&2) 73-76

Lavakare, N.A., & Hiswankar, S. (1995). Effect of Parent-directed intervention on the child's personality dimensions and parental approach towards the child. *Indian Journal of Applied Psychology*, Vol. 32, No. 1&2, 74-79.

Lerner, J. V., & Galambos, N. L. (1986a). Temperament and maternal employment. *New Direction for Child Development, 31*, 75-88.

Lerner, J. V., & Galambos, N. L. (1986b). Child Development and family change: The influences of maternal employment on infants and toddlers. *Advances in Infancy Research, 4*, 39-86.

Litovsky, V. G. (1986). *Maternal employment effects on perception of parental-child-rearing practices and on psychological adjustment during adolescence*. Unpublished doctoral dissertation, Syracuse University.

Litovsky, V. G., & Dusek, J. B. (1988). Maternal employment and adolescent adjustment and perceptions of child rearing. *International Journal of Family Psychiatry, 9*, 153-167.

Maccoby, E. E., & Martin, J. P. (1983). Socialization in the context of the family: Parent child interaction. In P. Mussen (Ed.), *Handbook of child psychology*. (Vol. 4, pp. 1-101). New York: Wiley.

Majeed, A., & Ghosh, E. S. K. (1979). *Relative effects of membership of social class and rural/urban background on cognitive style*. Unpublished study, Department of Psychology, Allahabad University, Allahabad.

Mak, A. S.(1994).Parental neglect and overprotection as risk factors in delinquency. *Australian Journal of Psychology*, 46(2), 107-111.

Malhotra, S., & Malhotra, A. (1985). Culture-conflicts and psychopathology in Indian children. *Indian Journal of Social Psychiatry*, 1, 48-53.

Martin, J. A. (1981). A longitudinal study of the consequences of early mother-infant interaction: A microscopic approach. *Monograph of the Society for Research in Child Development, 46* (serial No. 190).

Maslow, A. H. (1968). *Toward a psychology of being*. (2nd ed.). Princeton: Van Nostrand.

McEachern, L. V. H. (1973). An investigation of the relationships between self-esteem, the power motives or laissez faire home atmosphere. *Dissertation Abstracts International*, 3, 572, (A).

Mead, G. H. (1934). *Mind, self and society*. Chicago: University of Chicago Press.

Mehra, I. (1974). *Parental perception of selected behaviour in pre-adolescent children of two socio-economic groups*. Unpublished master's dissertation. University of Delhi, Delhi.

Mehrotra, N., & Anjula, P. (1992). An Analysis of temperamental and social adjustment problem of college students. *Indian Journal of Social Research, 33 (1) March*, 1992.

Menon, P. (1974). *Parental perception of selected specific behaviours in pre-adolescent children of two socio-economic groups.* Unpublished master's dissertation. University of Delhi, Delhi.

Miller, S. M. (1975). Effects of maternal employment on sex-role perception, interest and self-esteem in Kindergarten girls. *Dissertation Abstract International, 11*, 3.

Minturn, L., & Lambert, W. H. (1964). *Mothers of six cultures.* New York: John Wiley.

Minturn, L., Boyd, D., & Kapoor, S. (1978). Increased maternal power status: Changes in socialization in a re-study of Rajput mothers of Khalapur. *Journal of Cross-Cultural Psychology, 9*, 493-98.

Misra, G. (1990). Psychology of deprivation. In G. Misra (Ed.), *Applied social psychology in India*. New Delhi: Sage Publications.

Misra, G., & Tripathi, L. B. (1980). *Psychological Consequences of Prolonged Deprivation*. Agra: National Psychological Corporation.

Misra, G., & Tiwari, B. K. (1986). Environmental correlates of cognitive development. *Indian Journal of Applied Psychology, 24*, 41-52.

Misra, G., & Tiwari, B. K. (1992). Psychological differentiation in Indian children: Role of ecology, quality of schooling and home environment. *Indian Educational Review, 27*, 23-25.

Mishra, R. C., & Gupta, V. (1978). Role of schooling and exposure in perceiving pictorial sequence. *Psychologia, 21*, 231-36.

Mishra, R. C., & Gupta, V. (1983). Schooling exposure and the skill for pictorial comprehension. *Indian Psychological Review, 24*, 29-34.

Mody, S. N., & Murthy, V. N. (1988). The study of mental health of children of working mothers. *Journal of Personality and Clinical Studies, 4*, 161-164.

Moore, T. W. (1975). Exclusive early mothering and its alternatives. *Scandinavian Journal of Psychology, 16*, 256-272.

Morgan, M., & Grube, J. W. (1987). Consequences of maternal employment for adolescent behaviour and attitudes. *Irish Journal of Psychology, 8*, 85-98.

Mullener, N., & Laird, J. D. (1971). Some developmental changes in the organization of self-evaluations. *Developmental Psychology, 5*, 233-236.

Murray, H. A. (1938). *Explorations in personality*. New York: Oxford University Press.

Nanda, P. (1991). Opinions of children regarding their mother's employment. *Indian Journal of Behaviour, 15*, 5-12.

Nelson, C., & Keith, J. (1990). Comparison of female and male early adolescent sex-role, attitude and behavior development. *Adolescence, 25*,183-203.

Nelson, D. D. A. (1968). Study of school-achievement and personality adjustment among adolescent children with working and non-working mothers. *Dissertation Abstract International, 29*, 153-(A).

Ojha, H. (1977). Parental behaviour as perceived by authoritarian and non-authoritarian college students, *Psychologia, 20*, 49-53.

Ojha, H., & Pramanick, M. (1995). Parental behaviour as related to some personality traits of adolescents. *Psychologia*, Vol. 28, No. 1, 31-37.

Ojha, H., & Singh, R. (1988). Child-rearing attitudes as related to insecurity and dependence proneness. *Psychological Studies, 33,* 75-79.

Olweus, D. (1980). Familial and temperamental determinants of aggressive behaviour in adolescents: A casual analysis. *Developmental Psychology, 16,* 644-660.

Owen, M. T., & Chase-Lansdale, L. (1978). *Maternal employment and its relationship to peer competence of pre-schoolers.* Unpublished manuscript, University of Michigan, An Arbor.

Pahwa, N., & Khanna, P. (1991). A comparative study of nutritional status and personality traits of children belonging to working and non-working mothers. *The Asian Journal of Psychology and Education,* 24 (5-6).

Pal, R., & Sharma, A. (1981). A factor-analytical study of mother-child relation dimension of working housewives. *Indian Psychological Review, 20,* 29-34.

Paris, J., & Frank, H. (1989). Perception of parental bonding in borderline patients. *American Journal of Psychiatry,* 147, 1498-1499.

Parsons, J. E., Frieze, I. H., & Ruble, D. N., (1978). Intrapsychic factors influencing career aspirations in college women. *Sex Roles,* 4,337-347.

Passi, S. (1998). *Parents can make or mar child's personality.* An article in *Times of India,* New Delhi (daily).

Patterson, G. R. (1982). *Coercive Family Process.* Eugene: Castalia Press.

Pleck, J. H. (1984). Husband's paid work and family roles: Current research issues. In H. Lapata & J.H. Pleck (Eds.), *Research in the inter-weave of social roles, families and jobs,* (Vol.3). Greenwich, CT: J.A.I. Press.

Ponnuswami, S. (1977). Mother-child interactions and cognitive style. *Indian Journal of Psychology, 52,* 250-55.

Prasad, M.B., & Prasad, A. (1975). Social and emotional development of pre-school children of employed mothers.

Journal of Social and Economic Studies, 3, 73-87.

Pulkkinen, L. (1982). Self control and continuing from childhood to adolescence. In P.B. Baltes & O.G. Brim. (Eds.), *Life span development and behaviour* (Vol.4). New York: Academic Press.

Punia, S. & others (1995). Disciplinary technique for infant socialization in rural Haryana. Indian *Journal of Social Research, 36*, 27-34.

Query, J. M., & Kuruvilla, T. C. (1975). Male and female adjustment and maternal employment. *Adolescent, 10(39).*

Rai, G. C. (1979). A study of certain socio-psychological dimensions of child-rearing practices adopted by Indian mothers. *Psycholingua, 9*, 15-29.

Ransford, H. E. & Miller, J. (1983). Race, sex, and feminist outlooks. *American Sociological Review, 48*, 46-59.

Reddy, C. R. (1986). *Changing status of educated working women*. Delhi: B.R. Publishing Corporation.

Renner, V. (1970). Effects of modification on cognitive-style on creative behaviour. *Journal of Personality and Social Psychology, 14*, 257-262.

Richter, J., Eisenmann, M., & Richter, G. (1991). Perceived Parental rearing and state vs. trait aspect of depression. *Psychopathology, 24*, 25-30.

Rogers, C. (1964). Toward a science of person. In T.W. Wann (Ed.), *Behaviourism and phenomenology*. Chicago: University of Chicago Press.

Roland, A. (1978). Psychoanalytic perspectives on personality development in India. *Samiksha, 32*, 47-68.

Ronald, A. (1982). Towards a psychoanalytical psychology of hierarchical relationship in Hindu India. *Ethos, 10*, 232-253.

Romer, N., & Cherry, D. (1978). *Developmental effects of pre-school and school age maternal employment on children's sex role concepts*. Unpublished manuscript. Brooklyn College of the City University of New York.

Roodin, P. A. Broughton, A., & Vaught, G. M. (1974). Effects of birth order, sex and family size on field dependence and locus of control. *Perceptual and Motor Skills, 39*, 671-676.

Rosenberg, M. (1979). *Conceiving the self.* New York: Basic Books.

Ross, A. D. (1961). *The Hindu family in its urban setting*. Delhi: Oxford University Press.

Rossi, A. (1978). A biosocial perspective on parenting. In A. S. Rossi, J. Kagan, & T. K. Hareven (Eds.), *The family.* New York: W.W. Norton.

Rotter, J. B. (1954). *Social learning and clinical psychology*. New Jersy: Prentice-Hall.

Ruble, D. N., & Nakamura, C.Y. (1972). Task orientation versus social orientation in young children and their attention to relevant social cues. *Child Development, 43*, 471-480.

Sahoo, F. M. (1982). Affective sensitivity and cognitive style. *Indian Psychologist, 1*, 57-66.

Sahoo, F. M. (1986). *Affective sensitivity and cognitive style.* Agra: National Psychological Corporation.

Saksena, N. K., Agrawal, G., & Singh, S. B. (1977). Attitudes of working and non-working mothers towards child rearing practices. *Child Psychiatry Quarterly, 10*, 1-5.

Sandhu, R., & Bhargava, M. (1987). Background factors as determinants of children's perception of maternal acceptance. *Indian Journal of Current Psychological Research, 2*, 124-128.

Sanyal, S. (1998). In an article *Parents can make or mar child's personality* by Sudha Passi, *Times of India, New Delhi (daily).*

Saraswathi, T. S., & Dutta, R. (1988). Invisible boundaries: grooming for adult roles. New Delhi: Northern Book Centre.

Saraswathi, T. S., & Dutta, R. (1990). Poverty and human development: Socialization of girls among the urban and rural poor. In Misra, G. (Ed.), *Applied social psychology in India.* New Delhi: Sage Publications.

Saraswathi, T. S., Thakkar, D., & Kaur, I. (1979). Perceived maternal disciplinary practices and their relation to development of moral judgement in 10-13 yr. old Indian children. In L. Eckenseberger, W. Lonner, and Y.H. Poortinga, (Eds.), *Cross-cultural contribution to psychology*, (pp. 345-353). Lissee: Sweets and Zeitlinger.

Saraswathi, T. S., & Sundaresan, J. (1979). Parental disciplinary practices and development of moral judgement in children. *Social Change, 9*, 23-28.

Saxena, S. (1994). Happy home, happy child? *Social Welfare, 41 (4)*.

Scarr, S., & Hall, E. (1984). What's a parent to do? *Psychology Today, 18*, 58-63.

Scarr, S., Phillips, D., & McCartney, K. (1989). Working mothers and their families. *American Psychologist, 44*, 1402-1409.

Schachter, F. F. (1981). Toddlers with employed mothers. *Child Development, 52*, 958-964.

Schuck, J. R. (1974). The use of casual non-experimental models in aggression research. In J. DeWitt, & W. W. Hartup (Eds.), *Determinants and origins of aggressive behaviour*. The Hague: Mouton.

Scott, P. L., Yarrow, M. R., & Heining, C. (1962). Child rearing in families of working and non-working mothers. *Sociometry, 25*, 122-140.

Seth, M., & Khanna, M. (1978). Child-rearing attitudes of mothers as a function of age. *Child Psychiatry Quarterly, 11*, 6-9.

Seth, M., & Saksena, N. K. (1978). Attitudes of literate and illiterate mothers towards child-rearing. *Child Psychiatry Quarterly, 11*, 49-54.

Sharma, P., Saraswathi, T. S., & Gir, S. (1981). Role of parents and teachers in promoting social competence in children. *Child Psychiatry Quarterly, 14*, 134-137.

Sharma, S. (1971). Parental occupation and anxiety. *New Trends in Education, 2*, 21-24.

Shavalson, R. J., Hubner, J. J., & Stanton, G. C. (1976). Self-concept: Validation of construct interpretations. *Review of*

Educational Research, 46, 407-441.

Shulman, B. H. (1973). *Contributions to individual psychology.* Chicago: Alfred Adler Institute.

Singh, A., & Sharma, S. (1978). Disrupted father-son relationship and its relation to delinquent behaviour. *Asian Journal of Psychology and Education, 3*, 16-20.

Singh, M. B., & Kaur, S. (1981). Mother-child interaction in rural and urban areas. *Indian Psychological Review, 20*, 7-16.

Singh, L. B., & Fatmi, R. B. (1980). A relationship between social responsibility and parental discipline. *Asian Journal of Psychology and Education, 6*, 9-11.

Singh, S. N., & Sharma, N. (1975). Child-rearing practices of working and non-working women. *Manas, 22*, 113-119.

Singh, U. P., & Sowaid, M. (1976). The role of parental discipline in hostility, guilt and conflict over hostility. *Psychologia, 19*, 29-34.

Sinha, D. (1962). Cultural factors in the emergence of anxiety. *Eastern Anthropologist, 15*, 21-37.

Sinha, D. (1977). Some social disadvantages and development of certain perceptual skills. *Indian Journal of Psychology, 52*, 115-132.

Sinha, D. (1980). Sex differences in psychological differentiation among different cultural groups. *International Journal of Behavioural Development, 3*, 455-466.

Sinha, D. (1981). *The Socialization of the Indian child.* (Ed). New Delhi : Concept.

Sinha, D. (1982). Towards an ecological framework of deprivation. In D. Sinha, R. C. Tripathi, & G. Misra, (Eds.), *Deprivation: Its social roots and psychological consequences* (pp. 25-35). New Delhi : Concept.

Sinha, D. (1982). Socio-cultural factors and the development of perceptual and cognitive skills. In W.W. Hartup (Ed.) , *Review of child development research.* (Vol.6). Chicago: University of Chicago Press.

Sinha, D. (1984). *Manual for story-pictorial E.F.T. and Indo-African E.F.T.* Varanasi: Rupa Psychological Centre.

Sinha, D., & Mishra, R. C. (1987). A developmental study of psychological differentiation among rural and urban tribal children in relation to quality of schooling and religion. *The Creative Psychologist, 1.*

Sinha, D. (1988). The family scenario of a developing country and its implications for mental health: The case of India. In P.R. Dasen, J. W. Berry, and N. Sortorious (Eds.). *Health and cross-cultural psychology: Toward applications* (pp. 48-70). Newburry Park, California: Sage Publications.

Smokler, C. S. (1975). Self-esteem in pre-adolescent and adolescent females. *Dissertation Abstracts International, 35*, 3599(B).

Stein, A. H. (1973). The effects of maternal employment and educational attainment on the sex typed attributes of college females. *Social Behaviour and Personality, 1*, 111-114.

Stucky, M. F., McGhee, P. E., & Bell, N. G. (1982). Parent-child interaction: The influence of maternal employment. *Developmental Psychology, 18*, 635-644.

Suseela, K., Devi, R. N., & Dev Das, R. P. (1970). Child-rearing of employed and non-employed mothers. *Indian Journal of Home Science, 4*, 40-45.

Tandon, T. (1981). Process of transmission of values in the Indian child. In D. Sinha (Ed.), *Socialisation of the Indian child* (pp. 11-29). New Delhi : Concept.

Thornton, A., Duana F. A., & Camburn, D., (1983). Causes and consequences of sex-role attitudes and attitude change. *American Sociological Review, 48,* 211-227.

Tiwari, A. N., & Misra, G. (1977). A study of achievement motive in relation to prolonged deprivation. *Psychologia, 20*, 172-179.

Trimberger, R., & MacClean, M. J. (1982). Maternal employment: The child's perspective. *Journal of Marriage and the Family, 44*, 469-475.

Vanaja, M., & Vankatramaiah, S. R. (1990). Effect of marital satisfaction and employment status of mothers on behavioural problems of their children. *Indian Journal of Clinical Psychology, 17(1).*

Vandell, D. L., & Ramanan, J. (1992). Effects of early and recent maternal employment on children from low economic families. *International Conference on Infant Studies, 63*, 938-949.

Vyas, H. (1982). Education and cognitive styles: A case study of Gujarati children in Britain, Eastern United States and India. In C. Bagley and G. Varma, (Eds.), *Multicultural childhood.* Aldershot, U.K.: Gower Press.

Wadekar, A. J., & Palsane, M. N. (1987). Sex differences in child's perception of parent-child relations. *Journal of Psychological Research, 31*, 160-165.

Werkerle, C., & Wolfe, D.A. (1993). Prevention of child physical abuse and neglect: Promising new directions. *Clinical Psychology Review* 13(6), 501-540.

Wiggins, J. S., Renner, K. E., Cloré, G. L., & Rose, R. J. (1971). *The Psychology of personality reading.* Cambridge, Mass: Addison Wesley.

Willetts-Bloom, M. C., & Steven, L. N. (1994). The influence of maternal employment on gender role attitudes of men and women, *Sex Roles, 30*, 371-389.

Witkin, H. A. (1969). Social influences in the development of cognitive style. In D. Goslin (Ed.), *Handbook of socialization theories and research.* Chicago, Illinois: Rand McNally.

Witkin, II. A. (1976). *Socialization and ecology in the development of cross-cultural and sex difference in cognitive style.* Prepared for presentation at the 21st International Congress of Psychology, Paris.

Witkin, H. A., & Goodenough, D. R. (1977). Field dependence and interpersonal behaviour. *Psychological Bulletin, 34*, 661-689.

Witkin, H. A., & Goodenough, D. R. (1981). *Cognitive styles : Essence and origins.* New York: International University Press.

Witkin, H. A., Dyk, R. B., Faterson, H. F., Goodenough, D. R., & Karp, S. A. (1962). *Psychological differentiation.* New York : Wiley.

Witkin, H. A., Goodenough, D. R., & Oltman, P. K. (1979). Psychological differentiation: Current status. *Journal of Personality and Social Psychology, 37*, 127-1145.

Witkin, H. A., Oltman, P. K., Raskin, E., & Karp, S. A. (1971). *A manual for the embedded figures test.* Palo Alto: Consulting Psychologists Press.

Witkin, H. A., Cox, P. W., Fredman, F., Hrishikesan, A. G., & Siegel, K. N. (1974). *Field-dependence-independence and psychological differentiation.* Supplement No.1 (ETS RB-74-42). Princeton : Educational Testing Service.

Witkin, H. A., Lewis, H. B., Hertman, N. M., Machover, K., Meissner, P. B., & Wapner, S. (1954). *Personality through perception.* New York, Harper.

Wolfe, D. A., & Werkerle, C. (1993). Treatment strategies of child physical abuse and neglect: A critical progress report. *Clinical Psychology Review* 13(6), 473-500.

Zimmerman, I. L., & Bernstein, M. (1983). Parental work patterns in alternative families: Influence on child development. *American Journal of Orthopsychiatry, 53*, 418-435.

INDEX